the films of
Hal Ashby

CONTEMPORARY APPROACHES TO FILM AND TELEVISION SERIES

A complete listing of the books in this series can be found online at wsupress.wayne.edu

General Editor
Barry Keith Grant
Brock University

Advisory Editors
Patricia B. Erens
School of the Art Institute of Chicago

Lucy Fischer
University of Pittsburgh

Caren J. Deming
University of Arizona

Robert J. Burgoyne
Wayne State University

Tom Gunning
University of Chicago

Anna McCarthy
New York University

Peter X. Feng
University of Delaware

Lisa Parks
University of California-Santa Barbara

Frances Gateward
Ursinus College

Walter Metz
Montana State University

Thomas Leitch
University of Delaware

Christopher Beach

Wayne State University Press   Detroit

© 2009 by Wayne State University Press, Detroit, Michigan 48201.
All rights reserved. No part of this book may be reproduced without formal permission.

13 12 11 10 09   5 4 3 2 1

Library of Congress Cataloging-in-Publication Data

Beach, Christopher.
 The films of Hal Ashby / Christopher Beach.
  p. cm. — (Contemporary approaches to film and television series)
 Includes bibliographical references and index.
 ISBN 978-0-8143-3415-7 (pbk. : alk. paper)
 1. Ashby, Hal—Criticism and interpretation. I. Title.
PN1998.3.A7635B43 2009
791.4302′33092—dc22
                              2009004088

All photos courtesy of the Academy of Motion Picture Arts and Sciences.

"For What It's Worth," words and music by Stephen Stills © 1967 (renewed) Cotillion Music Inc., Ten East Music, Springalo Toones and Richie Furay Music. All rights administered by Warner-Tamerlane Publishing Corp. All rights reserved. Used by permission of Alfred Publishing Co. Inc.

Designed and typeset by Maya Rhodes
Composed in The Mix Black and Dante MT

CONTENTS

Preface   vii

1. Hal Ashby: New Hollywood Auteur   1
2. Hollywood Maverick: Ashby, the New Hollywood, and the 1970s   10
3. On the Road to Find Out: *The Landlord* and *Harold and Maude*   38
4. Once I Was a Soldier: Visions of the Military in *The Last Detail* and *Coming Home*   66
5. I Like to Watch: *Shampoo* and *Being There*   96
6. There's Something Happening Here: Music in Ashby's Films   118
7. A Director under the Influence: Ashby's Final Decade   143

Notes   159
Filmography   173
Bibliography   181
Index   189

PREFACE

When I was fourteen years old, I went to see an offbeat comedy called *Harold and Maude*. I knew nothing about the director—a man with the unpretentious name of Hal Ashby—and I was completely unprepared for what I was about to see. The film's brilliantly satirical love story, its haunting visual images, and its evocative musical score of songs by Cat Stevens combined to make it a thoroughly engrossing cinematic experience. In the following weeks, I found myself going back to see *Harold and Maude* a second and a third time. I was not alone in my fascination: the movie achieved cult status in cities like Montreal, Detroit, Boston, and Minneapolis. At the Westgate Theater in my hometown of Edina, Minnesota, the film was shown for 115 straight weeks, surpassing the record for a continuous run by any movie in the Minneapolis area.

An improbable yet entirely convincing story about a love affair between a twenty-year-old man and an eighty-year-old woman, *Harold and Maude* combines humor and pathos in a way that few movies in the history of American cinema have done successfully. It took risks, refusing to conform to Hollywood formulas of what a successful movie should be. And it announced the arrival of a director with both natural talent and creative vision.

By the time he directed *Harold and Maude*, Ashby was already a meticulous craftsman whose nuanced understanding of the filmic medium resulted in striking visual images, compositions, and sequences. Ashby's training as an assistant editor for such Hollywood legends as William Wyler and George Stevens, and his later experience as lead editor for Norman Jewison, had made him an exceptionally versatile and unusually creative director. A highly intuitive filmmaker, Ashby relied more on instinct than on strict plans or storyboards. The two directors with whom Ashby's work can best be compared are Robert Altman and John Cassavetes, both of whom are known for their individualized attempts to achieve a greater degree of spontaneity and creative freedom. Yet while both Cassavetes and Altman have received considerable critical attention over the past two decades, Ashby and his films have virtually disappeared from the regard of critics and film scholars.

This book, the first critical study of Ashby's filmmaking career, focuses primarily on his first seven films: *The Landlord* (1970), *Harold and Maude* (1971), *The Last Detail* (1973), *Shampoo* (1975), *Bound for Glory* (1976), *Coming Home* (1978), and *Being There* (1979). Ashby's last four films—*Second-Hand Hearts* (1981), *Lookin' to Get Out* (1982), *The Slugger's Wife* (1985), and *8 Million Ways to Die* (1986)—which are almost universally considered his least successful artistically, are discussed in the final chapter of the book.

The chapters of this study do not progress in a strictly chronological format: instead, they are organized around the analysis of thematic, generic, or formal similarities in groups of films. The first two chapters provide an overview of Ashby's filmmaking career. In chapter 1, I make a case for Ashby as "auteur," emphasizing his extensive training as a Hollywood film editor, his participation in the New Hollywood of the early 1970s, and his collaborative approach to filmmaking. Chapter 2 is a biographical survey of Ashby's most productive and successful decade, the 1970s, providing a context for the detailed discussions in later chapters of Ashby's most important films.

In chapter 3, I analyze Ashby's first two films as a director: *The Landlord* and *Harold and Maude*. In these films, both social comedies involving a young male protagonist, I trace the development of Ashby's art from the self-consciously experimental approach of *The Landlord* to the more polished but still highly personal style of *Harold and Maude*. The next two chapters examine the treatment of two important thematic concerns in Ashby's work. Chapter 4 concerns Ashby's treatment of the United States military, focusing in particular on *The Last Detail* and *Coming Home*, while chapter 5 analyzes the role of television and the mass media in two satirical comedies: *Shampoo* and *Being There*.

In chapter 6, I examine the crucial role played by the musical score in Ashby's films: through a comparison of the music in three films—

Harold and Maude, Shampoo, and *Coming Home*—I argue that music functions both as an important formal and aesthetic component and as a highly effective means of ideological commentary. In chapter 7, I assess Ashby's last four films in an attempt to understand the rapid decline in his career after *Being There*. Ashby's final film, *8 Million Ways to Die*, provides a fascinating case study of the director's largely failed attempt to resurrect his career by transforming a standard Hollywood crime film into a personal statement about addiction and recovery.

My understanding of Hal Ashby and his films has benefited greatly from conversations with the many people I have interviewed in the course of writing this book. These interviews, conducted in person, by phone, or in some cases by e-mail, are listed in the bibliography. I am grateful to all those who took the time to share their knowledge and insights about Ashby and his films with me.

I have also done extensive research in the archive of Ashby's papers at the Special Collections of the Margaret Herrick Library of the Academy of Motion Picture Arts and Sciences. Particular thanks go to Barbara Hall, Research Archivist, and Faye Thompson, Photograph Department Coordinator, for their help in accessing the collection, and to Bill Black and the Academy Film Archive for providing access to materials relating to Ashby's films.

I thank the American Film Institute for allowing me to use transcripts of seminars given by Ashby, and the UCLA Film and Television Archive for making available a 35mm print of *Second-Hand Hearts*, a film that is unavailable in any commercial format.

Finally, I thank Larry Reynolds, executor for the estate of Hal Ashby, for his assistance in this project and for his permission to quote from unpublished materials.

ONE

Hal Ashby
New Hollywood Auteur

> Hal Ashby was, without a doubt, the most committed editor I ever worked with.... He would of course move on to become one of the finest directors in (contemporary) American film.
> —Norman Jewison, *This Terrible Business Has Been Good to Me*

> Hal Ashby is now largely forgotten because he had the misfortune to die at the end of the '80s, but he had the most remarkable run of any '70s director.
> —Peter Biskind, *Easy Riders, Raging Bulls*

Hal Ashby was part of a generation of American filmmakers who collectively produced the phenomenon known as the New Hollywood. Ashby, Robert Altman, Peter Bogdanovich, John Cassavetes, Francis Ford Coppola, Brian De Palma, William Friedkin, Terence Malick, Paul Mazursky, Alan Pakula, Bob Rafelson, Michael Ritchie, and Martin Scorsese were, in their ensemble, as talented a generation of directors as has ever appeared in Hollywood. During the late 1960s and the 1970s, they transformed the way in which American films were made, dealing the final deathblow to the studio system as it had existed for several decades. Compared with the generation of filmmakers who

CHAPTER 1

preceded them, the directors of the New Hollywood commented far more directly on the historical, social, and cultural events of their time. In questioning the dominant myths and ideologies of mainstream American life, they foregrounded a profound sense of alienation from traditional values and attitudes.

During the 1970s, Ashby would direct a total of seven feature films, five of which *(Harold and Maude, The Last Detail, Shampoo, Coming Home,* and *Being There)* have since established themselves within the pantheon of significant American cinema. It is no exaggeration to claim, as Peter Biskind does in his book on the New Hollywood, that of any American director of the 1970s, it was Ashby who put together the most remarkable string of successful films.[1] Ashby's films present an unflinchingly honest portrait of America in the late 1960s and early 1970s, a period during which the need to express cultural tensions artistically brought a new vitality to the art of American filmmaking. Ashby's career as a film director lasted only about fifteen years, less than half as long as the careers of contemporaries such as Altman, Coppola, and Scorsese. Yet in that relatively brief span, Ashby's films made an important contribution to the cultural rhetoric of liberal post-sixties America. *The Landlord* critiques race relations in contemporary urban America; *Harold and Maude* articulates a resonant countercultural alternative to the institutions of bourgeois American life; *The Last Detail* takes aim at the dehumanizing experience of soldiers in the United States military; *Shampoo* offers a scathing portrayal of the American political system; *Coming Home* represents one of Hollywood's first attempts to deal with the devastating legacy of the Vietnam War; and *Being There* combines a satire of corporate and political mentalities with a prescient critique of the ubiquity of the media in everyday life.

Diane Jacobs, one of the first film scholars to delineate the New Hollywood generation in her book *Hollywood Renaissance,* included Ashby in a select list of the seven most important American directors of his era. Placing Ashby in the company of Altman, Coppola, Mazursky, Cassavetes, Ritchie, and Scorsese, Jacobs identified him as a major American filmmaker, "an artist, a superb storyteller [and] an auteur with a subtle but unmistakable personal touch."[2] The concept of auteurist cinema was popularized by critic Andrew Sarris, in his book *The American Cinema: Directors and Direction 1929–1968* and other writings.

Sarris defined the auteur as a "strong director [who] imposes his own personality on a film."³ In spite of Jacobs's classification, more recently, Ashby's career has not been granted such an elevated status: despite the significance of his accomplishments, Ashby has become the most neglected major American director of his era.

If it is true, as Peter Biskind remarks, that Ashby is "largely forgotten," it is not altogether clear why. While Ashby may not have been an auteur in the strictest sense, he was clearly an auteur in the more general sense proposed by Peter Lehman: "a filmmaker of substance who shapes and forms films with careful thought and attention to style, not just as window dressing but as integral to storytelling."⁴ In this book, I will attempt to make a convincing case for Ashby's career as that of a significant American director, and to place his accomplishments alongside those of contemporaries such as Altman, Coppola, Scorsese, and Cassavetes. It is clear that Ashby brought to his filmmaking not simply the technical skills needed to craft well-made Hollywood movies, but a strong social vision, a unique sense of artistry, and an extraordinary ability to direct actors.

Despite the considerable success Ashby achieved during the most productive decade of his career, critical assessments of his filmmaking have not always been kind. Ashby's detractors have argued that his method was too collaborative to be seen as that of a true auteur. David Thomson, for example, in his *Biographical Dictionary of Film*, described Ashby as "a sad casualty who depended on strong collaborators."⁵ Thomson gave screenwriter Colin Higgins credit for the "dark humor" of *Harold and Maude;* he attributed the success of *The Last Detail* to its writer Robert Towne and its star Jack Nicholson; and he dismissed Ashby's role in making *Shampoo*, describing it as "a film without any directorial personality." While it is true that Ashby made his best films with the help of very talented collaborators—including writers, actors, and cinematographers—the same could be said of many directors who attain auteur status.

Perhaps the most telling comparison is with Robert Altman. Altman has been more consistently cited as an auteur than any other American director of his generation and has been referenced extensively in discussions of American cinema of the past four decades.⁶ Robert Kolker, for example, calls Altman "one of the few American filmmakers to

CHAPTER I

confirm the fragile legitimacy of the auteur theory with such a visible expression of coherence in his work."[7] Ashby, on the other hand, has not achieved anything like the same auteur status, despite the fact that his best films are, in my opinion, just as strong as those of Altman.

Although Ashby's films of the 1970s received their share of praise, they have not to this point received the kind of serious critical and analytical consideration they deserve. In the eighteen years since Ashby's death, there has not been a single published book about his films or his filmmaking career. Other critical and biographical literature on Ashby is fairly limited. There has been one PhD dissertation (Ron Elwood, *How We Live: An Analysis of the Films Directed by Hal Ashby from 1970 to 1980* [1988]), as well as chapters on Ashby in critical/historical overviews of the period (see David Cook's *Lost Illusions* and Diane Jacobs's *Hollywood Renaissance*). Other books, such as Peter Lev's *American Films of the 70s* and Glenn Man's *Radical Visions: American Film Renaissance, 1967–75*, contain cursory discussions of individual films Ashby directed.

Unfortunately, the only extended biographical treatment of Ashby's career thus far is contained in Peter Biskind's 1998 book *Easy Riders, Raging Bulls*. Biskind's sensationalistic account of Ashby's life focuses on his drug use and obsessive, reclusive personality, rather than on his work. A thoroughly researched biography of Ashby is clearly needed in order to provide a more balanced account of his life. It is to be hoped that the forthcoming biography by Nick Dawson, *Being Hal Ashby: Life of a Hollywood Rebel*, will provide such an account.[8]

The vocabulary used to talk about a director like Robert Altman does not apply as readily in the case of Ashby. Film scholars look for distinctive patterns and repeated themes in the work of the filmmakers they discuss, and they show a marked preference for directors who, like Altman, insist on "coherence of form and content."[9] The desire to categorize certain "strong" directors as the sole authors or creators of their films is symptomatic of a Romantic conception of artistic production—one based on the belief that there is a central creative force behind any work of art.[10] The single-author model of filmmaking has been so dominant within the field of film studies over the past several decades that analyses of authorship as collaborative enterprise have been relatively rare.[11] As John Caughie suggests, the most common assumptions behind auteurist discussions of cinema are that "a film, though produced collectively, is . . . valuable when it is essentially the product of its director," and that the director's personality "can be traced in a thematic and/or stylistic consistency over all (or almost all) of the director's films."[12]

Based on these criteria, Ashby's status as an auteur is indeed questionable, although, as Thomas Elsaesser has noted, designating such status is a slippery slope, "a treacherous classification of the unclassifiable under the sign of unity."[13] Jack Stillinger is even more skeptical, arguing that "the idea of director as the author [of a film] will not hold up under scrutiny." Stillinger contends that "it is simply not possible for one person, however brilliant, to provide the entire creative force behind so complex a work as a motion picture."[14]

In fact, historical and biographical evidence fail to support the auteurist model in its most extreme formulation. Take as examples two of the most celebrated films in the American canon: *Apocalypse Now* (1979) and *Citizen Kane* (1941). It is impossible to imagine Francis Ford Coppola's *Apocalypse Now* without the contributions of John Milius (screenplay), Vittorio Storaro (cinematography), and Dean Tavoularis (production design), or Orson Welles's *Citizen Kane* without Herman Mankiewicz's original screenplay, Perry Ferguson's innovative art direction, and Gregg Toland's stunning cinematography, not to mention the music of Bernard Herrmann, the editing of Robert Wise and Mark Robson, and the performance of Joseph Cotten. Robert Carringer's discussion of the collaborative nature of *Citizen Kane* makes clear that "in a number of its most important visual features, *Citizen Kane* can be seen as a direct and logical extension of [cinematographer] Toland's previous work."[15]

Thomas Schatz also classifies Frank Capra as a largely collaborative filmmaker: "Capra's steady decline after leaving Columbia suggests that he was a filmmaker whose talents, personality, and working methods were best suited to a studio-based production process. His 'one man, one film' bombast aside, Capra may have been essentially a house director, a collaborative artist whose vision and artistry were inextricably wed to Columbia's 1930s house style."[16] Capra's primary collaborators at Columbia were Robert Riskin, who scripted seven of the eight films Capra directed from 1932–37, and cinematographer Joseph Walker, who served as director of cinematography on all of Capra's 1930s pictures.

A more nuanced approach might recognize several forms of auteurship. Some auteurs dominate nearly every aspect of their films (Charlie Chaplin), others work collaboratively but exercise tight control over their cast and crew (John Ford or Howard Hawks), and yet others work as true collaborators who keep a relatively low profile on the set (George Cukor). Yet even this kind of approach is too schematic to be of any practical use, since there are many possible permutations of each category. Within Ashby's own oeuvre, the environment in which he directed each film varied greatly. In the case of *Harold and Maude*, Ashby worked in an environment of almost complete artistic freedom, while in the case of *Shampoo*, he worked with a lead actor who was also the film's producer and co-writer.[17]

The precise circumstances under which Ashby interacted with writers, cinematographers, producers, cast and crew varied, and yet each film reflects, in significant ways, the personal stamp of its director. Ashby's collaborative method in his most successful films conforms quite closely to what Bruce Kawin proposes as the ideal filmmaking process: "It is not that the director issues instructions to everybody in sight and they then carry them out; rather, every creative member of the filmmaking team comes to share a vision of how the film ought to be, a vision that they may well identify with the desires of the director. They each do their part, and the parts are coherent because they are each fashioned in relation to an ideal of the whole."[18]

In fact, Ashby was strongly committed on both a theoretical and a practical level to the collaborative process of filmmaking. His method involved a spontaneous and at times even improvisational approach to acting and filming that required significant contributions by writers, actors, cinematographers, production designers, and editors. "Hal enjoyed the collaborative process of filmmaking more than anyone I've known," said Gordon Willis, who worked as Ashby's cinematographer on *The Landlord* before going on to a highly successful career shooting films for such directors as Coppola, Pakula, and Woody Allen. According to Caleb Deschanel, cinematographer on *Being There* and *The Slugger's Wife*, Ashby's collaborative approach was seen by some in the industry as the sign of an inability to exercise creative control over his films: "Hal's style of directing was off-putting to people who had this vision of a director as someone very much in charge, like Erich von Stroheim with his whip. But there is another kind of director who can create an atmosphere that is conducive to everyone feeling free to express themselves and do their best work."[19] According to David Hamburger, assistant director on *Being There* and *Second-Hand Hearts*, Ashby gave his actors "as much freedom as they could stand."[20]

Like his contemporary John Cassavetes, Ashby made it a priority to maintain a supportive and egalitarian atmosphere on the set. As a result, he was able to elicit highly naturalistic performances from his actors that exemplify the vitality and raw emotional honesty of which the New Hollywood cinema at its best was capable.[21] Ashby's style was not, however, devoid of guidance or direction. If he felt that an actor could not be directed in a particular scene, Ashby let him find his own way, for example, by giving him twenty takes.

Given the creative space in which to improvise and experiment, actors produced performances that were in many cases among the strongest of their careers: we need only think of Jack Nicholson in *The Last Detail*, Jon Voight and Jane Fonda in *Coming Home*, Warren Beatty and Lee Grant in *Shampoo*, David Carradine in *Bound for Glory*, and Peter Sellers in *Being There*. A number of actors interviewed for this book emphasized Ashby's supportive presence on the set. The remarks of Ronny Cox, who played the role of Ozark Bule in *Bound for Glory*, typify the feelings of many of these actors: "Hal would always make you feel secure. You would do a scene and he would be so positive. You were never under any obligation: if you had any kind of impulse, he encouraged you to go with it. I don't mean to imply that there was any sort of anarchy, because you knew that with that freedom came an awesome responsibility not to mess up what was going on."[22]

In addition to inviting the active participation of his cast and crew, Ashby encouraged them through internal promotions to explore their creativity in new ways: He promoted Michael Chapman from camera operator to cinematographer for *The Last Detail*; he moved Don Zimmerman from assistant editor to lead editor on *Coming Home*; he allowed editor Robert Jones to work as a writer on both *Coming Home*

CHAPTER 1

and *Being There*; he nurtured the career of Jeff Wexler by moving him from production assistant on *Harold and Maude* to head of his sound crew on several subsequent films.

If Ashby was an auteur—albeit one given to free-spirited collaboration rather than authoritarian control—we must ask why he has received such a relatively small share of critical and biographical attention. There are several probable causes for Ashby's lack of auteur status, first and foremost the fact that he was not strongly associated with a particular genre or type of thematic material. He worked in a number of disparate genres—a racial comedy, a wartime love story, a biographical drama, and a deadpan satirical farce—virtually reinventing himself with each film he directed. From the eccentricity of *Harold and Maude* to the minimalism of *The Last Detail*, from the sharply satirical *Shampoo* to the epic *Bound for Glory*, from the visceral drama of *Coming Home* to the surreal humor of *Being There*, Ashby was versatile enough to meet the requirements of each project. Such eclectic range, while it produced artistically excellent movies on vastly different subjects, tended to work against the requirement that an auteur leave an easily identifiable personal stamp on each of his films.[23] Ashby's visual style is, however, consistent in many of his films and includes a penchant for long takes, long shots rather than closeups, and the use of tableau shots.

Second, Ashby did not fit the mold of the typical New Hollywood director. The mythology that painted the New Hollywood director as young, brash, educated, and articulate—conforming to the popular image of "easy riders" and "raging bulls"—largely excluded a filmmaker like Ashby, who rose through the ranks as an editor within the traditional studio system and who began his directorial career at the relatively advanced age of forty. Ashby has often been cast as a primarily technical director, whose background as an editor and role as de facto editor on nearly all of his films supposedly made him less interested in story than in camerawork and editing.[24] This impression was encouraged by the fact that Ashby did not attend film school, did not write film criticism, and was relatively inarticulate in discussing his own films. According to Jerome Hellman, producer of *Coming Home* and *Being There*,

> Hal was much more intuitive than most directors: he wasn't a verbal guy. He was much more visual, and worked through feeling rather than words. He was more inclined to hang loose and let things happen. Hal was not cerebral, not particularly articulate. He wasn't a guy who would sit down and tell you what he thought. He would kind of go all around it and leave you to deduce what he meant. I felt that he had a machine inside his head that could see things, but that he had difficulty externalizing that in a way that other people could have access to.[25]

Ashby was by nature a reclusive, extremely private, and highly principled person. He rarely gave interviews, and outside of the effort he put into directing his films, he made practically no attempt to promote his own career. Whether out of a natural reticence or out of a contrarian wish to resist the pressures to "sell out," Ashby stolidly maintained his distance from the career-making institutions of Hollywood, to the point of refusing to attend the Academy Awards the year when he received his only nomination as best director. Over time, Ashby's reticence made it increasingly difficult for him to survive as a filmmaker. What began in the early part of his career as a refusal to indulge in self-promotion gradually evolved into a more destructive tendency. As his career progressed, Ashby developed an unyielding attitude toward those upon whom he depended for the financial backing of his pictures, constructing a wall of paranoia that separated those who performed the creative work of filmmaking and those responsible for financing and producing movies.

Finally, like many of his New Hollywood contemporaries, Ashby was blindsided by widespread changes in the film industry during the 1980s that altered the rules of filmmaking. According to Amy Holden Jones, editor of the ill-fated *Second-Hand Hearts*, "Hal made 1970s movies, and in the 1980s that left him out in the cold." Clearly, there is some truth in the assessment: Ashby worked far more effectively with the literate and countercultural scripts of the early 1970s than with the more mainstream Hollywood projects he was given later in his career. It is no coincidence that the often flaccid and uninspired films Ashby directed in the 1980s bear little resemblance to the masterful and prescient films he made in the 1970s.[26]

TWO

Hollywood Maverick
Ashby, the New Hollywood, and the 1970s

The fact is that filmmaking, although unquestionably predicated on profit and loss like any other industry, cannot be made to please solely the producer's image of the public.
—John Cassavetes, "What's Wrong with Hollywood"

It was a very different experience working with Hal. He did things his own way, and he was very hip, like an old beatnik. He was also very kind and understanding. Directing was not an industrial process for him. It was always a labor of love.
—David Carradine

The city of Ogden, Utah, is situated at the base of the Wasatch Mountains, an hour's drive north of Salt Lake City. The jagged peaks of the Wasatch, rising more than five thousand feet above Ogden, provide a spectacular setting that could serve as the backdrop for a Hollywood western. Ogden, established by the Mormons in the early 1850s and designed by Brigham Young, experienced rapid growth in the late nineteenth and early twentieth centuries, fueled by the arrival of both Mormon and non-Mormon settlers. By the turn of the century, Ogden was Utah's second largest city, an important rail hub and distribution center for the intermountain west.

William Hal Ashby was born in Ogden on September 4, 1929, less than two months before the stock-market crash plunged the United States into the Great Depression. Though Ashby rarely talked about his Utah childhood, the place most likely had symbolic significance for him. Indeed, the landlocked setting might be described as the antithesis of the Hollywood hills and the shores of Malibu. Ogden may have signified to Ashby the relic of a past to which he could never return, like the sad, empty house the young sailor Meadows tries to visit on his way to the brig in *The Last Detail*.

Ashby's parents were Mormon, respectable churchgoing people, if not particularly devout. Soon after the birth of their first two children, two daughters, James Ashby went to South Africa to serve on a church mission, where he stayed from 1915 to 1918, leaving his milk bottling operation and dairy store in the hands of his wife, Eileen. After his return, James fathered two boys: John ("Jack") in 1925 and William ("Hal") four years later. Ashby's early years were a subject he kept closely guarded. As Paul Frizler noted in his account of a 1978 interview with the director, Ashby was "unwilling to dwell on his unhappy childhood"—so much so, it seems that he made up or changed facts about his early life. Ashby told Frizler, for example, that he was born in 1932 (not 1929) and that his parents were non-Mormons.[1] He also claimed to have graduated from Utah State University, though he in fact never completed high school.[2] Ashby's reluctance to talk about his childhood and his efforts to create a new autobiography suggest a desire to bury his own past as deeply as possible, to distance himself from his family and from his Utah Mormon origins. After leaving Ogden at the age of eighteen, Ashby would return only twice: once in the early 1950s and again some two decades later for his mother's funeral.

Ashby's lack of personal revelation seems to have been a constant trait, even with those he considered close friends. Over the years, his refusal to discuss his personal life severely limited his relationships with those around him. "Hal never, ever, even in the most intimate moments, would reveal anything to me about his past," said Jerome Hellman, Ashby's producer on *Coming Home*. "I knew no more about him when he died than when I first met him."[3] According to David

CHAPTER 2

Hamburger, first assistant director on two of Ashby's films, "Hal never talked to anyone about his childhood: that was his problem with everyone. He made everyone feel like they were his favorite, but nobody could get past a certain point. The conversations I had with him were pretty close when they were about other people, but there was always that barrier when it came to talking about himself."[4]

This much we know: Ashby was healthy and well adjusted as a younger child. He was popular in school, even something of a ringleader among his peers, and he enjoyed outdoor games, especially football. On weekends, Hal often went hunting or fishing with his father. He was blessed with humor—the seed of what would become the finely honed sense of the comic evident in his films—as well as a mischievous nature sometimes bordering on rebellious. He was not an avid reader (his passion for literature would develop later in life), and he disliked school. "Hal didn't like to be told to sit down and listen," said his brother, Jack.[5]

Ashby's early childhood may not have been idyllic, but at least it was relatively calm. His behavior seems to have changed after his parents' divorce in 1935 and worsened after his father's suicide in 1942. Already confused and disturbed by the divorce, Ashby became "surly and difficult" after his father shot himself.[6] By the time he entered high school, Ashby was engaging in wild behaviors—at least by the standards of the Mormon community. He began hanging out with older kids, smoking cigarettes, and drinking beer. While most of Ashby's classmates were involved in extracurricular activities ranging from ROTC to drama club, Hal was remarkably uninvolved in school life, and his name does not appear on a single page of his junior-class yearbook other than under the mandatory class picture. Ashby also began dating girls: in the winter of his junior year, his girlfriend La Von Compton became pregnant, and as was customary in such instances at the time, they were soon married. A daughter was born in September 1947, just as Ashby should have been enrolling in his senior year of high school.[7]

At some point during the fall and winter of 1947, Ashby decided to leave Ogden for California, even though it meant abandoning his wife and baby daughter. Before hitchhiking out of town in the spring of 1948, Ashby informed his brother, Jack, that he was "going down to Hollywood to work in the movies." Ashby arrived in Los Angeles with no money and no prospects; over the next few years, he bounced from job to job.[8] In 1950, desperate for work, Ashby went to the California Board of Unemployment Office in Los Angeles to ask if there were any positions available at a movie studio. As it happened, there was a position operating a multilith copying machine in Universal's script department. Ashby took the job and then moved to a similar position at Republic Pictures. While at Republic, Ashby began to inquire how he might become a film director. The road most available to him, he was told, was editing. The following year he was accepted as an apprentice editor under the supervision of Robert Swink, an experienced Hollywood editor who had cut dozens of movies at RKO and Paramount, including several of William Wyler's films.

For a young man with limited skills and no high school diploma, the cutting room may have been the best place to enter the world of filmmaking. However, the road in Hollywood, then or now, does not usually lead from apprentice editor to Hollywood director. At that time, only a handful of film editors had made the transition to directing feature films, and even those few—Dorothy Arzner, David Lean, Robert Wise, and Mark Robson—had to learn a new set of skills. Working as an editor involves doing one task extremely well; a director, on the other hand, must have at least a basic understanding of every component of the filmmaking process, from writing, shooting, and editing to production design, acting, music, and special effects. Beyond that, a successful director needs a number of skills that have nothing to do with the technical aspects of filmmaking: working within a budget, dealing with producers and studio executives, smoothing the ruffled egos of actors, and supervising dozens of crew members. Where the job of an editor is relatively solitary—involving long hours spent either alone or with one or two others in the editing room—the job of a director is inherently social, requiring constant interaction with people both on and off the set.

In 1950s Hollywood, becoming an editor meant a long and tedious training: union rules required would-be editors to work for eight years as assistants before they were eligible to edit a feature film. Much of the work of an apprentice or assistant editor was mechanical, involving the mind-numbing task of rerolling, cutting, splicing, and cataloguing film. "What you have to do as an apprentice, I can tell you, is horrendous,"

CHAPTER 2

Ashby told Frizler. "Some good talent has gone down the tubes in the process."⁹ Ashby, who questioned authority, was a rebellious apprentice, frequently arguing with his mentor. Swink, however, accepted Ashby's outbursts, perhaps seeing in him the combination of drive and raw talent needed to survive such arduous training.

Ashby had gifts that made him ideally suited to editing film: meticulous attention to detail, a superlative memory for what was contained in a particular shot or a given take, and an unusually fine sense of both comic and dramatic timing. Ashby's eye for detail was legendary. While making *The Landlord,* after viewing the cut of a sequence by his editor Edward Warshilka, Ashby announced that there was an eyeblink in one shot. Warshilka went back to his Movieola, but, unable to find the eyeblink, he showed the footage to Ashby once again. "It's still there," Ashby told him. When Warshilka went back and looked at the sequence a third time, he discovered the beginning of an eye movement in one frame.

According to cinematographer Haskell Wexler, who worked with Ashby on a total of seven films, Ashby raised film editing to the level of a creative art: "Hal disciplined himself to let the film talk to him, and sometimes it would tell him little stories that were not in the script. Some people think of the editor as just putting the scenes together to make the film play better or faster, basically doing a jigsaw puzzle. But a true editor, which Hal was, may see that what we thought of as the ending of the film should really come at the beginning."¹⁰

During the late 1950s and early 1960s, Ashby worked on a number of films as an assistant editor—including William Wyler's *Friendly Persuasion* (1956) and *The Big Country* (1958); George Stevens's *The Diary of Anne Frank* (1959); Phil Karlson's *The Young Doctors* (1961); Wyler's *The Children's Hour* (1961); and Franklin Schaffner's *The Best Man* (1964)—before being hired as the lead editor on Tony Richardson's *The Loved One* (1965). Producer John Calley, who had hired Ashby to edit *The Loved One,* then introduced him to director Norman Jewison. Jewison was in urgent need of an editor, having inherited *The Cincinnati Kid* from Sam Peckinpah—who had been fired from the picture. Jewison was impressed by Ashby's credentials, and in particular by the fact that he had worked for William Wyler, an especially big name in Hollywood at the time.

Ashby, the New Hollywood, and the 1970s

By this point, Ashby had gone through a radical transformation in his appearance and lifestyle, adopting the countercultural persona that within a few years would come to define the New Hollywood. He had abandoned his conservative Brooks Brothers apparel in favor of Nehru jackets and sandals, grown his hair long, and begun to grow a beard. Ashby had also become politically active in the Civil Rights movement, the antiwar movement, and the farm workers movement. As Jewison describes him, Ashby was the embodiment of the 1960s hippie ethos: "He was the first real sixties guy I knew—tall, thin, wearing beads and sandals, smoking pot, his white-blond hair and beard long and scraggly."[11]

Jewison and Ashby had complementary backgrounds in the film industry: While Ashby had come up through the ranks as a Hollywood editor, Jewison had learned his craft in the electronic medium of television. Where Jewison had a well-developed sense of story and character, Ashby possessed an acute feeling for pacing and visual structure. Ashby quickly became a central creative influence on Jewison's films. "I immediately saw what a force Hal was," said Haskell Wexler. "I have to say, and not to take away from Norman, that Hal's contribution to Norman's films elevated Norman's directorial skill." Beyond their creative collaboration, Ashby and Jewison established an exceptionally close friendship. "I liked Hal because he had such a great sense of humor and was so cynical," said Jewison. "He had a very easygoing personality, he was quick to laugh and very mischievous and rebellious, which fit right into my camp. We also shared a lot of political feelings, although he was from Utah, and I was Canadian and from a very different background."[12]

After *The Cincinnati Kid*, Ashby edited or participated in the editing of three more of Jewison's films: *The Russians Are Coming, The Russians Are Coming; In the Heat of the Night;* and *The Thomas Crown Affair. The Russians Are Coming*—based on a novella by Robert Benchley about a Russian submarine that runs aground on a small island off the New England coast—was a topical, extremely funny take on US-Soviet relations at the height of the Cold War. Ashby's work on the film earned him his first Academy Award nomination for best editing.

While working on *The Russians Are Coming*, Jewison read a screenplay called *In the Heat of the Night*, which follows a black detective from

CHAPTER 2

Philadelphia who becomes involved in a murder investigation while visiting a small Mississippi town. A Hollywood film about race relations in the South was still a radical idea in the mid-1960s, but producers Walter and Harold Mirisch, who were financing the film, gave Jewison their full support. *In the Heat of the Night* became one of the most important Hollywood films of the 1960s—a document that marked the industry's growing political consciousness and earned Ashby his only Academy Award as either an editor or a director.[13]

Ashby's last two collaborations with Jewison were *The Thomas Crown Affair* and *Gaily, Gaily*. On *Thomas Crown*, Ashby acted as both supervising editor and associate producer, consulting with Jewison on such areas as casting, script development, and locations. *Gaily, Gaily*, on which he was associate producer, was an expensive period piece based on Ben Hecht's memoir of life as a cub reporter in 1910 Chicago. Though the film was a commercial flop, it established a relationship between Ashby and a young actor named Beau Bridges, who would be the star of his directorial debut, *The Landlord*. While on location for *Gaily, Gaily*, Jewison realized that he would not have time to direct *The Landlord*, and he offered Ashby the film. Thus Ashby's directorial career began in 1969, almost two decades after he had begun work as an apprentice editor.

Hal Ashby had the good fortune to become a Hollywood director at one of the most exciting moments in the history of American filmmaking. During the three-year period from 1968 to 1970, the New Hollywood movement that had begun in 1967 with *Bonnie and Clyde* and *The Graduate* crested in an American "New Wave" that would redefine American cinema. The list of films released during those years provides overwhelming evidence of a generational shift toward a group of younger directors, working both inside and outside the traditional Hollywood structure. The most influential films of the period included Peter Bogdanovich's *Targets* (1968); Martin Scorsese's *Who's That Knocking at My Door* (1968); John Cassavetes' *Faces* (1968); Bob Rafelson's *Five Easy Pieces* (1970); Brian De Palma's *Greetings* (1968) and *Hi, Mom!* (1970); Dennis Hopper's *Easy Rider* (1969); Haskell Wexler's *Medium Cool* (1969); Michael Ritchie's *Downhill Racer* (1969); Robert Downey's *Putney Swope* (1969); Paul Mazursky's *Bob & Carol & Ted & Alice* (1969) and *Alex in Wonderland* (1970); Robert Altman's *M*A*S*H* (1970); Frank

Ashby, the New Hollywood, and the 1970s

Perry's *Diary of a Mad Housewife* (1970); Richard Rush's *Getting Straight* (1970); Jerry Schatzberg's *Puzzle of a Downfall Child* (1970); and Stuart Hagmann's *The Strawberry Statement* (1970). If these films found much of their inspiration in the work of French New Wave directors like Jean-Luc Godard and François Truffaut, they were also a response to what Thomas Elsaesser describes as "a period of intense collective soul-searching, fuelled by open generational conflict and no less bitter struggles around what came to be known as 'race' and 'gender.'"[14] The filmmakers of the New Hollywood took as their primary responsibility to register the moral malaise of a nation dealing with social issues including the Vietnam War, the Civil Rights movement, and the emergence of feminism.

Ashby's directorial debut was clearly a response both to the social upheavals of the late 1960s and to the stylistic experimentation of the New Hollywood cinema. *The Landlord*'s darkly satirical story involves a young man from the wealthy suburbs of Long Island who purchases an urban tenement, intending to evict its black tenants. Beau Bridges was cast in the lead role of Elgar Enders. Lee Grant, who had worked with Jewison and Ashby in *In the Heat of the Night*, played Elgar's mother, and the stage icon Pearl Bailey played Marge, the matriarch of the tenement. Other excellent casting choices included Susan Anspach as Elgar's eccentric sister, Susie; Marki Bey as his mixed-race girlfriend, Lani; and Diana Sands as Fanny, the older woman Elgar impregnates during a one-night stand.

Norman Jewison would serve not only as the film's producer, but also as Ashby's mentor on his first directorial effort. Jewison was confident in Ashby's ability to direct the actors and get the shots he needed, but he was less sure of his protégé's ability to finish the movie on time and within the established budget: "I was very worried about him falling behind in the shooting, because I thought he would cover too much. He was an editor, always thinking about all the cuts, all the shots you need in order to make the scene."[15]

As Jewison had feared, Ashby began shooting huge amounts of film and falling behind schedule. In addition, the production ran into fourteen straight days of rain on Long Island, which set the schedule back even further. When Walter Mirisch came to the set to express his concern that the shooting was taking too long and would therefore put the

CHAPTER 2

First-time director Ashby with Beau Bridges on location in New York City during the shooting of The Landlord.

film over budget, Ashby replied that he was working as fast as he could. If Mirisch was not happy with the way things were going, Ashby said, he could replace him.

Another point of contention between Mirisch and Ashby involved the lighting of certain sequences. Mirisch complained that the film was too dark and that it was impossible to see the characters' eyes. Ashby explained that he and cinematographer Gordon Willis were trying to stylize the look of the picture: they wanted the ghetto footage to have a warm, dark feeling to contrast with the billowy, white-on-white sequences that they would be shooting on Long Island in a few weeks. "But this is a comedy," Mirisch insisted, "and if you want people to laugh you've got to show the characters' eyes." The argument went on and on, with neither side giving in; finally, Ashby ended the conversation by saying that while he understood Mirisch's position, he was going to make the film his own way. When Mirisch saw the white footage, he eased the pressure on Ashby. Ashby was able to finish the film in sixty-six days, only a few days behind schedule and about $400,000 over budget.

For a debut film, *The Landlord* is impressive both as a demonstration of Ashby's solid grasp of filmmaking technique and as an indication of his ability to work with actors. Bridges is uncannily convincing as the insouciant Elgar; Grant is brilliant as his daffy, castrating mother; and Bailey appears completely in her element as the matriarchal Marge. When the film was released in May 1970, it was well received by critics, who saw it as a remarkable effort by a first-time director. John Mahoney praised the "superb performances" Ashby had elicited from his cast as well as the director's sense of comic timing: "The film survives even when [Ashby] overworks a scene or overplays the show to take a flourishing bow."[16] Richard Harmet singled out the movie's "sharp, hilarious jabs at white pretentions," and found that it succeeded in blending comedy with "the poignancy of a young man's leaving to come to terms with life and himself," while Clayton Riley's review in the *New York Times* called *The Landlord* "a brilliant piece of cinema craftsmanship, rising above its sometimes politically incorrect commentary to display an awesome clarity in the orchestration of some living Blood rhythms."[17]

Ashby's next film, *Harold and Maude*, began as the senior thesis of a UCLA film school student by the name of Colin Higgins. Higgins's script was a black comedy involving a depressive young man who finds love and unconditional acceptance in a relationship with an eccentric woman old enough to be his grandmother. The screenplay had found its way to Robert Evans, head of production at Paramount, who bought it and put it into preproduction. The script Ashby shot stayed close to Higgins's original screenplay, which was set in Los Angeles. Ashby did make one important change: arguing that there were already enough movies depicting Southern California, Ashby pushed for a change of venue to either Boston or Northern California. Boston was Ashby's first choice, but since shooting on the east coast would have added to the film's budget, it was decided to shoot in the vicinity of San Francisco.

For a character-based film like *Harold and Maude*, proper casting was a major concern. Paramount had already spoken to the veteran stage and screen actress Ruth Gordon about playing the role of Maude, but Ashby insisted on choosing his own Maude, scheduling trips to both New York and London to meet with potential leading ladies. In New York, he met with several actresses, including Gordon, in his room at the Drake Hotel. When Gordon asked Ashby if he wanted her for the role, he told her that he was still thinking: he would be flying to London that night to interview some other actresses before deciding. Gordon was taken aback by Ashby's response, having assumed the role was hers for the asking. Ashby saw several more actresses before agreeing that Gordon was, in fact, the best choice.

For the role of Harold, Ashby auditioned about thirty young actors before narrowing the field to six finalists. In mid-December 1970, Gordon tested with the six prospective Harolds at Ashby's house in the Hollywood hills. One of the finalists was a young actor named Bud Cort. Only twenty-one, he already had a good deal of film experience, having appeared in two of Robert Altman's films, *Brewster McCloud* and *M*A*S*H*, as well as Stuart Hagmann's *The Strawberry Statement* and Jack Smight's *The Traveling Executioner*. Cort was the fifth actor to read, and Gordon felt that with him playing Harold the scene finally came to life: "We weren't actors remembering lines; Harold was really telling Maude."[18] Apparently, Ashby noticed the natural affinity between the two actors as well.

As he had when making *The Landlord,* Ashby surrounded himself with a highly supportive crew. Ashby's friend Chuck Mulvehill had originally been hired as production manager, but Ashby insisted he be promoted to producer. As art director, Ashby chose Michael Haller, who had been responsible for the innovative design of George Lucas's science-fiction film *THX-1138*. Along with Mulvehill, Haller was to become one of Ashby's most frequent collaborators, serving as production designer on six of the director's eleven films and visual consultant on two others.

Haller's contribution to *Harold and Maude* would consist primarily of scouting locations on the San Francisco peninsula, where the foggy weather provided the kind of misty, flat light that would help to create the film's otherworldly mood. The movie was filmed at various sites in the Bay Area. Maude's house was a converted antique railway passenger car on Oyster Point, and Harold's home was the Cameron Estate, a mansion valued at $7.5 million, or five times the film's total budget.

The biggest problem Ashby faced during the process of assembling the crew for *Harold and Maude* was finding a cinematographer. Ashby wanted to work with Gordon Willis again, but since Willis was part of the New York union local, the California local refused to let him work in California. Ashby next gave a copy of the script to Conrad Hall, but he was not interested, and his third choice, Haskell Wexler, was unavailable. Wexler recommended John Alonzo, a young cinematographer who had shot *Bloody Mama* for Roger Corman. Alonzo, one of the first Chicano cameramen in the guild, was a perfect choice for *Harold and Maude:* his impact can be seen clearly on the striking visual style of the film.[19]

The shooting for *Harold and Maude* was as relaxed as that of any film in Ashby's career. After spending the day shooting footage, the entire cast and crew would gather in the evening to watch the dailies. "Hal would sit up front on a mattress with the groupies and pot-smokers," recalled Ellen Geer, who played Harold's computer date Sunshine Dore. "The cameramen and crew would be in the back drinking beer, and everyone else would be somewhere in the middle." Throughout the shoot, Ashby was "very approachable, like an older hippie": "Hal let you do what you wanted in your scenes, and he got the humanity out of the script. He always followed his instincts."[20]

Sometimes, however, the working conditions became a bit *too* relaxed. When Paramount executive Peter Bart dropped in during the third week of shooting, he saw that the production had already fallen behind schedule. Ashby was shooting a scene at the Chasen house, and during the lunch break Bart took the director aside and handed him a one-way ticket to Los Angeles, telling him that "if he kept on getting stoned and losing days, he might as well use the ticket 'cause he wasn't going to stay on the movie."[21] Ashby took Bart's advice seriously, and the shooting remained on schedule from that point on.

Harold and Maude opened in mid-December 1971, amid a number of studio releases more appropriate, to the season. The week's top-grossing film was Disney's animated *Lady and the Tramp*, followed by the musical *Fiddler on the Roof* (directed by Ashby's former mentor Norman Jewison), and the Clint Eastwood vehicle *Dirty Harry*. Unsurprisingly, given the film's brand of morbid humor, *Harold and Maude* bombed.

CHAPTER 2

Few reviews of the film were positive. While Susan Stark of the *Detroit Free Press* and Charles Champlin of the *Los Angeles Times* bravely complimented the film, most critics' opinions ranged from negative to outright hostile. *Variety*, for example, dismissed *Harold and Maude* as "a tasteless offbeat comedy . . . that had all the fun and gaiety of a burning orphanage."[22]

After the disappointing opening, the studio began relegating *Harold and Maude* to the bottom of double bills. Ashby and Mulvehill were stunned by the negative reaction to the film. "[We] couldn't believe it," said Mulvehill. "The scripts and phone calls that had been coming in just stopped. . . . It was really a rude awakening."[23] The film's originality was immediately recognized by some viewers, however. In France, *Harold and Maude* was a major hit, and Cort won the Crystal Star award for his performance—only the third American actor to do so. The film played in French theaters for three years, the longest run any American movie had ever enjoyed in that country.

Over time, *Harold and Maude* began to develop a following in North America as well, playing especially well in college towns and smaller art-film houses. It played for 115 straight weeks in Minneapolis, seventy-two weeks in Detroit, ninety-two weeks in Boston, and 112 weeks in Montreal. Gradually, *Harold and Maude* began to be recognized as a highly original and brilliantly crafted work of cinema: in 1997 it was put on the National Film Registry's list of significant American films.

Harold and Maude may have not been well received, but Ashby was still a known quantity with two films under his belt, and in the early part of 1972, he entered discussions with MGM about directing a remake of *The Postman Always Rings Twice* (1946), to be called *Three-Cornered Circle*. Jack Nicholson, who had struck up a friendship with Ashby, had already been cast as the male lead, but a lead actress had not yet been cast. Nicholson and Ashby wanted Nicholson's girlfriend, Michelle Phillips, for the part, and Ashby did a screen test of Phillips in an attempt to convince the studio. Phillips tested well, but apparently not well enough for MGM executives, who told Ashby to find another actress. Rather than acquiesce to the studio's demands, Ashby and Nicholson walked away from the project.

It was not long before Ashby and Nicholson would have another

Ashby, the New Hollywood, and the 1970s

chance to work together. Gerald Ayres, a vice president for creative affairs at Columbia, had come across a novel called *The Last Detail*. The novel, by Darryl Ponicsan, involved a pair of petty naval officers—Billy "Bad-Ass" Buddusky and "Mule" Mulhall—who are assigned to take a young seaman from the Norfolk naval base to the navy prison in Portsmouth, New Hampshire. Ayres sent a copy to Nicholson, whom he felt would be perfect for the role of Buddusky, and he commissioned Robert Towne to write the screenplay. Robert Altman was Ayres's first choice to direct the picture, but when Altman declined, Nicholson suggested Ashby. Ayres agreed with the choice: "I thought this was a picture that required a skewed perspective, and that's what Hal had. He felt to me like a brother in the fraternity of the self-styled underground of the early 70s."[24]

Towne had finished the first draft of his script in November 1971, before Ashby became involved with the project. Though the script stays faithful to the spirit of Ponicsan's novel and to the overall story line, the end is very different. In Towne's version, Buddusky does not die, and Mule does not end up in prison. Instead, Towne wrote an ending more suitable for a Hal Ashby film: neither comic nor entirely tragic, it leaves the emotion of the final shot to the viewer's discretion.

Since the film relied so heavily on the performances of the three central characters, correct casting was as important as it had been for *Harold and Maude*. Nicholson's friend Rupert Crosse had been cast as Mulhall even before Ashby came onto the picture, but less than two months into preproduction, he was diagnosed with terminal cancer. On November 15, just days before shooting was to begin, Ashby cast Otis Young in the role. A Marine veteran who had served in the Korean War before beginning a career as a stage and television actor, Young was well cast as the world-weary African-American sailor. For the third lead, the part of Seaman Larry Meadows, Ayres and Ashby decided to cast an unknown actor. After several auditions, they settled on a tall, gawky actor named Randy Quaid, whose on-screen presence perfectly captured the awkward innocence of Meadows's character.

The actors, Nicholson in particular, responded brilliantly to Ashby's relaxed, improvisational style. As Nicholson's biographer Patrick McGilligan put it,

CHAPTER 2

> Where actors were concerned, Ashby's method was laissez-faire (the kind of method Jack preferred). The director set up the environment and let the actors do their jobs. Ashby had a visual simplicity whereby he let the scene more or less create itself. His style was to observe through an open frame and to let the actors move freely through that space. His close-ups were modest, his pullbacks and other camera moves unobtrusive. Almost patriarchal, Ashby would lean back in his chair on the set, saying nothing, watching.[25]

The film was shot on location between November 1972 and January 1973 in Washington, New York, Boston, Toronto, and other locales along the Atlantic coast. Michael Chapman, who would later shoot *Taxi Driver* and other films for Martin Scorsese, made his debut as cinematographer after working for five years as Gordon Willis's chief camera operator. Chapman's skilled camerawork, especially in hand-held shots, added the feel of a documentary to the film.

During postproduction, the studio's major issue concerned the film's language. Columbia felt the characters' language was so coarse as to keep the film from reaching as large an audience as it might otherwise. In fact, the film probably did contain more "language" than any Hollywood movie released up to that time, but Ashby felt that the dialogue as it had been written and shot was needed for an accurate portrayal of the characters and the situation, and he argued that removing a certain percentage of the swear words would do little to make the film more palatable. For screenwriter Robert Towne, the use of rough language also served a thematic purpose. "In the service you swear a lot precisely because you are impotent," Towne maintained. "When Columbia said wouldn't it be better to have twenty 'motherfuckers' instead of forty 'motherfuckers,' I said no, because then you'd lose the point that these men can't do anything more than swear. The repetitiousness is an index of their inability to do anything else."[26] Ashby convinced Columbia to preview the film in San Francisco with the language intact, and the audience liked the picture so much that the studio dropped its objections. The film was released in December 1973, exactly two years after the ill-fated opening of *Harold and Maude*.

With *The Last Detail*, Ashby achieved a style that was ideal for a small-budget, character-based film. He would allow his actors relatively free rein, knowing that his abilities as an editor would allow him to put together a tight, engrossing picture. *New York Times* critic Vincent Canby compared the film favorably to Cassavetes' *Husbands*, remarking that *The Last Detail* had "the sense of extraordinary life of Cassavetes' films without those great arid patches of actorish nonsense."[27] William Walling, writing for *Society*, noted the film's "structure of visual counterpoint": as the characters travel north and the weather becomes colder, "we experience simultaneously the growing warmth among the characters."[28]

The film would garner a number of nominations and win several awards, giving Ashby his first taste of the mainstream success he had always dreamed of achieving. Nicholson was nominated for both the Golden Globe and the Academy Award, losing out in both cases to Jack Lemmon for his performance in *Save the Tiger*. But Nicholson made a clean sweep of practically every other major award: best actor awards at Cannes, from the British Academy of Film and Television Arts (BAFTA), and from both the National Society of Film Critics and the New York Film Critics. Randy Quaid received nominations for best supporting actor from the Golden Globes, the Academy Awards, and BAFTA; and Robert Towne's screenplay earned nominations from both the Academy and the Writer's Guild and won the BAFTA award.

Ashby was approaching—if not yet quite part of—the elite company of A-list Hollywood directors. Clearly identified as one of the rising stars of the New Hollywood, he was known as a director who worked well within a darkly comic sensibility. During postproduction on *The Last Detail*, Ashby began talks with producer Saul Zaentz about directing *One Flew over the Cuckoo's Nest*. Zaentz and his co-producer Michael Douglas had commissioned Ken Kesey to write a screenplay based on his popular novel, and Ashby discussed the script with both Kesey and Douglas. By the early summer of 1973, however, the project appeared headed for trouble. Ashby received a worried letter from Kesey. "I fear for our project. The hit I get off Saul [Zaentz] is that he got popped a little harshly the last time out as a producer, which is causing him to want to play this hand a little closer to his belt."[29] Kesey was concerned that the vision the producers had of the film was too mainstream: the film, he felt, should be "madness communicating, not [just] a film about madness."

CHAPTER 2

Whatever creative differences existed between the producers and their writer and director were serious enough to break the deal: by late July, both Ashby and Kesey were off the picture. According to Peter Biskind, the problems with the film involved strained relations between Ashby and Zaentz. "Zaentz was the kind of creative producer Ashby hated. The director was too withdrawn and suspicious, refused to say how he would approach the book, so [Zaentz and Douglas] walked away [and] found Milos Forman." This explanation seems plausible enough: Ashby worked best with minimal creative interference from producers and studio executives and was able to work closely with certain producers on rare occasions. One of these was *Shampoo*, on which the producer Warren Beatty was also the co-writer and lead actor; another was *Coming Home*, where Ashby had a relatively harmonious collaboration with Jerome Hellman.

Around the time of Ashby's involvement with *Cuckoo's Nest*, Warren Beatty gave him a copy of the screenplay he had written with Robert Towne for *Shampoo*. The story is a modern adaptation of William Wycherley's restoration comedy *The Country Wife* (1675), in which the protagonist, a man named Horner, lets it be known throughout all of London that his doctor has rendered him a eunuch. As a result of this deception, the husbands trust Horner with their wives, allowing him free rein to seduce them. In discussing the possibilities for a screenplay, Beatty and Towne decided the contemporary equivalent to Wycherley's seducer would be a Beverly Hills hairdresser. Towne wrote his first draft of the script, at that point called *Hair*, in 1970 and showed it to Beatty. Beatty disliked Towne's script: he saw the film as needing a single strong female lead, which he thought should be played by Julie Christie, whereas Towne wanted to have two strong women's roles. (The final script ended up having three important female roles, played by Christie, Goldie Hawn, and Lee Grant). Beatty also wanted to introduce and develop a political subtext. After months of wrangling between the two writers, the project was put aside.

By 1973, when Beatty talked to Towne about reviving the idea of the film, he had formulated a more concrete idea of how to add the political element to the story: they would set the action of the film during the day and night of the 1968 presidential election. Beatty had originally considered directing the film himself, but by this point he had decided against it. He felt that as producer, star, and co-writer, he had enough responsibilities without also directing, and he thought that Ashby's liberal politics, his unique comic sensibility, and his relatively unobtrusive use of the camera would make positive contributions to the film.[30]

In late November 1973, Beatty, Towne, and Ashby spent six days in the Beverly Wilshire Hotel putting together a script based on the existing drafts Towne and Beatty had created. While Ashby contributed some of his own ideas, his primary role was that of a mediator between the other two men, both of whom had strong creative visions and equally strong egos. "We had a volatile time," remembered Towne. "Hal was in the middle, and thank God he was. We'd talk about it, and then I'd go into the next room and write ferociously and come out. We were all a little thrown by the surprising quality of the work, and the speed."[31] During their discussion sessions, Beatty continued to push for a more political statement, while Towne resisted, seeing the movie more along the lines of a light-hearted social farce like Ingmar Bergman's *Smiles of a Summer Night*. As the debate grew more heated, Beatty became more stubborn, insisting that Towne's story was not sufficiently political. The final result, it is generally agreed, was about half Towne and half Beatty.

As the director of *Shampoo*, Ashby headed a production team that was as accomplished as any that could have been assembled at the time. The cinematographer, László Kovács, had shot such New Hollywood films as Peter Bogdanovich's *Targets*, Dennis Hopper's *Easy Rider*, Robert Altman's *A Cold Day in the Park*, and Bob Rafelson's *Five Easy Pieces;* the production designer, Richard Sylbert, had worked with Sidney Lumet, Mike Nichols, and Roman Polanski; and the editor, Robert Jones, had been Ashby's collaborator on *The Last Detail*. The cast was equally strong, with Beatty, Julie Christie, Goldie Hawn, Lee Grant, and Jack Warden in the major roles.

Later, Ashby admitted to difficulties working with Beatty, who as both producer and lead actor exercised a great deal of control over the production: "Many times it wasn't easy. It was difficult because I was working with an actor who was also the producer of the film, and we spent a little bit of time trying to differentiate between [those roles], never with much success."[32]

CHAPTER 2

Those present on the set of *Shampoo* had differing impressions of the dynamic between the two men. "I wasn't aware of tension on the set," said assistant director Art Levinson. "Hal was very quiet, but I think he handled it well. I didn't feel any division." Others, however, remembered the situation very differently. According to editor Robert Jones, "Everybody on the set except me was with Warren, and it was tough on Hal. I felt a lot of tension on the set: Warren and Towne would be off whispering in one corner of the set, and Hal would be sitting in the other corner." Haskell Wexler, who visited the set occasionally, remarked: "Hal was like an office boy on that film, and he wasn't used to being that way. Warren chewed Hal up and spit him out."[33] At times, Beatty would insist on doing a scene his way first before allowing Ashby to get the takes he wanted. What prevented Ashby from throwing up his hands in despair was his knowledge that he could ultimately craft the film he wanted in the editing room, no matter how much Beatty tried to control the shooting.

The film remains one of Ashby's best, the fortunate result of the collaboration between Beatty, Towne, and Ashby, not to mention the highly talented cast and crew. *Shampoo* was not only Ashby's first significant commercial success, but also the greatest critical triumph he had enjoyed to this point in his career. The film earned over $40 million domestically and another $15 million overseas, making it the top grosser in the history of Columbia up to that time. Reviews touted Ashby as a talented director of comedy and compared the style of the film to the work of Altman and Mazursky. Vincent Canby of the *New York Times* called *Shampoo* a "witty, revolutionary, foul-mouthed comedy-of-manners cast in the fairly conventional frame of a story about the comeuppance of a small-town Casanova."[34] In *New York*, Judith Crist described it "the *La Dolce Vita* for the 1970s . . . a black-tinted comedy that touches memorably and painfully at the roots of our moral malaise." Even critic Pauline Kael, not generally a fan of Ashby's directorial style, considered the film "the most virtuoso example of sophisticated kaleidoscopic farce that American moviemakers have ever come up with."[35]

Shampoo would receive a number of nominations and awards. The screenplay was nominated for an Academy Award—losing, however, to Frank Pierson's script for *Dog Day Afternoon*—and it took the prize for best screenplay from both the National Society of Film Critics and the Writer's Guild. Beatty, Hawn, and Christie all received Golden Globe nominations, though none of them was similarly honored by the Academy. Jack Warden was nominated for best performance as a supporting actor, and Lee Grant was nominated for and won the Oscar for best supporting actress.

Ashby's fifth film, *Bound for Glory*, was based on the autobiography of legendary folk singer Woody Guthrie. Guthrie's life was a subject that held a great deal of interest for Ashby. Like him, Guthrie had risen from modest origins to achieve artistic success. Further, he was a countercultural icon: a social activist with populist, anticorporate politics. As in *Shampoo*, Ashby would have the opportunity to frame a larger political statement within the story of a single individual.

Ashby's most difficult task in making *Bound for Glory* was finding an actor to play Guthrie. Ashby and the film's producers, Harold Leventhal (Guthrie's longtime business manager) and Robert Blumofe, asked several actors—including Jack Nicholson, Dustin Hoffman, and Robert de Niro—before settling on David Carradine. Carradine, known primarily for his work in the *Kung Fu* television series, had a reputation for being moody and difficult. Ashby, however, was convinced that he was right for the role, and he was able to convince the executives at United Artists to let Carradine play the part.

The other question mark was the film's location. Robert Getchell's script focused on a four-year period in Guthrie's life, from 1936 and 1940, covering the "Okies'" migration to California and Guthrie's beginnings as a songwriter. Ashby originally intended to shoot the entire film in the area around Pampa, Texas, the town in the Texas panhandle where Guthrie lived before moving to the west coast. By the 1970s, however, Pampa had become too prosperous to serve as the Depression-era location Ashby required, and he asked production designer Michael Haller to find a more suitable site. Haller scouted possible locations in Texas, Oklahoma, Kansas, and Colorado before deciding to use several small towns in central California. The storefronts of 1930s Pampa were shot in the town of Isleton, near Stockton, while the town's residential area was created from the town of Allensworth, near Bakersfield. Haller's crew also built a realistic migrant workers' camp in the Stockton area.

CHAPTER 2

While shooting the camp scenes, Ashby had the seven hundred extras playing the migrants live in the camp for ten hours each day so that they could absorb the psychological patterns of the people they were portraying.

Haller's painstaking attention to detail helped create the accurate look of the film. For the scenes involving cars, Haller used beat-up automobiles from 1924 to 1934, and for the scene in which Guthrie tries to unionize the women meatpackers, he found a packing plant in Walnut Grove that still used original 1930s equipment. A Depression-era trolley was restored for the scene in which Guthrie rides the trolley to the radio station. The dramatic dust storm near the beginning of the film was powerfully recreated by special effects director Sass Bedig, using forty tons of specially mixed dust propelled by airplane engines that could whip up seventy-five-mile-per-hour winds. All of these design elements were captured by Haskell Wexler's brilliant cinematography, which would earn him an Academy Award.

If *Bound for Glory* went far beyond the standard Hollywood biopic in its state-of-the-art cinematography, special effects, and production

David Carradine rehearses a song in the character of Woody Guthrie, as cinematographer Haskell Wexler and camera operator Garrett Brown look on.

design, its most important innovation was the use of the Steadicam in a feature film. The Steadicam, a camera stabilization system invented and operated by Garrett Brown, allowed the camera operator to run, climb steps, and move swiftly over rough terrain without the jerking and bouncing of regular hand-held cameras. The most spectacular use of the Steadicam in *Bound for Glory* occurs in a scene that takes place in a migrant camp. The camera cranes down to find Carradine sitting on an old car and then continues down to the ground, where the cameraman steps off the crane and follows Carradine under tents and through narrow passageways and crowds of migrants. Brown, who planned and performed the shot, described the historic event:

> No one had ever taken a camera off a crane and made this kind of combination shot. I was pretty nervous about the crane shot, because I had never seen an object like that before, much less been on one. We had a rehearsal, and then we did one take. On the first take, Carradine didn't recognize this object and didn't see a camera anywhere and wasn't sure when he was supposed to start. Then we did two more takes, and then everyone was waiting to see if this was any good. I had no idea whether it had worked or not. We had a spectacular screening of the footage two nights later, and when the shot went by everybody stood up and applauded and made a big fuss over me and Haskell. What was amazing was that Ashby had allowed this to happen without ever seeing this machine.[36]

All this innovation came with a considerable price tag. Originally set at $4.4 million—already three times the cost of *Harold and Maude*—the budget of *Bound for Glory* continued to swell as shooting went on, finally wrapping after 118 days. The production used 120 different sets as well as hundreds of extras, and Ashby ended up shooting an extraordinary 800,000 feet of film. The total cost of the production was close to $10 million, a high-budget film by the standards of the mid-1970s. Unfortunately, spending more money did not translate into a creating a commercially successful film: despite its visual beauty and a striking performance by Carradine, *Bound for Glory* was a major disappointment at the box office, failing to engage audiences in the way Ashby's last three movies had. When the film opened at the end of October 1976, it played to mostly empty houses.

Critics, however, generally praised *Bound for Glory*, singling out its acting, direction, and cinematography in particular. Joseph McBride called it "a majestic film, the most ambitious film made in the United States since *The Godfather Part II*, and one of those rare pictures that are made with the lavish resources, meticulous care, and concern for epic breadth that characterize the way the great Hollywood movies used to be made."[37] Diane Jacobs called *Bound for Glory* "an exhilarating film, as American in its own rootless way as the other great and more homely saga of westward-movers, John Ford's *The Grapes of Wrath*."[38] Most critics agreed that Ashby had elicited a particularly fine performance from Carradine. According to McBride, Carradine's performance contains "charm and sensitivity, yet with an undercurrent of mangy meanness and animal ferocity—in sum total one of the few convincing portraits of an artist ever put on the screen." Carradine's Guthrie is a "reserved, uncertain, slowly developing twentieth-century folk artist whose evolution can be detected in small increments emerging in the course of experience."

A number of critics, however, found that *Bound for Glory* suffered from a lack of dramatic intensity. Vincent Canby, while lauding Carradine's "dry, haunted performance," commented that the screenplay failed to match "the intensity and drive of its largely mysterious central character."[39] Stanley Kauffman found the film "stilted and dated," concluding that "it all stews in warmed-over Steinbeck sauce."[40] Pauline Kael complained that while *Bound for Glory* had "the visual beauty of a great movie," it missed the mark by overly glorifying Guthrie.[41]

In fact, the film must be judged at least a partial failure: while it contains a number of memorable scenes, *Bound for Glory* lacks the tight narrative structure that had marked each of Ashby's previous efforts. The film did manage to collect six Academy Award nominations—for best picture, adapted screenplay, cinematography, editing, musical score, and costume design—but Ashby was disappointed that it only took home only two awards, for Leonard Rosenman's score and Wexler's cinematography.[42]

In July 1976, Ashby began preproduction on *Coming Home*, a drama about the experience of soldiers returning from the Vietnam War. *Com-

ing Home is set in 1968, just after the Tet Offensive, a moment when the sense of excitement and optimism about America's role in the conflict is tipping into disillusionment. Specifically, the film is the story of Sally Hyde, the wife of a Marine captain, Bob Hyde, who begins an affair with a paraplegic veteran. But in a more general sense, it is the story of the devastating effects of the war on its soldiers and their families.

Ashby saw the role of the paraplegic, Sergeant Luke Martin, as ideally suited to the talents of Jack Nicholson, but Nicholson was preparing to direct and star in his comic western *Goin' South*. When both Al Pacino and Sylvester Stallone also turned the part down, Ashby decided to cast Jon Voight in the role, even though he had been thinking of Voight for the supporting role of Bob Hyde. Moving Voight to the role of Luke was the most important casting decision Ashby made on *Coming Home*, and one of the wisest casting choices of his career. Voight put himself body and soul into the role and ultimately turned in the most riveting performance of the year.

Between July and November 1976, Waldo Salt wrote two drafts of the script, and he was beginning work on a final draft when he suffered a heart attack. Only weeks before shooting was to begin, Ashby brought in his former editor Robert Jones to finish the script. "We had three or four scripts," Ashby told journalist Rick Honeycutt, "an ending that didn't work, and the first thirty or forty pages that weren't any good."[43] Of all Ashby's films of the 1970s, *Coming Home* was made with the roughest script. Much of the film's dialogue was either written at the last minute or improvised by the actors themselves: Ashby estimated that eighty percent of the dialogue was written by the actors.[44] Before filming the climactic confrontation scene, Bruce Dern, Jane Fonda, and Jon Voight did several improvisations, recording the dialogue on a tape recorder and then transcribing it before shooting. In Voight's final speech to the high school, the scene was cut together from semi-improvised takes in which different dialogue was used.

The film opened in February 1978 to both good box office and favorable reviews. Charles Champlin noted how "the movie effectively translated a changed national consciousness into credible and touching personal terms," while Jack Kroll praised the acting performances as well as Wexler's "masterful" cinematography, which provided "a luminous dramatizing of detail."[45] *Coming Home* was to be Ashby's most highly awarded film. If it had not been for the release that summer of another Vietnam film, Michael Cimino's acclaimed *The Deer Hunter*, *Coming Home* might have won even more awards than it did. When the Academy Award nominations were announced, it was clear that the two films would be competing for the major Oscars: *The Deer Hunter* had nine nominations, *Coming Home* eight. *Coming Home* won in three categories (as compared with five for *The Deer Hunter*), but they were significant ones: best original screenplay, best actor (Voight) and best actress (Fonda). The film was also nominated for six Golden Globe awards, and won in the categories of best actor and best actress in a dramatic role. Voight made a clean sweep of the major awards that year, also winning the best actor award in Cannes, as well as the awards from the Los Angeles Film Critics, the National Board of Review, and the New York Film Critics.[46]

In April 1978, feeling that he needed a change from working with established film studios, Ashby signed a multipicture deal with Lorimar Productions, the company that produced the popular television shows *The Waltons* and *Eight Is Enough*. For Ashby, working with a new production company like Lorimar presented the possibility of greater creative freedom. It also appealed to Ashby that Peter Bart, who had worked on *Harold and Maude* while at Paramount, had recently been installed as president of Lorimar's film division.

Ashby's deal with Lorimar involved developing a number of screen properties that he would either direct or produce. Two projects already in development were *The Hamster of Happiness* (released as *Second-Hand Hearts*) and *Being There*. Feeling that idle time was lost time, Ashby decided that he would shoot the two films for Lorimar back to back: his plan was to finish shooting *Hamster of Happiness* by October 1978 and then take a week off before beginning principal photography on *Being There*.

In July 1978, Ashby began shooting *Second-Hand Hearts,* an offbeat romantic comedy starring Robert Blake and Barbara Harris. *Second-Hand Hearts* was a road movie with a script by Charles Eastman involving the misadventures of two eccentric characters, Loyal Muke and Dusty Dinette, who discover love and happiness in the course of their drive from Texas to California. By the time he directed *Second-Hand Hearts,* Ashby had made six films, all of them artistically successful, and there was no reason to think this one would be any different. Eastman's script was quirky, but it was the kind of narrative that appealed to Ashby: the story of a down-and-out misfit who discovers himself. It was also the kind of low-budget, character-oriented, off-center comedy that, like *The Landlord* and *Harold and Maude,* suited Ashby's sensibility so well. With his friend Robert Blake and Barbara Harris in the lead roles, and Haskell Wexler as cinematographer, it seemed like a project with good prospects for both artistic and commercial success. The film, however, was to be Ashby's first failure, both commercially and aesthetically.[47]

In the late fall of 1978, after completing photography on *Second-Hand Hearts,* Ashby turned his attention to *Being There.* Based on a screenplay by Jerzy Kosinski, adapted from his 1971 novel, the film would star Peter Sellers as Chance the Gardener, a naive simpleton who ends up being courted by the Washington power elite. Like *Coming Home, Being There* had a long gestation period. Kosinski wrote his first draft of the screenplay in 1971, the same year the novel was published. Discussions of the project with his friend Roman Polanski and with American director Sidney Lumet went nowhere. Meanwhile, Peter Sellers had wanted to play the role of Chance ever since he read the novel in the early 1970s. Sellers saw the character of Chance as an ideal vehicle for his acting talents, and he felt the movie would represent a significant departure from the Pink Panther films and other comedies he was making at the time. Sellers approached Ashby about the possibility of directing a film version of *Being There* when they met in London in 1973. Finally, in early 1978, British producer Andrew Braunsberg became involved in the project when Kosinski contacted him about putting together a deal for the movie, and Braunsberg asked Ashby if he would be interested in directing. Ashby agreed to do the film with Sellers in the lead role.

What Ashby saw in Kosinski's script was the same kind of satirical, absurdist humor he had responded to in Colin Higgins's screenplay for *Harold and Maude.* The film would be a witty critique of the media-driven political culture of contemporary America: Chance, who has learned practically everything he knows by watching television and repeating the words and gestures he sees on the screen, becomes a figure of power and influence in Washington through his connection with

CHAPTER 2

Ashby directs Peter Sellers as Chauncey Gardiner in Being There.

the billionaire industrialist Benjamin Rand, played by a perfectly cast Melvyn Douglas.

Ashby sensed from the start that *Being There* would be an important movie. He was right: when the film appeared in theaters in early 1980, it earned $11 million in domestic box office—very respectable for a movie that had cost $7 million to produce. After *Shampoo* and *Coming Home*, it was Ashby's third most commercially successful film. The film also won its share of awards. Sellers won the Golden Globe for best actor in a comedy, best actor from the National Board of Review, and a special achievement award from the London Critics Circle. Melvyn Douglas made a clean sweep of the awards for best supporting actor, including the Oscar, the Golden Globe, and awards from both the Los Angeles Film Critics and the New York Film Critics. Caleb Deschanel, who had been hired as director of photography when Haskell Wexler was unavailable, won the cinematography award from the National Society of Film Critics, and the screenplay, written by Kosinski and an uncredited Robert Jones, won awards from both the British Academy and the Writer's Guild. By the end of the 1970s, Ashby had established himself as one of the most talented, innovative, and capable directors in Hollywood. Ashby's string of successes was nearly unprecedented: there may be no other case in the history of American filmmaking of a director achieving such consistently impressive results in his first seven films.

During the 1980s, Ashby's career declined rapidly for reasons that will be discussed in the final chapter of this book. The four films released between 1981 and 1985 (*Second-Hand Hearts, Lookin' to Get Out, The Slugger's Wife,* and *8 Million Ways to Die*) represented an unbroken string of failures, redeemed in some cases by moments of inspired filmmaking, but rarely rising above a level of mediocrity that is difficult to reconcile with the consistently high quality of his earlier work. When Ashby died in December 1988, after losing a months-long battle with cancer, he became the first director of his generation, and the first major figure of the New Hollywood, to pass away.

THREE

On the Road to Find Out
The Landlord and *Harold and Maude*

When you sit down with a group of people and talk about the great American directors, nobody ever mentions Hal Ashby, but he was one of the greatest. All his pictures have tremendous soul, and he had a huge range. He was a wonderful storyteller: he challenged us with the stories he told. A lot of the subjects he took on were tough ones. He thought that if the truth needed to be told, it was time for him to hold up the mirror. No one could intimidate him.
—Beau Bridges

Hal had great respect for the image, for the reinforcement of storytelling ideas visually.
—Gordon Willis

Ashby's first two films as a director, *The Landlord* and *Harold and Maude*, are social comedies that focus on young male protagonists. Both films also reflect, through narrative and characterization, the sense of confusion and alienation that marked the late 1960s and early 1970s. The central characters of these films suffer from a sense of personal and social dislocation. Elgar, in *The Landlord*, is a naive innocent with little understanding of the world, while Harold is a social misfit unable to adjust to what society requires of him. Both young men still live with their parents, who in both cases create a home environment that is constrictive, infantilizing, and psychologically destructive. Both films are concerned with psychically rootless characters who are in one way or another trying to make new homes for themselves. In their own ways, both *The Landlord* and *Harold and Maude* encourage breaking through a stifling code of traditional values to discover a more open and spontaneous means of interacting with the world.

The characters that appear in these early films display a striking degree of neurosis. In *The Landlord*, as in *Harold and Maude*, the nuclear family is primarily responsible for the protagonist's problems. Elgar flees his narcissistic and overprotective mother and his racist, domineering father for the urban black ghetto. During the course of the film, he evolves from a naive border-crosser in search of adventure to a more fully politicized individual in search of a new community. Similarly, Harold in *Harold and Maude* seeks independence from his domineering upper-class mother by embracing the alternative lifestyle and progressive ideology of the eccentric Maude, a woman nearly four times his age.

Despite the similarities of theme and character between the two films, they are so different in their underlying tone and stylistic vocabulary that they might easily appear to be the work of two separate filmmakers. Both *The Landlord* and *Harold and Maude* use satire to critique an affluent and hypocritical American society, but where *The Landlord* feels at times as though it wants to beat the audience over the head with its message of social hypocrisy and racial inequality, *Harold and Maude* is a far more quirky, lyrical, and aesthetically successful film, a film that perhaps more than any other expresses the originality of Ashby's vision.

The Landlord is the story of Elgar Enders (Beau Bridges), a charming but ineffectual rich kid, who at the age of twenty-nine still lives in his parents' Long Island mansion. Treated like an adolescent, with a mother so self-involved that she can neither remember his birthday nor imagine why he would want to move out and make his own life apart from her suffocating influence, Elgar buys a tenement brownstone in an African-American neighborhood in Brooklyn—the first genuinely

CHAPTER 3

independent act of his life. He intends to evict the brownstone's current tenants and renovate the building for his own personal use. This attempt to assert his independence and to shock his conservative family into some recognition of their own racist complacency produces mixed results: His mother (Lee Grant) is alarmed at the idea that her son is considering such a plan, but she is too preoccupied with her leisure activities and charity events to pay much attention. His father (Walter Brooke), a conservative businessman, is unable to fathom why Elgar would even contemplate such a venture.

When Elgar first visits his new property, he arrives in a white Volkswagen convertible, looking ridiculously out of place in his white suit and a pink tie. Rather than being welcomed by his tenants, he is chased down the street by a gang of local men. On his second visit, he encounters Marge (Pearl Bailey), the eccentric matriarch of the building, who appears in the hallway and points a shotgun at him, accusing him of being a "white rapist." When Marge learns that he is in fact the new landlord, she quickly becomes more accommodating, especially when he produces a rent-book showing that most of the tenants are behind in their payments. Among the other tenants are Fanny Copee (Diana Sands), an attractive black woman who lives with her husband Copee (Louis Gossett Jr.) and their young son, as well as Professor Duboise (Melvin Stewart), a racial militant and teacher in a school for the neighborhood children. Fanny, a former "Miss Sepia" beauty queen, uses her charms to distract Elgar from the fact that she runs an illegal hair salon out of her apartment; Copee, however, threatens Elgar with a bow and arrow, and the landlord is forced once again to flee the premises.

Elgar then visits a black nightclub, where he meets Lanie (Marki Bey), an exotic dancer. Elgar at first assumes that Lanie is white, but she explains to him that she is of mixed racial background. The next day, as Elgar begins making repairs on his tenement, Lanie comes to visit him. Elgar shows her his somewhat grandiose plans for renovating the building. When he returns to his parents' house, he tells his mother that he is in love with a "negro." At a fund-raising party, Elgar introduces Lanie to his family, but none of them suspects that she is non-white.

In the second half of the film, events begin to spin out of control. After a "rent party" at which Elgar gets very drunk, he and Fanny have a one-night stand, during which Fanny becomes pregnant. When Copee finds out about her pregnancy, he threatens Elgar with an ax, but he breaks down before inflicting any harm on Elgar and is taken away to a psychiatric hospital. Fanny has the baby and decides to put it up for adoption, asking Elgar to make sure the adopting parents are white, so the baby can grow up "casual, like her daddy." Instead of putting the baby up for adoption, however, Elgar decides to raise her himself. In the final scene, Elgar appears at Lanie's apartment building, holding the baby they are presumably to raise together.

Ashby was well aware of the potentially explosive racial politics of *The Landlord*, and as he told an audience at the American Film Institute, making an accurate and believable film about the experience of African-Americans was his priority: "All through my life I've had a very close kinship with blacks. But I still knew that I wasn't black, so there were obviously a lot of things I wouldn't have any idea of.... I worked a lot with Diana [Sands] and Lou [Gossett] and Mel [Stewart] and whoever else was into it.... We did a lot of improvising in order to get a lot of the feeling in that sense, because I wanted it to be as honest as it could be."[1]

Despite Ashby's sensitivity to the racial issues raised by *The Landlord*, some African-American viewers took umbrage at the film. One night, at a screening of the film at the Occidental Life Insurance Building in Los Angeles, several black audience members criticized Ashby for not having Copee kill Elgar in the climactic scene in which he attacks him with an ax. While it seems clear that such an outcome would not have been possible in any Hollywood film of the late 1960s, much less a comedy, it is important to recognize the less than satisfying ideological implications of the scene as it appears in the film. The decision to have Copee suffer an emotional breakdown rather than kill Elgar—a decision Ashby discussed with the actor Lou Gossett—preserves the possibility of a comic resolution to Elgar's narrative, but at the same time, it forecloses any liberation on the part of the building's black residents from the kind of racial and social oppression they have suffered for decades. The black man, Copee, is disempowered (in the next scene he is literally tied down to a stretcher in the ambulance that will take him away), while the white man, Elgar, is allowed to continue his social "education." A later scene, in which Elgar is humiliated by Professor Duboise in an empowerment class for black children, only partially redresses the harm created by Elgar's attempt to evict the tenants from the building, his impregnation of Fanny, and Copee's subsequent breakdown. Though Elgar does donate the building to Fanny and her husband at the end of the film, this gesture may be a case of too little, too late. The film itself addresses this issue directly: When Elgar tells Professor Duboise that he does not need the money he might gain by selling the tenement, the professor sarcastically replies, "Did [Fanny] need another baby, too, Mr. Enders?"

Perhaps the most obvious connection between *The Landlord* and Ashby's later films is his use of satire and dark humor. Satire would continue to be one of Ashby's most effective tools in later comedies like *Harold and Maude, Shampoo,* and *Being There.* In *The Landlord,* the satire is less effective than in Ashby's other comedies, because it is directed only at the white family, thus creating an awkward tonal imbalance between the treatment of the white and black characters. While the African-American characters are generally treated with respect—even Copee maintains his dignity—the foibles of the upper-class white family are heightened to the point of ridicule. In the Long Island scenes, satire is nearly eclipsed by parody, so exaggerated are the Enders in their stereotypical WASP attitudes and pastimes.[2] They wear white, play croquet, shoot skeet, and espouse the attitudes of a ruling class totally out of touch with the realities of contemporary America. Their business interests include the manufacture of napalm, deodorant, insecticides and tobacco, and their racial attitudes range from paternalism to outright bigotry.

Though the brand of humor in Ashby's comic films varies from film to film—from the parodic wit of *The Landlord* to the black humor of *Harold and Maude* to the farce of *Shampoo*—all of his films present a form of humor that is tinged with a darker mood, threatening at any moment to veer off into less comforting territory. It is a difficult balance to maintain. While *The Landlord* is generically a comedy, it grows less and less comic in tone as the story progresses: in its final act, it contains both an unwanted pregnancy and an enraged black man threatening to kill the white protagonist with an ax. When the end of the movie reunites Elgar with Lanie and establishes the possibility of a successful family structure, the comic resolution feels forced, especially since there has been relatively little in the narrative that would lead us to believe that Elgar would choose to raise a baby or that Lanie would agree to do it with him.

The problematic tone of *The Landlord* originates with its source material. It is clear from the different drafts of the screenplay that Ashby and others involved in the project were concerned about the tone of the film. Bill Gunn's original screenplay was less comic than the finished film and considerably harder-edged in its depiction of urban racial tensions: it contained references to a white vigilante group that patrolled urban neighborhoods, and it ended with a violent sequence in which Elgar's tenement is burned down by a crowd of angry black men. Even in the final version of the film, some of the situations are too fraught with serious implications to be funny. In the early scene, for example, in which Marge accuses Elgar of being a "white rapist," we understand that the charge, given his innocuous appearance and the fact that he has arrived in a white Volkswagen Beetle filled with potted plants, is ludicrous and, considering the context, perhaps darkly humorous. Yet later in the film, after Elgar has impregnated Fanny and attempted to evict his black tenants in order to create a luxury condominium for himself, we are clearly asked to make a connection between his actions and the rapes, both literal and metaphorical, perpetuated on black people by white men throughout American history. In this case, an ostensibly comic moment is undermined by subject matter that forces us to think about the underlying social tensions in a serious way. While such layering may have been Ashby's intention, the resulting tonal conflict is confusing for the audience.

Another similar example involves the incident in which Elgar's mother, tipsy, lends Marge her charge card to buy material for curtains to decorate Elgar's building. Later in the film, she demands the return of the card when she discovers that Marge has been using it for other acquisitions. This discovery, treated as a comic plot point within the film, comes disconcertingly close to reinforcing the stereotype of African-Americans as dishonest or untrustworthy, a stereotype it seems the film is otherwise attempting to overcome.

Nevertheless, there are a few moments in the film where the humor works effectively and unambiguously. During the dinner party at the Enders', for example, the racist attitudes of Elgar's family—and Elgar's attempts to provoke a reaction from them—are wittily juxtaposed with

CHAPTER 3

the obsequious behavior of the black servants.³ Elgar, upset by his family's obvious disapproval of his plan to buy a tenement in a "colored neighborhood," tells his sister's fiancé, Peter Cootes (Robert Klein), that his family are all octaroons and that the black servants, Heywood and Edith, are "our poor dark relations." This "revelation" brings out the unspoken political and racial tensions that have been lying just beneath the surface of the dinner party, provoking the following interchange:

> Mr. Enders: Elgar! Would you please explain your conduct at the dinner table tonight?
>
> Mrs. Enders: Yes, darling, come on, apologize.
>
> Elgar *(indicating Peter)*: He makes napalm and deodorant.
>
> Peter *(oblivious to the intended insult)*: And insecticide.
>
> Mr. Enders *(to Elgar)*: You lazy, no-good liberal!
>
> Heywood: Should I serve the fish, Mr. Enders?
>
> Mr. Enders *(surprised by Heywood's sudden appearance)*: What? Oh, yes, Heywood, bring in the fish, please. *(To Elgar)* Let me tell you something, Mr. Lincoln. If you march into this house with an armful of pickaninnies from this business venture of yours, the only thing you can expect from me is a swift kick in the ass!
>
> Edith: Mr. Enders, you forgot to finish your soup!
>
> Mr. Enders: I'm just too upset, Edith. Edith, bring in some of that wonderful trout of yours. I think that will help everything.
>
> Edith: Yes, sir.
>
> Heywood *(offering more soup to Elgar)*: Mr. Elgar, you sure love Edith's cold potato soup. You want some more, sir?
>
> *Elgar stands up, takes the soup tureen from Heywood, and pours the white soup over Heywood's head.*

During the scene, Heywood's performance in his role of the shuffling Sambo (played wonderfully by Stanley Greene), and Edith's as the accommodating Black Mammy, border on blackface minstrelsy (a connection made clearer by the reversal when Heywood's face is "whitened" by the soup). The scene ends with Heywood, his head and shoulders still covered in soup, continuing to serve the meal. When Mrs. Enders tells him to "knock it off"—suggesting that his behavior is self-consciously mocking the social dynamics of the situation—he stares back at her, this time without the obsequious smile on his face. The message is clear: African-Americans are willing to play the roles assigned to them by rich whites up to a point, but they can only be pushed so far. It is a lesson that Elgar himself will learn during the course of the film.

If it can be argued that Ashby has a recognizable directorial style, it would be difficult to identify it based on his first film. *The Landlord* is an uneven work, in which moments of inspired filmmaking alternate with less successful passages.[4] The film displays a firm grasp of technique, yet it feels at times like the work of a young director trying too hard to establish his unmistakable personal style. Ashby's use of methods such as disjunctive montage, repeater shots, and straight-to-the-camera monologues might have been effective in creating a unique look for the film, but they also serve as stagy devices that draw audience attention away from the story. They are techniques Ashby would fortunately abandon before making another film.

The Landlord was, in spite of its inconsistencies, an innovative and daring debut for Ashby, and it represented a stylistic departure from the films he had edited for Norman Jewison. As Darren Hughes notes, "Ashby's skills as an editor, now freed by his creative control over the picture, are on display from the opening moments, as he crosscuts between high contrast footage of a racquetball game and the softer, more natural tones of the African-American neighborhood, a visual motif that continues throughout the film." *The Landlord* was the first of a number of successful collaborations between Ashby and a series of talented cinematographers. Ashby worked closely with Gordon Willis on developing a visual style for the film, just as he would with John Alonzo, Michael Chapman, Haskell Wexler, and Caleb Deschanel in his later films. Willis—who was just beginning a career that would include Coppola's *Godfather* films, as well as several films for Woody Allen—helped Ashby to create what they both saw as an appropriately cutting-edge style for the film. According to Willis:

CHAPTER 3

> Hal and I had many discussions about what things should feel like, but I always did what I thought was appropriate, and he always gave me great support for that. Hal and I would usually agree on shots and scene layout. The interpretive level seemed appropriate as far as Hal and I were concerned. I think the only people who perceived the camera work on *The Landlord* as experimental were the studio people and [the producer] Norman Jewison. Norman was a main-line thinker, and he didn't care much for Hal's or my shooting approach. Hal had cut for Norman, but that's very different from directing and delivering images that Norman and the Hollywood mentality were not used to dealing with. The only thing I can say is it didn't fit in the studio mold.

The most consistent visual device Ashby uses in the film is the contrast between the underexposed footage of the ghetto scenes and overexposed footage of the scenes at the Enders' Long Island mansion. According to Willis, this "visual placement of the story" was his idea, but it was one Ashby both embraced and defended. Willis's lighting emphasizes the surface shine of the Enders' world and the sense of mystery and hidden danger in the tenement. The world from which Elgar comes is bright and cold, permeated with light and made to look as sterile as a deodorant commercial. The colors of the ghetto, on the other hand, are heavy and dark, suggesting a place to be feared but at the same time a place that is warm and human. In his more mature films, Ashby might have found this use of such obvious visual cues heavy-handed, but it is nevertheless effective in *The Landlord,* a film that contrasts race, class, and geography.

Another aspect of *The Landlord* that appears to have been experimental was Ashby's editing style. As a former editor, Ashby was unusually exacting in his choices in the editing room and uniquely attuned to the impact of editing on the rhythmic, tonal, and narrative dimensions of a film. In analyzing Ashby's editing style, we can look at a number of different factors, including the overall pace (as quantified by average shot length), the variations in the pace of cutting, the use of crosscutting between one narrative line and another, the use of non-classical editing techniques, and the interaction between the editing and the camerawork (camera angles, camera movement, composition of shots).

The Landlord and *Harold and Maude*

Diane Jacobs called *The Landlord* "the jerkiest of Ashby's films," an accurate observation if we understand that "jerky" means the edits are faster and more noticeable than in Ashby's other films. In fact, the editing rhythm of *The Landlord* is much faster than that of any other film Ashby made, though it is not particularly fast for films of the period.[5] *The Landlord* has an average shot length (ASL) of 7.6 seconds. While considerably shorter than the ASLs of Ashby's subsequent films, this length was about average for the late 1960s.[6]

While average shot length is a useful starting point for understanding the overall pacing of a film, it tells us very little about particular scenes or sections of that film. For example, *Harold and Maude* has an above-average ASL of ten seconds, but what is striking in the film is less the average length of the shots than the degree to which Ashby varies the editing rhythm of the scenes, balancing extremely long takes with much shorter takes and, in the last five minutes of the film, with the use of a rapid cross-cutting montage. Varying the shot length in this way can be used for dramatic effect: longer takes lend more relative importance to the shot, giving the viewer time to think about the composition of the shot and about what is happening visually and dramatically within it. Longer takes also allow the filmmaker to create and sustain a particular mood or feeling, to maintain the focus on a dramatic moment, or to highlight visual aspects of the film.

In general, Ashby's editing style tended toward longer takes rather than fast cutting. With the exception of *The Landlord*, Ashby's films range from a low ASL of ten seconds for *Harold and Maude* to over fourteen seconds for *The Last Detail*.[7] In other words, his average shots last significantly longer than those of typical Hollywood films. Given Ashby's training as an editor on the films of William Wyler and George Stevens, both filmmakers who favored the long take, it is perhaps not surprising that Ashby would also tend in that direction. Long takes played to Ashby's strengths as a director: they allowed his actors more space in which to develop their performances; they provided a more naturalistic or documentary feel (particularly in films like *The Last Detail* and *Bound for Glory*); they foregrounded the visual aspects of each shot (especially the kinds of static, composed shots of which Ashby made extensive use); and they permitted him to exploit the fluidity and

CHAPTER 3

lyricism of the filmic medium rather than heightening the sense of excitement, action, or speed.

In the case of *The Landlord*, what makes the film feel "jerky" is the editing rhythm in different parts of the film. The pace varies considerably from scene to scene, from the more rapid cutting during the rent-party sequence to the much slower cutting in other sections. Ashby's predilection for using a syncopated shot duration as one of his primary tools in establishing rhythm and mood is already evident in *The Landlord;* the difference between his editing style here and in his later films will be merely a matter of degree, as the shifts in editing speed become more subtle. Two good examples of this rhythmic approach to editing can be found in *Bound for Glory*. In an early part of the film, the fast cutting of a fight in the boxcar of a moving train is followed by a very long take of Woody and Slim sitting on top of the train. Later in the film, a very long Steadicam shot of Guthrie walking through the migrant camp is followed by a quickly cut montage of people in the camp. Similarly, in *Being There,* Ashby speeds the editing rhythm when Chance appears on the *Gary Burns Show.* In this scene, as Ashby cuts frequently to the reactions of those watching the show on television, the usually slow pacing of the film accelerates to match the audience's fanatical interest in Chance as a media celebrity.

Diane Jacobs notes that in *The Landlord* the syncopated rhythm created by longer scenes followed by much shorter scenes "meshes nicely with Elgar's own offbeat temperament." While this rationale is a plausible explanation for Ashby's editing style in the film, it is also possible that Ashby, the prize-winning editor, is displaying his prowess in the cutting room by showing more flashy editing techniques in his directorial debut than he would in his later films.

Several sequences in *The Landlord* display particularly skillful editing. One of the most striking is the film's opening sequence, during which Ashby uses dramatic shifts in rhythm as well as extensive cross-cutting to present the contrasts—between white and black, suburbs and city, wealth and poverty—on which the entire film will be based. In a brief shot, we see a classroom of white children, one of whom is Elgar as a boy, being asked by their teacher, "How do we live?" Rather than hear the answer to the question, however, we cut to a long shot of Elgar reclining barefoot in a lawn chair in front of his parents' Long

Island mansion. In a shot that anticipates many of the highly composed tableau shots of Ashby's later films, Elgar is positioned just left of center (perhaps a sly reference to his perceived sense of his own political position) on a wide expanse of lawn, the corner of a swimming pool just visible in the right-hand corner of the frame. As the camera moves in to a medium-long shot, an older black servant dressed in a white waiter's uniform (the Enders' butler Heywood) comes out from the house to the right of Elgar, carrying a glass of lemonade on a tray, walks behind Elgar, and hands him the glass. Elgar thanks Heywood, who goes back toward the house.

As Elgar sips his drink, smacking his lips with satisfaction, we cut to a medium close-up of a well-dressed African-American man on an urban street running to hail a taxi. After viewing the man's failed attempt to get a taxi to stop, we return to the shot of Elgar, who begins speaking directly to the camera: "It's just that I get the feeling that we're all . . . like a bunch of ants." We then cut away from Elgar again to an exterior shot of a barbershop in an urban African-American neighborhood, followed by another shot of the man attempting to hail a taxi. As we see the frustrated man mouth the word *motherfucker,* we cut back to a medium shot of Elgar, who continues his monologue: "Everybody wants his own home, and I've never had a place of my own."

At this point, Ashby begins cross-cutting more rapidly between shots of dilapidated tenements; a game of squash between two white men dressed identically in white shoes, shorts, and tennis shirts; and close-up shots of Elgar, now bare-chested and drinking from a bottle of juice, framed against a white background. As the credits roll and the music of the song "Brand New Day" begins—the song's upbeat lyrics ironically juxtaposed against the stark visual images of the ghetto—Elgar explains his plans for the building he has just bought, his comments gradually revealing the rather unsavory nature of his project: "I want to get all the goddamn tenants out. It's an old goddamn house—lots of molding. I want to rip out all the floors all the way to the skylight . . . and hang this big goddamn modern spectacular psychedelic son-of-a-bitching light from the ceiling!" The contrast provided by Ashby's editing throughout the opening sequence helps the viewer understand that the film's tone is satirical: only a member of a privileged social class could be so out of touch with contemporary society as to contemplate

CHAPTER 3

such a grandiose use of the tenement with such perfect disregard for its current occupants.

If the shooting and editing of *The Landlord* were markedly different from Ashby's later films, his use of mise-en-scène is typical of what would become his signature style. Ashby often uses mise-en-scène to create comic or ironic contrasts. In the scene at the charity costume ball, for example, when Elgar's father corners him in the bathroom to question him about the apartment building, the camera is placed at hip level behind another man whose guns and holster are placed in the foreground, ironically contrasting Mr. Enders's statement, "Let's have a civilized conversation."

Another brilliant example of mise-en-scène occurs when Elgar and his sister (played by Susan Anspach) are smoking marijuana in the foreground, while their father is shooting skeet in the background. Ashby begins the sequence with a carefully composed tableau: a medium shot of Elgar and Susan on a first-floor balcony—Elgar to the left of the frame and Susan to the right—reveals Mr. Enders and Heywood, their backs to the camera, viewed in the space between the siblings. As we observe the primary action in the foreground—Susan smoking a joint while Elgar sprays air freshener to cover up the smell—our eyes are drawn repeatedly to the action in the background, highlighting the generational divide between Elgar and his parents.

While the mise-en-scène sets the tone, the dialogue contributes another layer of irony. Susan has just told Elgar she is proud of him for moving into a black neighborhood. "I think somebody's got to begin to integrate," she says. "I can't: I just don't have the stomach for it." As Susan continues to praise her "devil-may-care, revolutionary brother" for his plans to buy the tenement (presumably unaware of his intention to evict all its black tenants), Ashby cuts to a medium-long shot of Mr. Enders and Heywood, now viewed from the front. Heywood takes the skeet from a box and throws them into the air. Mr. Enders shoots. Then we cut back to Susan and Elgar, as Susan continues to characterize Elgar as a political activist: "I mean, have your people planned any marches or rallies anywhere, anything like that?" As she asks Elgar not to talk to her new fiancé about politics ("the napalm and all that"), we hear the sounds of Mr. Enders's gun firing in the background.

This scene displays Ashby's considerable talent for combining dialogue, mise-en-scène, framing, editing, and sound, and it highlights many of the contradictions the film as a whole seeks to expose. The culture clash between a leisure-class existence based on the demeaning labor of African-American domestics and a rhetoric of sixties liberal politics can, as we have seen, be very funny; it can also, as Elgar comes to discover, be deadly serious.

Like Elgar Enders, the protagonist of *Harold and Maude* is a wealthy, disaffected young man. Harold Chasen is a wealthy twenty-year-old who lives with his mother in their Northern California mansion. Harold is obsessed with death: he drives a hearse instead of a normal car, and his favorite activities are attending funerals and staging fake suicides. Harold's behavior appears to be a desperate attempt to gain the attention of his emotionally cold and manipulative mother (Vivian Pickles), who generally ignores him and goes blithely about her business. Every attempt by Mrs. Chasen to "normalize" Harold is met with a gesture of rebellion. For example, when she gives him a new Jaguar sports car, he transforms it into a miniature hearse.

In her desire to find a suitable girlfriend for Harold, Mrs. Chasen signs him up for a computer dating service: three dates are sent in rapid succession to the Chasen mansion, but none of them lasts more than a few minutes. While attending a funeral for fun, Harold encounters Maude (Ruth Gordon), an eccentric seventy-nine-year-old woman who appears to enjoy funerals as much as he does. When Maude attempts to strike up a friendship with Harold, he is initially cautious, but eventually he is won over by her vitality and unconventional charm. Harold begins to visit Maude at her home, an abandoned railroad car filled with memorabilia she has collected over the years. Maude exposes Harold to the joys of music, art, and philosophy, and opens him up to the pleasures of the senses. As they drink elderberry wine, eat ginger pie, play music, and spend quiet days in the country, Harold begins to develop strong feelings for Maude. At the same time, he becomes aware of Maude's dramatic past: she has been, among other things, a political radical and a concentration-camp prisoner.

In the meantime, Harold's mother, having failed to find a girlfriend for him, decides that he should join the military. Mrs. Chasen enlists the aid of Harold's Uncle Victor (Charles Tyner), a retired army officer whom she describes as General MacArthur's "right-hand man"

CHAPTER 3

(although he has, ironically, lost his right arm). While Uncle Victor attempts to convince Harold of the virtues of a military life, Harold and Maude devise a plot to keep Harold out of the army. When Victor takes Harold on a visit to a home for old soldiers, Maude plays the part of an antimilitary activist whom Harold pretends to murder in a fit of patriotism. Victor, realizing that Harold is too psychopathic even for a career in the army, gives up on Harold as a prospective soldier.

By this point, Harold has fallen deeply in love with Maude. When he informs his mother of his intention to marry, Mrs. Chasen first thinks it is another of Harold's practical jokes; when she realizes he is serious, she promptly sets up appointments with the psychiatrist, the priest, and Uncle Victor, all of whom are appalled and repulsed by the idea of Harold's romantic and sexual involvement with a woman four times his age. Harold is undeterred, and he decides to propose to Maude on her eightieth birthday. During their celebration of her birthday, however, he discovers that she has taken an overdose of sleeping pills and is awaiting her own death. An ambulance rushes Maude to the hospital, where the doctors are unable to save her. Before she dies, Maude tells Harold that she loves him and that he should "go out and love some more." In the final sequence, Harold drives his Jaguar minihearse through the rainy countryside. He drives up a dirt road to a cliff, and we watch as the car plunges over the edge to the rocky beach below. The camera then pans up to the top of the cliff to reveal Harold still alive.

Both as a social satire and as a romantic comedy, *Harold and Maude* feels more assured than *The Landlord*. Where many of the comic moments in *The Landlord* seem forced—the slapstick of Elgar being chased down the street while carrying a potted plant is one obvious example—Ashby's direction of *Harold and Maude* is perfectly calibrated to bring out the already pointed satire of Colin Higgins's screenplay. The film's satire is directed both at social institutions—the church, the military, and psychiatry—and at the upper-middle-class values represented by Harold's smugly self-involved mother.

In one of the most effective dialogue scenes of the film, Mrs. Chasen is filling out a computer dating form for Harold. While Harold sits silently nearby, his mother answers the questions on the form as if it were she and not Harold who is applying for the service: in the process,

The Landlord and *Harold and Maude*

she reveals her conservative ideology and prudish attitudes. In the early part of the questionnaire, Mrs. Chasen's answers make clear that she has little understanding of Harold's personality. For example, when she comes to the question, "Do you often get the feeling that perhaps life isn't worth living?" she hesitates, deciding to put down "Not sure." As Mrs. Chasen continues to read the questions aloud and answer them, growing increasingly less aware of Harold's presence in the room, Harold removes a revolver from a felt-lined case and loads it.

> Mrs. Chasen: Do you believe in capital punishment for murder? Oh yes, I do indeed. In your opinion, are social affairs usually a waste of time? Heavens, no! Can God influence our lives? Oh yes, absolutely, yes! Does your personal religion or philosophy include a life after death? Oh, yes indeed, absolutely. Did you enjoy life when you were a child? Oh yes, you were a wonderful baby, Harold. Do you think the sexual revolution has gone too far? It certainly has! Do you find the idea of wife-swapping distasteful? I find the *question* distasteful.

At this moment Harold, having already pointed the gun at his mother without her noticing, moves it slowly toward his own forehead and pulls the trigger, falling backward in his chair as if he has been shot. The gun is, of course, loaded with blanks. Almost without missing a beat, Mrs. Chasen continues her monologue: "Harold, please! Do you have ups and downs without obvious reasons? That's you, Harold!"

The mise-en-scène, with Harold framed in a tableau shot between two family portraits and matching candelabra, and Mrs. Chasen sitting primly at her desk, adds to the humor of the scene, which is both ironic and morbid. The crisp editing, alternating shots of Harold and his mother in their increasingly isolated spheres, also contributes to the effectiveness of the scene.

We see a similarly satiric use of dialogue in the scenes between Mrs. Chasen and the young women who come to the house to meet Harold. The first date, Candy Gulf, is a good-natured but rather vapid college student majoring in "poli-sci" with a minor in "home ec." As she tells Mrs. Chasen, she studies political science because she wants to know "what's going on," but rests confident in her knowledge that if a career in poli-sci doesn't work out, "I can always fall back on my home-ec."

CHAPTER 3

The second date, Edith Phern, whose last name Mrs. Chasen is unable to pronounce, is a file clerk for a feed distribution company. "She supplies the whole southwest with chicken feed," Mrs. Chasen grandly informs Harold, her prim articulation of the sentence barely concealing her disdain for the enterprise. "Well, not exactly the *whole* southwest," Edith replies with false modesty, as Harold reaches into his blazer, takes out a hatchet, and pretends to chop off his arm.

The third young woman, a would-be actress named Sunshine Dore, seems the best match of the three for Harold: rather than running away after Harold's demonstration of hara-kiri, Sunshine is inspired to perform the suicide scene from *Romeo and Juliet*. The meeting ends abruptly, however, when Mrs. Chasen enters the room, accompanied by the butler carrying drinks, to find Sunshine lying on the floor with Harold holding a bloody knife. "Harold—that was your last date!" Mrs. Chasen proclaims, more upset by Harold's failure to find a suitable match than by the possibility that he has just murdered a young woman. Ashby ends the scene with a directorial flourish, as he cuts from Mrs. Chasen and the butler framed in the doorway to Harold dropping the knife, and then back to Mrs. Chasen dropping her glass of lemonade. The visual rhyme between the two shots is elegant and unobtrusive, but it displays the confidence Ashby has gained as a director in his second film.

The interactions between Harold and his mother, as well as the three scenes with the girls from the dating service and the scenes with Uncle Victor, are some of the most memorable comic moments in any American film of the period. While the satire of the military (which I will discuss in more detail in chapter 4) is the most pointed in the film, other institutions are satirized as well. The clergyman is characterized as a ridiculous, ineffectual, and sexually frustrated man. The psychiatrist, who venerates Sigmund Freud, recites platitudes to Harold in his sterile office and has no notion of how to help the confused young man with his real problems. Even the way in which the furniture is arranged in his office—two chairs set virtually parallel to one another and an analyst's couch against a far wall—seems to discourage authentic communication and individual identity. The police officer who tries to arrest Maude and Harold is vindictive, stupid, and ultimately powerless. The interchangeability of the film's male authority figures is cap-

The Landlord and *Harold and Maude*

tured by the decor of their offices: Uncle Victor sits beneath a picture of General MacArthur, the priest sits beneath one of the Pope, and the psychiatrist has a prominently displayed picture of Freud.

Several comic sequences had to be cut from the final film. One excised sequence contained a sight gag involving a fake head: In one of his many attempts to shock his mother, Harold arranges to have a silver serving dish brought to the dining room table with what appears to be Harold's head on it. Afterward, Harold takes the head to his room and puts it on a headless dummy. When his mother comes into his room, she begins talking to the dummy: "Now listen up, Harold. Your computer date will be coming and it would be nice if you got yourself ready." During Mrs. Chasen's dialogue, we cut to Harold in the closet watching her talk to the dummy. Mrs. Chasen continues, still oblivious to the fact that she is not addressing the real Harold: "Well, I've got to go to the ballet with the Fergusons. . . . You're looking a little pale, Harold; try to get a good night's rest."

This scene may have been too broadly comic for Ashby's tastes, but it clearly illustrates the way in which Mrs. Chasen is integral to much of the film's humor. She is the epitome of the wealthy suburban mother, concerned only with material comforts and social status, and incapable of engaging with her son in any meaningful way. Mrs. Chasen shares these traits with Mrs. Enders in *The Landlord*. The relationship between Harold and his mother echoes that of Elgar and his mother in more exaggerated form. Mrs. Enders, though she is willing to engage with her son to a certain extent, antagonizes him to such a degree that he threatens to throw her out of his apartment; Mrs. Chasen takes so little notice of Harold that he resorts to fake suicides in order to attract her attention.

Like *The Landlord*, *Harold and Maude* occasionally moves into a mode more accurately described as parody rather than satire. This parodic level of the film can be seen, for example, in the sequence involving Sunshine Dore, whose pretentious persona and acting style (she refers to her body as "my instrument," and takes her stage name from her acting teacher) are a blatant parody of the overly theatrical style Ashby was always intent on avoiding in his own films. The police officer who attempts to arrest Harold and Maude appears to have been taken right out of a television movie. Similarly, the scene between Harold and Uncle Victor parodies both the archetypal scene of the veteran recounting his "exciting" war experiences to a young recruit ("Only one thing kept going through my mind: Kill, kill, for Joe and Mac and all the rest of the guys!"), and the gung-ho enthusiasm of a naive young soldier ("the taste of blood in your mouth . . . another man's life in your sights!").

Subtle, and not so subtle, allusions can also be found to other films. The scene of Harold and his mother in the swimming pool, for example, would clearly have reminded viewers of the scenes of Benjamin Braddock in his swimming pool in Mike Nichols's *The Graduate* (1967). The same scene in *Harold and Maude* also contains a cinephilic reference to Billy Wilder's *Sunset Boulevard* (1950), another film about a relationship between a younger man and an older woman, in which a dead man is seen floating in the pool of a Beverly Hills mansion.

Like *The Graduate* and *Sunset Boulevard*, Ashby's comedy concerns the love affair of a younger man with an older woman, but *Harold and Maude* takes an idea from the school of social realism and pushes it to the border of absurdity. The affair between Benjamin and Mrs. Robinson is treated in a relatively straight fashion: Mrs. Robinson (Anne Bancroft), while a member of Benjamin's parents' generation, is still a conventionally attractive woman. The relationship between the two might be subversive, but it is hardly taboo. In contrast, the relationship between Harold and the nearly octogenarian Maude is presented as clearly outside the acceptable limits of American society. In fact, as the characters in the film denounce Harold's decision to marry Maude, so did the studio refuse to include a scene showing Bud Cort and Ruth Gordon involved in any form of sexual activity.

Where Dustin Hoffman's Benjamin is a version of the handsome and sexually potent young American male, Cort's Harold is a neurotic and desexualized figure whose awkward body language and pale, masklike face denote the antithesis of mainstream Hollywood masculinity. The allusion to *The Graduate* signals Ashby's sense of kinship with the kind of New Hollywood filmmaking exemplified by Nichols's film, but it also evokes a distinction between the more conventional satire represented by *The Graduate* and the subversive message of *Harold and Maude*. While *The Graduate* satirizes a particular kind of upper-middle-class suburban mentality, *Harold and Maude* uses its biting humor to question a far wider range of American beliefs and institutions.[8]

Examining *Harold and Maude* as parody reveals its destabilizing effect—an effect that made the film both anathema to mainstream audiences and an enduring hit on the art-house and cult-film circuit. The film also stands out in comparison to most Hollywood movies because of its emphasis on performance. *Harold and Maude* is not merely a film that contains brilliantly original performances by its actors,[9] but one that foregrounds various types of performance by the characters themselves within the diegetic narrative.

The characters in *Harold and Maude* share a constant need to perform, and as performers they can be divided into three groups. Harold's performances, at least in the first half of the film, take the form of fake suicides—non-verbal performances that dramatize his own desperately unhappy situation. Maude's performances, mostly given for Harold's benefit, include singing, dancing, and storytelling, all of which enhance the viewer's sense of her life-affirming and self-confident persona. We have a sense of Maude as someone who has always been most comfortable in front of the male gaze: whether that of her sculptor friend Glaucus or for the painter of the portrait of her as Leda that hangs on the wall of her house.

The minor characters, including the three computer dates, the psychiatrist, the priest, Uncle Victor, and Harold's mother, are also involved in one way or another in acts of performance. Harold's dates perform for both Harold and his mother, assuming the role of socially poised young women who will be both desirable to Harold and acceptable to Mrs. Chasen. The third and final date, Sunshine Dore, takes her performance at the Chasen mansion literally, acting out the death scene from *Romeo and Juliet* after watching Harold perform hara-kiri. Harold's psychiatrist performs, rather unimaginatively, his prescribed role as psychoanalyst, while the priest performs as a guardian of morality, and Uncle Victor acts out the role of the patriotic war hero.

Harold's primary audience is his mother, Mrs. Chasen, whose rigidly proper persona it is Harold's goal to destroy. While he does manage to crack her facade in a few instances, Mrs. Chasen always recovers enough to perform to perfection her own role as the controlling and infantilizing mother. In the dinner party scene toward the beginning of the film, for example, Mrs. Chasen repeatedly humiliates Harold in front of her dinner guests, first telling him not to play with his food,

CHAPTER 3

then recounting a story about how he was a sickly baby, and then ordering him to eat his beets. With *Harold and Maude*, the uncomfortable dinner party becomes a signature scene in Ashby's films, reminiscent of the dinner scene at the Enders' house in *The Landlord*, and to be repeated again in the nearly unbearable dinner scene at the Bistro in *Shampoo*. A slightly different version of the dinner scene also occurs in both *Bound for Glory* and *Coming Home:* Woody is most uncomfortable during his candlelight dinner with Pauline; and Sally's obvious nervousness during her dinner with Luke prompts him to ask if this is "have a gimp over for dinner night." In each of these scenes, the dinner party becomes an archetype representing an artificial, repressive social environment that exacerbates the characters' sense of social alienation until "acting out" becomes their only possible response.

The most striking diegetic performances in *Harold and Maude* are Harold's fake suicides. We witness no less than seven suicides or self-mutilations during the course of the film, three of them during visits by his computer dates and the other four performed purely for the benefit of his mother. In Ashby's films, actions often substitute for dialogue as a means of communication: in *Harold and Maude*, Harold's fake suicides become spectacular instances of non-verbal communication, physical attempts to communicate with the world around him. Where all the other characters in the film—Maude, Mrs. Chasen, Uncle Victor, the priest, and the psychiatrist—use language and rhetoric in articulate (if unoriginal) and often highly coded ways, Harold, inarticulate, uses physical gestures in the place of words.

This distinction is brilliantly illustrated in the first scene of the film. In the long opening shot, we see Harold descend slowly into a darkened room, light candles on a piano, step onto a piano bench, and slip his head into a noose. When his mother walks into the room, she throws an arch glance at Harold hanging by his neck, shrugs, and picks up the telephone to make an appointment with the hairdresser.

Mrs. Chasen's performance style signals to the world that she is above nearly everyone in it, including her "crazy" son. As I have established, Harold's performances are directed at his mother, but also at a spectator located outside the frame of the film: a fact demonstrated clearly in the shot in which, after one of the computer dates has left,

Harold, normally expressionless, looks directly into the camera and smiles conspiratorially at the audience.

Like most of Ashby's successful films—*The Last Detail, Shampoo, Coming Home*, and *Being There*—*Harold and Maude* has a straightforward linear narrative, avoiding any subplots that might distract from the central story. The simplicity of the plot and its symbolic structure of conflict and resolution contributes to the film's success. Several critics have noted the mythic, fairy-tale structure of the narrative. Darren Hughes comments: "As with the fairy tale, the moral of *Harold and Maude* is ultimately less important than the telling of the tale itself. The pure joy of Ashby's story-telling frees the film to transcend its often banal symbolism and preachy didacticism, creating a filmed world that, like that of Wes Anderson, Ashby's most gifted disciple, allows for the possibility of grace and childhood wonder in a fallen, cynical world."[10]

The film further suggests the fictional world of a fairy tale through its use of binary oppositions, such as youth and age, nature and culture, and life and death. The film's ending carries the symbolic force of a fairy tale: one character dies so that another can be reborn. We can also note the film's triadic structures, which correspond to a common pattern in the fairy tale plot: there are three dates (each with a corresponding fake suicide), three funerals that Harold and Maude attend, and three authority figures (priest, general, and psychiatrist) who attempt to advise Harold about his relations with Maude in three successive scenes.

The film uses parallels and oppositions between the two protagonists as a primary structuring principle. Harold is obsessed with death and destruction: he dresses in black and spends his time attending funerals, faking suicides, and watching buildings being demolished. Like Harold, Maude enjoys funerals; however, she is drawn to them not for their evocation of death but as part of "the great circle of life." She is also linked to Harold by her passionate rejection of the rules and regulations that govern mainstream American society. Though the two characters are also linked by Maude's real suicide at the end of the film, while Harold represents the death wish, Maude represents the life force. Despite her age, her lack of money, and her difficult past (including incarceration in a Nazi concentration camp), Maude is passionate

CHAPTER 3

Harold (Bud Cort) and Maude (Ruth Gordon) are kindred spirits, despite their difference in age.

about living life to its fullest. She wears bright colors, drives cars and even motorcycles with abandon, and spends time painting and modeling nude for her artist friend Glaucus. She breaks into pet shops to free canaries and transplants a sick tree from the city to the forest. The film charts Harold's progress as he moves closer to Maude's outlook, to the point where at the end of the film he can live on without her tutelage and still embrace hope.

Ashby's increasing assurance as a director between his first film and his second is clear in the stylistic choices he makes for *Harold and Maude*. As Stuart Samuels suggests, Ashby's directing style in his second film is both more straightforward and more effective than in his debut: "There are no long tracking shots or far-out angles or whiz-bang cutting. The film is fluid. The editing never gets in the way of the story." *Harold and Maude* is a visually beautiful film. If *The Landlord* established Ashby's ability to tell a story in bold visual terms, *Harold and Maude* displays his capacity to create a unique visual poetry that enhances the narrative and takes the viewer into a deeper meditation on love, life, and death. This visual poetry, brilliantly combined in postproduction with Cat Stevens's lyrical soundtrack, is created through Ashby's elegant use of lighting and camerawork. In collaboration with his cinematographer John Alonzo, Ashby decided to shoot most of the film on overcast days, avoiding direct sunlight whenever possible. As a result, the outdoor scenes have an ethereal quality that distinguishes the film's visual palette from that of most Hollywood films.

As he had in *The Landlord*, Ashby created in *Harold and Maude* a different visual look for scenes that focused on different characters. Though the contrast is far more subtle than in Ashby's first film, Harold's sequences appear colder and crisper, while Maude's scenes are warmer and softer. Ashby wanted not just the lighting but the style of the camerawork to be different for shooting the two characters, reflecting their very different personalities. As Alonzo put it, "Hal told me [that] all the sequences with Harold in his home should have a certain sort of sterility; sort of clear, clean, pure, no diffusion. The angles were to be more symmetrical; sort of meat and potatoes. And every time we ended up with Maude, it would have a slight craziness to it, just a little kookiness, a little tip (of the camera) up, a little tip down, a little diffusion."[11]

Some of the credit for the visual style of *Harold and Maude* also belongs to production designer Michael Haller, whose choice of location adds immeasurably to the film's effectiveness. Ashby and Haller set up many locations as a series of contrasts: Harold's palatial mansion, decorated in a tastefully conservative style and dominated by darker colors, contrasts visually with Maude's home, a converted railroad car filled with fanciful knickknacks and colorful works of art. Another significant contrast is established by the fact that many of the scenes between Harold and Maude take place in outdoor and pastoral settings, while the scenes between Harold and his mother take place primarily indoors.

In the first funeral scene, for example, Maude appears in a long shot, sitting against a tree and eating an apple. In the last funeral scene, we see Maude in a long shot leading the parade of mourners from the gravesite and between a row of tombstones. Among the mourners, only Maude and a young child wear brightly colored clothing, and Maude's yellow umbrella contrasts with the somber black umbrellas

CHAPTER 3

of the others. As Cat Stevens's "Tea for the Tillerman" plays on the soundtrack, Maude walks jauntily toward the camera, giving a casual wave to one of the attendants as she passes. Harold, in contrast, wears a black raincoat, walks in the center of the crowd, and keeps his head down and his hands in his pockets.

Ashby's use of the camera to frame his shots is far more apparent in *Harold and Maude* than in *The Landlord*. In one sequence toward the end of the film, Ashby films three successive scenes in which Uncle Victor, the psychiatrist, and the minister each express similar attitudes toward the union between Harold and Maude. The scenes are rendered more effective by Ashby's use of virtually the same camera angle and framing device in each case. First we see Uncle Victor behind his desk with a photograph of Richard Nixon in the upper right-hand quadrant of the frame; then, in a similar shot of the psychiatrist, we see a picture of Sigmund Freud in the upper left quadrant; finally, we see the minister with an image of the Pope in the upper right of the frame. In a crescendo of absurdity, the reactions of the men become increasingly violent, culminating in this outburst from the priest: "The thought of your firm young body commingling with the withered flesh, sagging breasts, and flabby buttocks, makes me want to vomit!"

The use of such tableau shots is an important signature of Ashby's visual style in the film.[12] In the first of two scenes between Harold and his psychiatrist, for example, they sit side by side in black leather chairs, turned at a forty-five-degree angle toward each other. The second scene begins with a medium close-up of Harold lying on the psychiatrist's couch, only his head and torso visible, and then we cut to a medium shot from behind the two chairs we saw in the previous scene, with Harold framed between them. The psychiatrist sits in the chair on the left, his back to the camera, and Harold, we now see, is lying on the couch backward, his feet on the headrest. Ashby then cuts to a frontal shot of the psychiatrist, speaking to Harold with the empty chair to his left. This complex, stylized series of shots within a scene in which the characters themselves do not move creates an oppressive atmosphere, while at the same time suggesting the emptiness of the doctor's "treatment" and reiterating Harold's refusal to play by the accepted rules of conduct. Later, at Harold's house, two limousines are shown parked at the same angle to each other as the two chairs in the psychiatrist's office, echoing the earlier shot and implying a similarity between the lifeless machines and the doctor and his patient. All of these shots serve as a visual representation of the static or frozen quality of Harold's life.

Another trademark of Ashby's films, apparent in both *The Landlord* and *Harold and Maude*, is a minimal use of close-ups, especially extreme close-ups, and the frequent use of the long shot. Ashby often uses the long shot to capture moments of heightened narrative or emotional resonance, for example in *The Last Detail*, when Bad-Ass and Mule chase Meadows in the snowy park; in *Shampoo*, when George watches Lester and Jackie drive away; in *Coming Home*, when Bob undresses before his suicide; and in *Being There*, when Chance walks across the water. The extreme long shot is used with particular effectiveness in *Harold and Maude*, both during the scene in which we first see Maude at the funeral and again at the end of the film when we see Harold's car accelerate over the cliff.

The third technique that defines Ashby's style in *Harold and Maude* is his use of the long take. One effective use of the long take, which serves to reinforce the tension between Harold and his mother, appears in the scene of the two characters in the swimming pool. The sequence begins with a shot taken from the bottom of the pool of Harold, fully clothed, lying facedown in the water. As the strains of Tchaikovsky's First Piano Concerto rise up, we cut to Mrs. Chasen, who stands at the other end of the pool, slowly removing her sunglasses and bathrobe. In a single shot that lasts nearly a minute, she enters the pool and begins to swim down the center lane, moving in an unhurried breaststroke past Harold, who has apparently drowned. As she swims by him, Mrs. Chasen casts a quick glance at her son, and then raises her eyebrows and continues on.

Ashby also contrasts long takes with takes of various lengths and angles, at times to help structure the film's narrative. For example, the credit sequence with which the film opens is a leisurely scene composed of an extremely long single take, while the film's final scene includes a rapidly paced montage sequence. At other moments, Ashby varies shot lengths and camera angles to heighten the force of the narrative. For example, after Harold's interview with his computer date Edith, we see her Volkswagen Beetle driving away from the front of the Chasen mansion in a beautifully composed, almost painterly shot. From there,

CHAPTER 3

Ashby cuts to an interior shot of Harold and his mother, the distance between them accentuated by the extremely high angle of the shot. As Mrs. Chasen informs Harold that she has instructed Uncle Victor to induct him into the military, we cut to a shot of Mrs. Chasen from behind Harold's back: she is framed, in yet another of the film's tableau shots, by a large stone fireplace and two embroidered footstools. Ashby then cuts to a medium close-up, high-angle shot of Harold, listening with his arms crossed, and then to a medium close-up, low-angle shot of Mrs. Chasen, punctuated by her delivery of the line, "And I hope they have more luck with you than I." Ashby angles these last two shots to reinforce the relative power positions of the two characters: the camera looks slightly down on Harold and slightly up at his mother.

Here and elsewhere in the film, as in *The Landlord*, Ashby's talent for mise-en-scène is striking. During a sequence near the middle of the film that begins at a building demolition site, we see a long shot of a wrecking ball, a telephoto shot of a crane scooping up a pile of debris, and then a medium shot showing Harold and Maude having a picnic in the midst of the destruction. During their dialogue, there is another cut to a long shot of the bin dumping out the debris. Another medium shot then shows Maude in a greenhouse looking at rows of potted plants, followed by a shot of both Harold and Maude in another part of the greenhouse amid a forest of lush hanging vines. The movement on the visual plane from destruction to progressive stages of growth matches Maude's dialogue about liking "to watch things grow," as well as her earlier reference to the circle of life and death. At this point, a long shot establishes another scene between the two characters, this time at a lake with a field of dandelions nearby. As we move to a series of medium close-up shots, the song "Where Do the Children Play?" begins to play. The camera then pulls back to reveal that they are in fact in a cemetery, with rows of gravestones in orderly rows as far as the eye can see.

Ashby achieves much of his visual and narrative style through his editing. The most striking editing in *Harold and Maude* takes place in the montage sequence with which the film ends. In this sequence, Ashby intercuts three narrative events: Harold and Maude's arrival at the hospital after Maude's suicide attempt, Harold's agonizing wait for news of her death, and his high-speed drive up the California coastline. In

The Landlord and Harold and Maude

the original screenplay, the scene of Maude's admission to the hospital involved several pages of dialogue while Harold went through the red tape of getting her admitted. The filmed version, a cross-cut montage of the hospital scenes and Harold driving, is far more effective, both in terms of the visual style and the narrative pace of the film.

Accompanied by Cat Stevens's song "Trouble," and by the roaring engine of Harold's Jaguar hearse, the final sequence contains nineteen shots of Harold in the hospital and twelve shots of him driving his car. The shots of Harold in the car are sequenced in such a way as to tell their own visual narrative: the first three shots are in a rainstorm, the next three are on rain-slicked roads, the next two on dry roads with an overcast sky, and the final four on a sunny day. In the final shots, no longer intercut with the hospital scenes, we see the car accelerating up to the cliff's edge, flying off the cliff, and crashing onto the beach below. A slow upward tilt of the camera reveals that Harold is standing on the cliff, alive and well. He walks away from the camera, playing the banjo that Maude gave him and dancing a little jig as he moves slowly away, out of the left side of the frame.

According to Edward Warschilka, one of the editors of the film, three different endings were shot for *Harold and Maude*. In the first version, the final shot stayed with the car lying on the beach; in the second, the shot panned out from the car to the ocean. The third version of the ending was the one ultimately used in the film: after showing the car hitting the beach, the shot travels back up the cliff to reveal Harold playing his banjo. Even after Ashby decided to use the most upbeat of the three endings, he hesitated about including the jig that Harold dances at the end. In a note to studio executive Robert Evans, he noted that "the happy happy [ending] always seemed to lessen [Harold's] real feelings for Maude." In the final cut, however—perhaps under pressure from Evans and Peter Bart to give the film a happier ending—Ashby decided to put Harold's jig back into the ending of the film. The decision to include the jig was probably the right one: the film is generically a comedy (albeit a very dark one), and although the dance may lessen our sense of Harold's sadness at Maude's death, it also reinforces the film's central theme of rebirth. The final sequence of *Harold and Maude* remains as evocative a piece of filmmaking as can be found in any movie of the era: a fitting ending to a highly original film.

FOUR

Once I Was a Soldier

Visions of the Military in *The Last Detail* and *Coming Home*

> In the original cut of *Coming Home*, my character stayed in Vietnam and became this gung-ho guy. But that's not the direction the film ultimately went. I think Hal wanted to show the politics, but he wanted to show them more through the situation of the paraplegics and through the marriage crumbling, rather than by showing the gung-ho soldier returning.
> —Robert Ginty

In 1978, two major Hollywood releases depicted the devastating effects of the Vietnam War on American soldiers and their communities at home. Hal Ashby's *Coming Home* focuses on the physical and emotional traumas caused by the war: the wounds of one central character have left him a paraplegic, while two other characters are driven to suicide by the psychological effects of their tours of duty. Michael Cimino's *The Deer Hunter* tells the equally traumatic story of a group of young men from a small Pennsylvania town who are sent to Vietnam, fall into the hands of the Vietcong, and are forced to play a brutal form of Russian roulette. While both films represented important contributions to America's discussion about its involvement in the war, they were very different movies. Where *Coming Home* was a per-

Visions of the Military in *The Last Detail* and *Coming Home*

sonal drama expressing a deep disillusionment with the war and with the United States government's treatment of its returning soldiers, *The Deer Hunter* was a high-budget epic that seemed unsure what position it should take on the war.

Though *Coming Home* and *The Deer Hunter* were the first major Hollywood films of the 1970s to focus explicitly on the Vietnam War, American films had been making oblique references to the conflict since the beginning of the decade. Robert Altman's *M*A*S*H* (1970) used the Korean War as an allegory for what was currently happening in Southeast Asia, while Ralph Nelson's *Soldier Blue* (1970) used the massacre of a Cheyenne village to symbolize events two years earlier in the Vietnamese village of My Lai.[1]

The Vietnam War had changed American culture in profound ways: the war had served since the late 1960s as a focal point for the growing dissatisfaction of the American public with its government's political and economic policies. Many American films of the late 1960s and early 1970s were on some level responses to the Vietnam experience. In a group of deeply pessimistic films that Christian Keathley has labeled the "post-traumatic cycle," New Hollywood filmmakers represented the experience of Vietnam without explicitly referring to it. The appearance between 1969 and 1976 of such films as John Schlesinger's *Midnight Cowboy*, Bob Rafelson's *Five Easy Pieces*, Robert Altman's *Nashville*, Martin Scorsese's *Taxi Driver*, Francis Coppola's *The Conversation*, Steven Spielberg's *The Sugarland Express*, John Boorman's *Deliverance*, Roman Polanski's *Chinatown*, Alan Pakula's *The Parallax View*, Arthur Penn's *Night Moves*, and Sidney Lumet's *Dog Day Afternoon* indicates "the onset of [a] trauma resulting from a realization of powerlessness in the face of a world whose systems of organization—both moral and political—have broken down."[2]

Under the shadow of what was happening in Vietnam, the optimistic energy of the counter-cultural movements of the 1960s had begun to drain away, and the films of the period registered a loss of confidence and a moral malaise: "America's lengthy involvement in the war in Vietnam and the impingement of that experience on the national consciousness served as the focus point for this breakdown of confidence. . . . The overwhelming feelings of disaffection, alienation, and demoralization that permeate these films are, in a sense, a displaced

CHAPTER 4

repetition of the intense trauma suffered by the Vietnam generation."[3]

Ashby's 1973 film *The Last Detail* belongs on Keathley's list of films in the post-traumatic cycle. Despite its silence on the subject of the war itself, the themes of *The Last Detail* resonate within the historical context in which the film was created. Aside from the fact that any film about the United States Navy released in the early 1970s would have suggested immediate and painful associations with the war, the film's cynical outlook and resignedly pessimistic tone cast it as a somber reflection on the demoralizing effect of the war on both the United States military and the general populace. The story concerns a young sailor, Meadows (Randy Quaid), who is being transported to the brig by fellow sailors Buddusky (Jack Nicholson) and Mulhall (Otis Young), after being sentenced to eight years for stealing forty dollars from a charity box, and is clearly an allegory for the thousands of American lives wasted, damaged, or destroyed during the Vietnam era.

This same theme would appear as the direct focus of *Coming Home* five years later. Viewed on its own, *Coming Home* might appear as an aberration in Ashby's career, a project that fell into his hands more by accident than by design and that owed less to Ashby's own thinking about the war than to the political commitments of his collaborators. When viewed in conjunction with *The Last Detail*, however, *Coming Home* can be appreciated as part of Ashby's larger goal of critiquing the American political, social, and economic systems that both initiated and prolonged America's involvement in the war.

The Last Detail is the least hopeful of Ashby's films. In contrast with a film like *Harold and Maude*, which suggests that, despite the repressive influence of contemporary social institutions, the possibilities of life remain almost limitless, *The Last Detail* depicts lives that are narrowly constricted. Although the film contains comic elements, it is essentially tragic: the mixture of futility and desperation conveyed by Robert Towne's screenplay is reinforced by both the visual and the aural dimensions of the film.

As Diane Jacobs describes it, *The Last Detail* is a "bleak-looking film, full of green and yellow military/motel colors, of quick dissolves from one gray landscape into another, of tight framing in which anything beyond the proximate looks blurred and unreal."[4] Ashby and his cinematographer, Michael Chapman, made a conscious decision to give

Visions of the Military in *The Last Detail* and *Coming Home*

Buddusky (Jack Nicholson), Meadows (Randy Quaid), and Mulhall (Otis Young) form a temporary friendship as they head north in The Last Detail.

the film the look of documentary footage such as that shown on the nightly television news. The gritty, realistic look of the film—very different from the visual style of Ashby's first two films—was accomplished by a combination of location shooting, naturalistic lighting, and the extensive use of handheld shots.

The physical setting is crucial to the visual style and thus to the tone of the film: Ashby is less interested in creating symbolic contrasts between settings—as he did in *The Landlord* and *Harold and Maude*—than in emphasizing the consistency and monotony of the locales as the characters travel north from Norfolk to Washington, New York, Boston, and Portsmouth. Most of the film takes place in oppressive and physically restrictive indoor settings: bus and train stations, buses, trains, and cramped motel rooms. Physical space, or the lack of it, becomes a motif in the film. Seated on the back row of the bus from Norfolk, Meadows is squeezed between Buddusky and Mulhall. When the sailors look for a restaurant in Washington, they reject the first place

CHAPTER 4

they find, ostensibly because it is too crowded (though the real reason may have more to do with the upscale nature of the eatery, the social class of the three sailors, and the fact that Mulhall is black). Later, in the hotel room where a long section of the film takes place, Buddusky and Mulhall struggle to make room for the fold-up beds where they will sleep. When the three men attempt to visit Meadows's mother in a grim blue-collar neighborhood in New Jersey, the front door opens to reveal a cramped, tawdry interior.

Even outdoors, the movie rarely provides a view of open spaces. The most notable exception to this lack of space is the park where the three men have a picnic together before Meadows is to be delivered to the brig. We feel a gripping sadness as the three freezing men stand around the small, smoky fire they've made in a grill in the snowy park. The scene starts with a slow pan over the sailors cooking hot dogs. The camera reveals the scene cautiously and delicately, capturing the sad beauty of the grey-brown leaves and then focusing on the freezing men. Then follows the tragic-comic detail that the men have bought no buns in which to put their hot dogs. This scene, so evocatively written, acted, and shot, is typical of Ashby's films, in which the moments most loaded with emotion are also those most tinged with irony, balanced between the tragic and the comic.

It is, perhaps, the very openness of the park that inspires Meadows to make his final desperate attempt to escape. Throughout the film, the possibility of Meadows escaping his two "chasers" emphasizes themes of space and movement. At first he is handcuffed, though Buddusky removes the cuffs on the bus, citing a regulation that seems at least partly invented for the occasion: "The navy feels that on certain kinds of vehicular transport, the prisoner shall have the use of both his hands, to protect hisself in case of an accident." Once Meadows is free of the handcuffs and his companions begin to relax their vigilant watch over him, Meadows makes two attempts to escape: one rather pitiful attempt on the train, where he is easily caught, and the other more serious attempt at the park, where his capture is correspondingly more violent.

The final scenes of the film occur at the Portsmouth brig itself, a place that will literally confine the young sailor Meadows for the next eight years, or six years if, as Buddusky suggests, he is lucky enough to

Visions of the Military in *The Last Detail* and *Coming Home*

be released early for good behavior. The shot selection and mise-en-scène in this final sequence are among the most effective in the film. After they enter the building, Meadows, who shows signs of the struggle in the park, is taken brusquely away by two marine guards, one holding each arm, and run up a slim staircase with a barred door at the top. The treatment of Meadows by the marine guards is a silent parody of Buddusky and Mulhall's detail, as if their rather leisurely trip up to Portsmouth were compressed into a few agonizing seconds. As Meadows moves up the stairs, his head bowed and his back to the camera, he is transfigured from a young sailor just beginning to assert his personality to a faceless and anonymous prisoner. When he passes through two sets of iron gates, the shot continues to follow the action in a low-angle shot from the bottom of the stairs as we hear the loud clanking sounds of the gates opening and closing; Ashby then cuts back to a high-angle shot of Buddusky and Mulhall watching helplessly from below.

In the next scene, when they are asked by the marine lieutenant if Meadows made any attempt to escape, Buddusky and Mulhall are torn between their sense of loyalty to Meadows and their desire to save their own necks.

> Marine O.D.: Where did you get the idea that strapping on an arm-band and a sidearm gives you the right to abuse a prisoner? They teach you that in the Navy, or was that your idea of a good time?
>
> Buddusky: I guess.
>
> Marine O.D.: You guess what, sailor?
>
> Buddusky: Nothing.
>
> Marine O.D.: Nothing?
>
> Buddusky: Nothing, sir.
>
> Marine O.D.: Did the prisoner offer any resistance?
>
> Mulhall: No, sir.
>
> Marine O.D.: Did he try to escape?
>
> Buddusky: Not exactly.
>
> Marine O.D.: That's a little vague, Buddusky. Either he did or he didn't: which is it? [*Buddusky looks at Mulhall for guidance.*] You don't have to look at him for the answer. Which is it?

CHAPTER 4

> Buddusky: He didn't.
> Marine O.D.: He didn't what.
> Buddusky: He didn't try to escape.
> Marine O.D.: He didn't try to escape, *sir*.

Robert Towne's brilliant dialogue captures the absurdity of the situation, in which the marine officer is more interested in humiliating Buddusky and Mulhall than in finding out the truth about their treatment of Meadows. Mulhall and Buddusky will win a small victory over the marine at the end of the scene when they remind him that he failed to "pull a few copies" of the paperwork before returning it to them. But while this incident allows them to maintain their sense of dignity—"I know my goddamn job better than anybody else in the goddamn Navy," Bad-Ass proclaims defiantly to Mulhall as they leave the premises—it cannot bring them any lasting sense of fulfillment.

It is significant that in the final scene of the film, Buddusky and Mulhall never mention Meadows. Any thoughts or feelings about the physical and spiritual journey they have taken with Meadows must be repressed so that they can continue with their military lives, governed by an endless series of details that are not under their control.

> Buddusky: Where are you going?
> Mulhall: Norfolk.
> Buddusky: I mean now.
> Mulhall: I don't know. Stop off in Baltimore, maybe. You?
> Buddusky: Back to New York, I guess.
> Mulhall: See you in Norfolk.
> Buddusky: Yeah. Maybe our fucking orders have come through.

As the two men talk, they are shown in medium close-up in a loose tracking shot. Then, as they move past the camera and begin walking away, the camera becomes stationary, framing the sailors in the center of the shot as they walk, in an unintentional lockstep, down the curving street until they disappear behind a house. As if to emphasize the marching rhythm that the two men, even on furlough, cannot seem to

Visions of the Military in *The Last Detail* and *Coming Home*

escape, an instrumental arrangement of "Anchors Aweigh" begins to play.

The soundtrack—which consists of jaunty renditions of traditional military tunes such as "American Patrol," "Last Detail March," "Washington Post," and "Anchors Aweigh"—reinforces the film's themes of institutional constriction and monotony. The loud, bright songs not only serve as an ironic commentary on the tragic nature of Buddusky and Mulhall's detail, but they also emphasize, through their associations with military life, the imprisonment of the two men in their careers as navy "lifers." Though the words of "Anchors Aweigh" are never sung in the film, the most commonly heard verse can be read as an ironic commentary:

Anchors Aweigh, my boys, Anchors Aweigh.
Farewell to college joys, we sail at break of day.

The lyrics of "Anchors Aweigh" provide a class commentary on the lives of Buddusky and Mulhall—who will never go to college and whose only home is the Norfolk naval base—and also allude to the 1945 MGM musical of the same name. *Anchors Aweigh* starred Gene Kelly and Frank Sinatra as two sailors on liberty in Los Angeles. The film is most famous for a dance number involving Kelly and an animated Mickey Mouse. The movie represents Hollywood's typically sentimental portrayal of the armed services. As Lawrence Suid suggests, *The Last Detail* "created an image of the modern Navy that was strikingly different from portraits created in earlier peacetime films of the 1930s or in the innumerable musicals and comedies of the 1940s and 1950s."[5] Unlike such films as *Anchors Aweigh*, *The Last Detail* conveyed a much darker and more ambivalent message: that "military regulations counted for little [and] sailors spent their time drinking and womanizing,"[6] not to mention the more disturbing fact that an eighteen-year-old sailor could be locked in the brig for eight years for being caught in the act of stealing forty dollars.

Ashby had already lampooned the American military in *Harold and Maude*. That film's satirizing of the American military establishment, in the form of Uncle Victor (Charles Tyner), spoke clearly to a generation that was questioning America's participation in the war. Uncle Victor,

CHAPTER 4

who has lost his right arm in battle, is nevertheless described by Mrs. Chasen, straightfaced, as "General MacArthur's right-hand man." She alludes here to an earlier, more popular war, an allusion that might have seemed almost quaint in 1971, as does Victor's sentimental celebration of the Revolutionary War hero Nathan Hale. Victor's ridiculousness is further emphasized by the fact that, at the pull of a lever, the empty right sleeve of his uniform automatically snaps into a salute, rendering him an automaton, a metaphor for the reflexive obedience required by the military. Standing next to a photograph of Richard Nixon, Victor gives Harold a pitch for the military life:

> It's a great life: There's action, adventure, advising. You get a chance to see the war first hand! And there are plenty of "Saigai" girls. It'll make a man out of you, Harold. You'll travel the world, put on a uniform, and take on a man's job. You'll walk tall, with a glint in your eye and a spring in your step. And the knowledge in your heart that you are working for peace, and are serving your country, just like Nathan Hale! Now that's what this country needs: more Nathan Hales! Harold, I think I can see a little Nathan Hale in *you*.

Throughout Victor's speech, we hear in the background the sounds of soldiers marching, loading rifles, and firing, as if to undercut the romantic tone of Victor's portrayal of the military with a more realistic version of what Harold's life as a soldier would be like. The line about "Saigai girls," spoken sotto voce and barely intelligible, was presumably Ashby's attempt to allude to Vietnam without incurring the objections of the studio. Later, Victor tells Harold he wants an "enemy worth killing" and "a war this whole country can support": "Now why in hell did we give up on the Germans? 'Cause the damn politicians in Washington chalked them up on our side, the wars ever since have been a national disgrace. Hell, look at history! Why, the two best wars this country ever fought were against the Jerries! I say get the krauts on the other side of the fence where they belong."

During Uncle Victor and Harold's visit to the home for retired veterans, Victor tells Harold that "this country has been too harsh in its outright condemnation of war" and that there are "many material advantages brought about by a crisis-and-conflict policy." As he speaks, a

Visions of the Military in *The Last Detail* and *Coming Home*

blind man with a cane passes by, and another old soldier collapses and lies helpless on the grass. If the satire is obvious, its implications are clear: American military policy is both blind and invalid. In another ironic moment, we cut from Victor's dialogue about the advantages of the military life—"the Army takes care of you, and you've got a buddy for life"—to the face of his black chauffeur, looking cynically in the rear-view mirror.

In *The Last Detail*, the critique of the military may be less blatantly satirical than in *Harold and Maude*, but it is no less effective. Buddusky, the chief chaser of the detail, is a wild spirit who seethes with anger at the military system in which he has spent his life working with little to show for it. In Darryl Ponicsan's novel, Buddusky is far more intellectual, a reader of philosophy; in Towne's screenplay, he is depicted as a typical navy "lifer." Mulhall, a black petty officer with no illusions about the possibilities available to him outside the navy, wants to finish the detail as quickly as possible. In the novel, Buddusky and Mulhall feel so alienated from the navy after dropping off Meadows that they decide to stay in Boston and go AWOL. When they try to sell their guns at pawnshops, they are turned down by the pawnbrokers. The sailors decide to drop their guns, holsters, and belts into a mailbox and get drunk. In the course of their arrest by two navy officers, Buddusky is knocked on the head and killed. Mule is subsequently sentenced to a military prison for three years.

In his screenplay, Towne decided to tone down the novel's ending, placing less emphasis on the dramatic elements of the plot in order to heighten the plebian aspect of the characters:

> I wanted to tell a story about typical people, not atypical people. Without saying it or trying to be pushy about it, I wanted to imply that we're all lifers in the navy, and that we will go along and be helpful to someone if our kindness or our courtesy doesn't cost us too much and it flatters our vanity. . . . We'll get the kid laid, we'll buy him a few drinks, we'll let him have a good time if that makes him think more of us, but we won't risk our neck. And all we'll do is feel a little guilty and cover it up by saying, "I hate this chicken-shit detail." . . . Those on the detail were no better than they ought to be, and no worse. But they were not particularly courageous. Nobody is.[7]

CHAPTER 4

Changes made in the script by Towne and Ashby emphasized both the war and the antiwar movement. Ashby's comments make clear that connecting the events of the film to the ongoing war was always a priority in the filmmakers' minds:

> In essence, [the film] deals with the military and military justice, and what a lot of shit all that is; it doesn't profess to give any answers, but it lays it all out, and that's something that's always intrigued me. We're not saying that he did something wrong in Vietnam that he's being called on the floor for, but he did something wrong here, and it's still military justice in the way that they respond. It deals with guys who are lifers in the service, and how they respond. It's about bondage.[8]

As in the novel, in Towne's original script the sailors meet Buddusky's ex-wife Charlotte and stay in her apartment while they are in New York. In the shooting script, the sailors instead meet a woman named Donna, a member of a pacifist Buddhist sect, who invites them to a party at her apartment and encourages Meadows to escape to Canada. Donna's offer to help the young sailor "get away" and to set him up with fellow Buddhists in Toronto alludes to the ongoing effort by those opposed to the war to subvert the draft of American men who would be just about Meadows's age. The chant Donna performs in aid of Meadows's escape suggests the presence of an active peace movement.

In general, the party at Donna's evokes the radical split that has developed in wartime between these enlisted men and an antiwar counterculture of which they are only vaguely aware. In fact, the young white liberals seem to have the war on their minds to a far greater extent than the three sailors. Mulhall is pressed by a man at the party to give his opinion of Richard Nixon and his policies, to explain why there are so few black officers in the navy (the answer is that a recommendation from a white man is needed), and to express his feelings about being sent to Vietnam. Mulhall's reply is one of the most revealing moments in the film: "Man says 'go,' gotta do what the man says. We're living in this man's world, ain't we?" Mulhall's cynicism, a verbalization of the sentiment expressed in non-verbal form by the black chauffeur in *Harold and Maude,* is an honest response to an awkward social situation.

Visions of the Military in *The Last Detail* and *Coming Home*

It is also a comment about the role of navy lifers and the rigid nature of social class.[9]

The release of *The Last Detail* in 1973 was an indication that Vietnam had made possible a new kind of film about the military. The background of the war—along with the breakdown of the Production Code in the 1960s—introduced a climate of greater realism in depictions of military life consistent with the brutally honest depictions of other parts of American society in New Hollywood films. Indirect references to the war and its cultural legacy can be found throughout *The Last Detail*. During the sequence at the hotel, for example, there is a scene in which Buddusky, after consuming several beers, attempts to teach Meadows how to be a signalman. As he begins his lesson, we hear the sounds in the background of a war film on television. Mulhall complains to Buddusky that he is interrupting the movie, and as the sounds of explosions and gunfire continue, Buddusky sits down next to the television, looks in the direction of the screen, and takes a puff on his cigar. For a moment, we see both the earnest face of a helmeted World War II soldier on the television, and Buddusky's clown-like face, his white navy hat pulled down over his eyes. Darren Hughes suggests that this scene can be read as "an ironic reminder of the 'good war' that precipitated America's disastrous involvement in Southeast Asia and that helped define masculinity and heroism for men of Bad-Ass and Mule's generation."[10]

Ashby made *The Last Detail* without cooperation from the United States military, an experience he would later repeat in making *Coming Home*. According to Lawrence Suid, the navy "adamantly refused to cooperate with the producers of *The Last Detail*." Producer Gerald Ayres made several efforts to procure military assistance, including a visit to the Norfolk naval base and letters to various military officials. The navy, however, decided it could find "no benefit" in assisting with the making of the film. The Navy Office of Information wrote Ayres that "no minor modification of the script can produce an acceptable film for the Navy," and that "you would have no plot left by the time you altered your script sufficiently to get our cooperation."[11]

The absence of military cooperation does not seem to have affected Ashby's ability to make a highly convincing film. The depiction of the three sailors, and of the military regulations and protocol that deter-

CHAPTER 4

mine their lives, was accurate enough to give the film the ring of truth, certainly more so than other Hollywood films about the military that had been made up to that time. Determined to make the film as realistic as possible, Ashby and Chapman managed to film a few shots of the entrance to the Norfolk Navy Base. This "stolen" footage so successfully gave the illusion of the opening scenes taking place on the base that one might assume Ashby had gotten the assistance of the navy in making the film.

The project that became *Coming Home* began as the brainchild of actress Jane Fonda. Dubbed "Hanoi Jane" by those who disliked her radical politics, Fonda was by the late 1970s as famous for her antiwar efforts as for her acting. By the time *Coming Home* was made, she had formed the Anti-War Troupe with actor Donald Sutherland, co-produced the documentary film *F.T.A.* (officially an acronym for "Free the Army" but more privately known as "Fuck the Army"), traveled to the "enemy territory" of North Vietnam, and been a leading member of the Indochina Peace Campaign (IPC), an organization concerned with bringing the war to the American consciousness prior to the 1972 presidential election. At one of the group's events, Fonda made the acquaintance of Bruce Gilbert, a young organizer for the California branch of the IPC. According to Gilbert, "We all agreed that if we could make any movie we wanted, it would be a movie about Vietnam, because it was the defining conflict of our lives. We came up with the idea of a triangle love story, which would allow Jane to be a pivot-point for two men who go to Vietnam: one who loses his body to regain his mind, and the other who comes back whole of body but whose mind becomes too brittle and breaks."[12]

The result was a screenplay, co-written by Gilbert and Nancy Dowd, for a film to be called *Buffalo Ghost*.[13] The screenplay, which bore only a general resemblance to the final script of *Coming Home*, concerns a woman, Marilyn Beaumont, who lives on a South Dakota army base and is married to a sergeant who is sent to Vietnam. When Marilyn's husband returns from his tour of duty, he has developed a drinking problem and has become emotionally distant, preferring the company of his war buddies to that of his wife. Marilyn has also changed over time, having established a close connection with a paraplegic veteran.

Visions of the Military in *The Last Detail* and *Coming Home*

The story ends tragically: Marilyn's husband attempts to drive home after getting drunk at a local bar, and he is killed while driving down the wrong side of a divided highway.

Nearly everyone who read the screenplay agreed that it was far too long and unworkable as a film. Dowd subsequently left the project, and Fonda and Gilbert approached veteran screenwriter Waldo Salt and asked him to rewrite the script. By choosing Salt, the author of a number of Hollywood films, including *Midnight Cowboy, Serpico,* and *The Day of the Locust,* the filmmakers made a strong political statement: Salt had been blacklisted in 1951 after refusing to testify about his Communist affiliations before the House Un-American Activities Committee and consequently had been denied work in the film industry for more than a decade.

Salt was fascinated by the concept of a "homefront" film, but he was not impressed by the script of *Buffalo Ghosts* and was not interested in rewriting it. Salt told Fonda and Gilbert that he would only work on the script if he could write it from scratch, basing it on interviews with Vietnam veterans and their families. As Salt began to hammer out ideas for story and character, he recorded interviews with veterans, including amputees and paraplegics. One of the men Salt interviewed was Ron Kovic, whose life story would later serve as the basis for Oliver Stone's *Born on the Fourth of July*.[14]

Salt wrote a first draft of *Coming Home* during the summer of 1976, and he had completed a second draft in November before succumbing to a heart attack. Both the beginning and the ending of Salt's script were very different from what they would be in the final film. The screenplay began with the funeral of Captain Bob Hyde's father, a highly decorated naval officer, thus establishing Bob's military background. However, in the shooting script, Bob's backstory would be removed, and the focus of the opening scenes would be on Sergeant Luke Martin and the other paraplegics in the hospital.

The most controversial section of Salt's script was the violent and melodramatic ending. After having returned from Vietnam, humiliated by a self-inflicted injury and disillusioned by Sally's affair with Luke, Bob begins to suffer from "post-Vietnam syndrome." Flashing back to Vietnam, he takes a cache of weapons and ammunition he has hidden in the house, dresses in camouflage, and holes up at a vegetable stand

CHAPTER 4

in the hills (presumably mistaking it for a Vietnamese village), where he takes hostages. Luke contacts Bob and tells him that he and Sally are coming up to get him, but while Bob is waiting for them to arrive, he kills a hostage and sets the stand on fire. When he sees Sally and Luke, Bob mistakes them for Vietcong and runs down to the freeway, where he is killed by the oncoming traffic.

Ashby knew he would need another ending for the movie, particularly in light of the fact that Bruce Dern, who was playing the part of Hyde, was strongly opposed to the ending Salt had written.[15] Ashby agreed with Dern that the violent ending was overly familiar and that it might also prove offensive to Vietnam veterans. "Every vet we showed the script to complained about that ending, about how they were always being depicted as totally crazy," Ashby told journalist Rick Honeycutt.[16] By the end of February, Ashby had written a new ending for the screenplay. Rather than going crazy and dying violently, Bob would simply walk down to the beach, remove his marine dress uniform and his wedding ring, and swim out to his death in the Pacific Ocean. Ashby's ending was diametrically opposed to that of the original script: in a sequence that is more lyrical than violent, we see the waves breaking over Bob's head as he gradually disappears from view.

Coming Home was one of the first filmed narratives to deal in a serious way with the effects of the Vietnam War on the United States; it was also a groundbreaking film about the experience of paraplegic veterans as they attempted to reenter American society. The film has been read in a number of contexts: as a melodrama about the plight of veterans returning from war; as a treatment of the psychological and sexual problems of paraplegics; as a critique of the gung-ho nature of American militarism; and as a feminist portrait of a woman's evolution from repressed military wife to socially and sexually liberated individual. The film is, in fact, all of these things.

Coming Home has also often been compared to other "homecoming" movies, including Delmer Daves's *Pride of the Marines* (1946), William Wyler's *The Best Years of Our Lives* (1946), and Fred Zinnemann's *The Men* (1950). *Pride of the Marines*, the first in the cycle of World War II homecoming films, is the story of blinded Marine Al Schmid (played by John Garfield), a hero from the battle of Guadalcanal, who resists returning to his loved ones because he wants "nobody to be a seeing-

Visions of the Military in *The Last Detail* and *Coming Home*

eye dog for me." After undergoing extensive psychological treatment, Schmid gradually comes to accept his disability, resumes his place in society, and is awarded the Navy Cross. The better-known *The Best Years of Our Lives* involves three American servicemen who return to the fictional Midwestern town of Boone City after the war, each finding his life irrevocably changed by his experience in the military. Homer Parrish (Harold Russell), a navy signalman, has lost his hands and becomes distant from his family and fiancée; Fred Darry (Dana Andrews), an Air Force captain, returns to a dead-end job as a soda-jerk and a loveless marriage to a cheating wife; and Al Stephenson (Fredric March), a middle-aged infantry sergeant during the war, finds it difficult to resume his duties as a husband, father, and bank loan officer.

As an editor on several of Wyler's films of the 1950s and early 1960s, Ashby was certainly familiar with *The Best Years of Our Lives*, and its melodramatic story and complex character structure were a partial inspiration for *Coming Home*. But the film to which *Coming Home* is most clearly indebted is *The Men*. As Sergeant Luke Martin, Jon Voight creates another version of Marlon Brando's character, Lieutenant Ken Wilozek. Like Wilozek, Martin is a paraplegic who begins the film in a state of bitterness, rejecting life and resisting all attempts at rehabilitation, but who gradually realizes that he can be reintegrated into society. Just as the character played by Theresa Wright in *The Men* pierces the shell of Brando's depression and self-loathing, Jane Fonda's character in *Coming Home* draws Voight's character out of his isolation and bitterness.

Ashby's film differs from *The Men* and other homecoming films, however, in two important respects. First, it goes far beyond previous homecoming or homefront films in its political message: the implicit arc of the film's narrative is not simply that of successfully reintegrating the wounded soldier into society, but of leading him to a rejection of the social consciousness that sent him to war in the first place. Where the rage felt by Brando's character in *The Men* is expressed in personal terms ("Why did it have to be me?" he asks his doctor), Luke Martin's anger in *Coming Home* becomes increasingly political during the course of the film, evolving from frustrated self-pity to a coherent antiwar position.

We hear the first articulation of Luke's politics in the statement he

CHAPTER 4

makes to television reporters soon after his arrest for chaining himself to a marine recruiting depot: "If we want to commit suicide, we have plenty of reasons to do it right here at home. We don't have to go to Vietnam to find reasons to kill ourselves. I just don't think we should be over there." By the end of the film, when Luke makes his speech to the high school, this antiwar position has become part of a personal biography that links Luke's own experience as a paraplegic veteran with a more general critique of American military ideology:

> I know some of you are going to look at uniformed men and you're going to look at all the films and you're going to think about the glory of other wars and think about some vague patriotic feeling and go off and fight this turkey too. And I'm telling you it ain't like it is in the movies. . . . I *wanted* to be a war hero, man. I *wanted* to go out and kill for my country. And now I'm here to tell you that I have killed for my country, or whatever, and I don't feel good about it. . . . I'm here to tell you it's a lousy thing, man. I don't see any reason for it. . . . And I'm just telling you there's a choice to be made here.

The difference between the political message articulated by *The Men* and *Coming Home* also explains the different levels of cooperation each film received from the armed services and the Veterans Administration. While *The Men* received full cooperation from both the Army and the Veterans Administration, institutions that saw the film as a means of informing the American people about the government's efforts to rehabilitate wounded soldiers, *Coming Home* received cooperation from neither the marines nor the VA. In fact, the Marine Corps Office of Information went so far as to recommend that the Pentagon refuse to assist the production, and the VA concluded that the script exploited paralyzed veterans and was "very offensive" to them.[17] As in the case of *The Last Detail*, the government refused to provide locations for filming, and the scene of Bob Hyde running on a military base had to be improvised by the filmmakers, who boosted Bruce Dern over the wall of an installation and photographed him running with a telephoto lens mounted on a car outside the base.

The second important difference between *Coming Home* and earlier homecoming films involves its treatment of women. In the nar-

Visions of the Military in *The Last Detail* and *Coming Home*

rative of Sally Hyde, a marine captain's wife whose evolving political consciousness and changing social values during her husband's tour of duty in Vietnam bring about an irreparable rift in their marriage, we see a distinct contrast with the women characters of previous homecoming films. Films such as *The Best Years of Our Lives* and *The Men* situated their women characters within a narrative focused almost entirely on the social integration of their male counterparts. The character of Sally Hyde, in contrast, is allowed to function as one of the film's protagonists and even to receive a political education about the unacceptably high cost of the war for soldiers and their families.

The question most often raised in critical appraisals of *Coming Home* is to what extent the film offers a coherent and well-articulated position on the war. Vincent Canby set the tone for many subsequent dismissals of the film's political message in his *New York Times* review. Suggesting that the film is more about the sexual relationship between a paraplegic veteran and a repressed military wife than about the reality of the war in Vietnam, Canby wrote, "*Coming Home* is more about Freud, perhaps, than about the war." Not all critics agreed with this assessment. Michael Arlen saw the film as an "achingly accurate representation of Vietnam"; *Los Angeles Times* columnist Peter Arnett considered it "an honest attempt to come to terms with the war in Vietnam"; and *Time* magazine's Frank Rich called it "a devastating vision of the nation's social history."[18] Nevertheless, most academic critics have tended to follow Canby's lead in dismissing the film's political relevance. David James criticized *Coming Home* for "rewrit[ing] the invasion of Vietnam as erotic melodrama."[19] Michael Anderegg claimed that the film "sanitizes politics, substituting sentimentalism and unobjectionable compassion for obvious victims for any kind of broader commitment to social justice" and that political issues in the film are "quickly, and with a complete absence of subtlety, reduced to the personal."[20]

The mixed critical reception of *Coming Home* may be attributed, at least in part, to the fact that most of those involved in making the film were reluctant to take a public stand about its politics. Jon Voight's statement to Janet Maslin that he "never wanted *Coming Home* to be a film that advanced any particular political viewpoint" is somewhat difficult to accept at face value.[21] Equally suspect is producer Jerome Hellman's claim that he, Fonda, and Ashby "didn't want to make a political movie."[22] In fact, Hellman would later admit in his *American Film* interview that the film "is intended to express a point of view about the futility and waste of this particular war," a position that is not only political but polemical.[23]

Haskell Wexler remembers that all of those involved in making the film were against the war: "We wanted to make a film which recognized that it was an unjust war: it was unjust to Americans, as well as to Vietnamese." But while *Coming Home* touched on highly charged political issues, the film could have been more direct in its commentary, Wexler admits: "We could have pressed the point a little further, a little more into the causes rather than just the results."[24]

Jane Fonda was even more outspoken in her criticism of the film's failure to take on the politics of the war directly: "It hardly deals with Vietnam too much, I regret," she complained to Joel Kotkin of *New Times*.[25] "We were not able to do everything that we wanted to," she told Richard Turner. "I would have liked to have seen the movie much more rooted in the Tet Offensive period in Vietnam. It was only hinted at. But we just couldn't find a way to do it that wouldn't come across as laying a message on people."[26]

Nevertheless, there is no doubt about the film's political viewpoint: the traditional ideals of heroism and patriotism are profoundly questioned throughout the movie. Ashby uses dialogue, mise-en-scène, and editing to help communicate this perspective. If the film's most frequently cited scene is that of Luke's speech to the high school, a less melodramatic expression of the film's political viewpoint is the Fourth of July picnic. The sequence is divided roughly into three parts: a game of wheelchair football, accompanied by the Rolling Stones' "Jumpin' Jack Flash"; a speech by a World War II veteran serving as a spokesman for the Veterans of Foreign Wars, which is intercut with shots of paralyzed veterans engaged in a variety of activities; and finally, a brief scene in which Bill Munson—Vi's brother and a patient at the VA hospital—breaks down while trying to sing a song for Vi, Luke, and Sally.

The speech by the VFW spokesman, a sentimentalized reminiscence about the meaning of the Independence Day holiday, seems particularly retrograde within the context of the film:

> When it got dark, the band would play "The Star-Spangled Banner,"

Visions of the Military in *The Last Detail* and *Coming Home*

and the fireworks would start up, and I'd start thinking about how brave those men were that fought in the revolution. I'd dream about those men, how they went to war for our freedom. I guess that's when I decided to be a soldier, seeing the sky lit up with those rockets. I enlisted when I became of age. I served in Europe in World War II and was involved in the liberation of dozens of towns. As I passed through them, as I saw the faces of the people, I realized I had fulfilled my dream. I had become one of those men who had gone to war for freedom. I sure wound up doing what I wanted to do, and that's what July Fourth means to me.

If the speech itself can be read as a rather benign example of the kind of patriotic American rhetoric often heard at such events, Ashby creates ironic contrasts through his use of editing and mise-en-scène that serve to undermine the speech's simplistic and predigested message. As the VFW spokesman speaks about the playing of the national anthem, for example, we cut to a group of paralyzed veterans passing a joint around. As the speaker opines on "how brave those men were who fought in the revolution," the camera shows the expressionless face of Bill Munson, whom we already know to have been severely traumatized by the experience of the Vietnam War, and who will later commit suicide in the VA hospital. When the speaker tells us that he enlisted when he first came of age, we cut to a shot of the paraplegic former high-school-football star Luke Martin, and then to the emaciated figure of another wounded veteran, presumably a quadriplegic. Finally, as the speaker declares that he became "one of those men who had gone to war for freedom," we cut to three consecutive shots of African-Americans vets. The second of these men holds a puppet of a Vietnamese peasant, as if to suggest that that this war, too, involves a people's revolution.

As in his exploration of the military in *Harold and Maude,* in *Coming Home* Ashby contrasts the nationalistic rhetoric surrounding the Revolutionary War and World War II with the very different cultural legacy of Vietnam. Unlike the VFW spokesman, these young paraplegics and African-American veterans do not feel that they have "fulfilled [their] dream[s]" by going to war. Living in a society divided by class, race, and physical ability, one that refuses to accept the experience of paraplegic

CHAPTER 4

Vietnam veterans as part of its glorified vision of history, their survival depends on a more detached and ironic attitude toward both the war and the nationalistic ideology that supports it.

The film's opening sequence is also a strong denunciation of American participation in the war. In the scene, a group of disabled veterans is engaged in a rap session around a pool table at the VA hospital. Shot with a handheld camera that evokes the feeling of a documentary more than that of a traditional Hollywood film, the scene introduces Luke Martin in a setting that de-emphasizes his identity as the actor Jon Voight, establishing a verisimilitude that sets the tone for the rest of the film. Voight plays the role of an observer in the scene rather than an active participant. He has no dialogue and is placed at a distance from the camera. The other veterans discuss the question of how they might justify the war to themselves and to others. "Some of us need to justify to ourselves what the fuck we did there," one of the men says. "So if we come back and say what we did there was a waste, what happened to us was a waste, some of us can't live with it. . . . How many guys do you know who can make the reality and say, 'what I did was wrong and all this other shit was wrong, man,' and still be able to live with themselves because they're crippled for the rest of their fucking life?"

The next dialogue we hear in the film occurs in the scene between Bob and his friend Dink on the rifle range. Their naiveté—expressed as gung-ho optimism as they prepare to go to war—is cast in stark relief against the combination of disillusionment and critical detachment we have just heard from the paraplegic vets:

> Dink: Word is it's turned into a hell of a war over there, captain.
>
> Bob: We're going there, pal! We're in Nam. "Combat City"!
>
> Dink: I am ready, really ready! I'll pop some rounds with you, captain.
>
> Bob: How's Vi taking to your leaving?
>
> Dink: Sometimes I think she hates everything military. But she stands behind me. She knows I want it more than anything else. What about Sally?
>
> Bob: She's OK. I don't think she really understands it all, but she accepts it.
>
> Dink: Can't ask for a hell of a lot more than that, now, can you?

Visions of the Military in *The Last Detail* and *Coming Home*

The aggressively cavalier and chauvinistic attitude of the two men—who assume that winning the war in Vietnam will be no more complicated that shooting a bull's-eye on the rifle range—is diametrically opposed to the grim reality of the war as presented by the wounded veteran in the opening scene, and later articulated by both Luke and Bob himself. The seeming disconnect between the lived experience of the returning veterans (who see their presence in Vietnam as a "waste") and the naive expectations of those preparing to leave for Southeast Asia is further reinforced by the subsequent scene at the officer's club. When Bob's friend Earl informs him that a mutual acquaintance was killed on the streets of Saigon, Bob is outraged: "That's an embarrassment, you know that! Makes us look like the goddamn B-team." Instead of expressing sorrow over the death of a fellow marine, Bob can only express scorn for the soldier, whose death represents an "embarrassment" to the military rather than a human tragedy. Bob's use of sports metaphors for the fighting in Southeast Asia continues throughout the scene. After Earl informs him that "word is from on top that Charlie shot his wad at the Tet Offensive and it's just a matter of a mop-up thing," Bob remarks that he is experiencing "competitive nervousness" about the prospect of heading to the front: "I feel like I'm going off to the Olympic Games, representing the United States," he says excitedly, as we see a close-up of Earl's wife whispering to Sally how sexy Bob is.

The painful irony of the scene depends on the fact that we know as we watch that the war will continue, that tens of thousands of American soldiers will die in Vietnam over the next five years, and that many more will suffer both physical and psychological injuries. Bob himself is completely naive about the realities of war, seeing Vietnam only as an opportunity to enhance his macho image and possibly gain a promotion. As Andrew Martin suggests, Bob is "pathologically locked into male fantasies of a heroic manhood which can only be legitimated on the battlefield." However, his experience in war will destroy these fantasies, leaving him an empty shell of his former self.[27]

The scene at the Officer's Club also sets up an ironic contrast with the scenes toward the end of the film, after Bob has returned from Vietnam. Before leaving, Bob boasts that he will bring Earl a "commie AK-47" as a souvenir, but all he will really bring home is the shame of a self-inflicted leg wound. Sally jokes that when Bob is promoted to

CHAPTER 4

major, she will have to lengthen her skirts and wear a girdle, when in fact, Bob will fail to gain a promotion, and Sally will adopt an appearance and lifestyle more suited to life outside the base. Similarly, Earl's vision of a coming-home party for Bob in three months' time—complete with a "side of beef, a case of Jack Daniels [and] . . . a couple of congressmen"—contrasts with Bob's actual homecoming party, a humiliating disaster attended only by Sally and Vi. Bob is more interested in getting drunk on the martinis Vi has prepared than in discussing his experience in the war, and he leaves after only a few minutes, unwilling to explain the details of his injury to the two women.

Bob's macho attitude extends to his married life as well. In one early scene, he sings the Marine Hymn as he prepares to make love to Sally, conflating military pride with sexual prowess. During the act itself, however, we see Sally, underneath Bob, staring at the camera as Bob satisfies himself. Sally, we later learn, has never had an orgasm, and it is with the paraplegic Luke that she finally has her first one. Bob's macho and insensitive attitude toward Sally is a motif throughout the film, from his sense that his wife does not need to "understand" the war as long as she "accepts" it, to his later annoyance at her for taking a job at the VA hospital and changing her hairstyle. Even at the beginning of the film, Sally is to some degree aware of the dismissive attitude the Marine Corps takes toward officers' wives. She jokes to Vi, "If the Marine Corps wanted you to have a wife, they would have issued you one."

When Vi and Sally meet two men at a disco and return with them to their hotel room, Ashby provides another commentary on wartime relations between men and women. Vi, distraught over the suicide of her brother, Bill, seeks some form of sexual adventure, but she suffers an emotional collapse after performing a go-go dance in the men's hotel room. The men, rather than showing any concern for Vi, display only frustration that they failed to "score." As James Conlon suggests, such predatory male behavior is also a commentary on "the soldierly ego in all its insidious forms," including its relations to women.[28] We see the counter-example to such treatment of women in Luke's relationship with Sally, which is based on mutual respect, understanding, and communication.

In the hotel scene, Ashby's mise-en-scène provides a silent com-

Visions of the Military in *The Last Detail* and *Coming Home*

mentary. When Sally and Vi leave the hotel and see Luke speaking on television after his arrest, the television is sitting on top of a *Playboy* magazine. Although Sally and Vi do not appear to notice this fact, it is clearly intended to draw a connection between the war and a form of exploitative sexuality. This connection is reinforced later in the film when Bob, several hours after leaving his homecoming party, returns with several men from the base. The men, already drunk, show little respect for Sally or her home. Their sexist jokes and boorish behavior can be seen as a commentary on the toxic effect the war has had on American soldiers. Viewed in this light, Luke's action at the marine recruiting office can be seen as a protest not simply against the war, but against a whole range of militaristic and chauvinistic attitudes that, unchecked, can lead to a debasement of the relationship between the sexes.

After Bob's return from Vietnam, the details of Bob and Sally's married life are set against his experience of the war—the atrocities he has

Militarism threatens domesticity in this emotionally charged scene between Sally (Jane Fonda) and Bob (Bruce Dern) in Coming Home.

CHAPTER 4

either seen or possibly committed himself. In the scene at the Hong Kong hotel, Bob shuns any physical contact with Sally. He has been rendered impotent by his wartime experience and responds defensively to her attempt to give him a massage by making insulting remarks about the attentions he imagines she is bestowing on the men at the VA hospital. Toward the end of the film, we again see the domestic and the military intertwined. When Sally suggests that Bob start a barbecue for dinner ("It's been a long time since you've lit a barbecue, hasn't it?"), Bob's hint of a smile suggests an ironic connection with his wartime experience, which presumably included torching Vietnamese villages. As Jeremy Devine suggests, the scene indicates the extreme distance between the two characters at this point in the film: "Dern's response is lost on Fonda as she and Vi go off to get the groceries for dinner. Her return to simple domesticity will not work any more than his return to civilian life."[29]

As in the hotel scene with Sally and Vi, the mise-en-scène conveys symbolic messages about the war throughout the film. When Sally first visits Vi's house, the television screen shows an American flag while the national anthem plays. When Vi intends to turn off the television, Sally asks her to leave it on. As the anthem plays, Sally turns away, as if the patriotic music has touched an emotional core; when asked about her reaction, she tells Vi that she is "superstitious" about the anthem and the flag, particularly on the night of Bob's departure. In the next shot, Vi places her hand carelessly on a folded American flag draped over the banister, but while Vi goes downstairs to get a beer, Sally picks up a corner of the flag and looks at it almost tenderly. As Sally replies to Vi's question about whether she intends to move off the military base, we see in the background a blown-up photograph of a naked man seated in the lotus position.

Here, the mise-en-scène accentuates the cultural divide that exists between the straight-laced Sally and the more bohemian Vi, and more generally between those who, like Sally, accept the military way of life and those who, like Vi, have begun to question it. This cultural gap between Sally and Vi will narrow considerably during the course of the narrative, as Sally becomes increasingly disaffected toward the other wives on the base and dissatisfied with the treatment of the wounded veterans at the hospital. The clearest moment in Sally's growing awareness comes when she asks the women in charge of the base newspaper to print an article about the wounded veterans at the hospital. When the women decline, saying that the paper is basically a gossip sheet rather than a forum for airing serious issues, Sally leaves the room in disgust—the first step of her evolution toward greater political awareness.

The change in Sally is apparent when she visits Bob during his R & R in Hong Kong. Her new assertiveness is first made clear in the scene at the bar in which she chastises Dink for his behavior toward Vi. When Dink expresses anger that Vi has not flown to Hong Kong to see him during his five-day leave, Sally asserts that if he wants her badly enough, he should marry her, saying sarcastically, "Women and dogs: you've got to have a license to show you're the owner." Later, in the hotel room, Ashby's mise-en-scène accentuates the growing distance between Bob and Sally. The size of the room emphasizes the emotional distance between the two characters, while the room's bare furnishings suggest the increasing emptiness of their relationship. As the scene begins, Sally is sitting on the bed on the left side of the frame, while Bob, isolated on the right side, walks toward the camera, nervously swinging his military dog-tag as he relates a disturbing incident involving his men's conduct in the war. When Sally crosses the room to embrace him—literally crossing over the cinematic space dividing them—Bob turns away from her and lies facedown on the bed. When she tries to massage him with Tiger Balm, he once again rejects her attempt to establish physical contact.[30]

Another symbolic use of mise-en-scène occurs later in the film. When Bob goes to meet Luke at his apartment building, he finds him giving a swim lesson to a young man. The message is clear. Luke, the paraplegic ex-marine, has found a way to help young people by coaching them in swimming; Bob, the able-bodied (if lightly wounded) marine captain, is metaphorically drowning in anger and self-pity.[31]

Here, as in many scenes of the film, Ashby's editing creates suggestive parallels between the film's characters. As we see Bob entering the apartment complex, we hear Luke off-camera delivering a line about a swimming race, and we cannot help but associate Luke's words with the image of Bob. "When that gun goes off," Luke tells the young man, "you gotta uncoil like a spring, you gotta . . . release." The verbal image

CHAPTER 4

of a gun "going off" is associated with the visual image of Bob, reinforcing our sense of Bob as a career soldier who knows no other way of life—after his return from Vietnam, Bob keeps a chest full of weapons and ammunition in his garage. In this scene, we also sense impending violence—the possibility of Bob either "going off the deep end" or "going off half-cocked," a mood that anticipates the scene in which Bob threatens Sally and Luke with a loaded weapon. Bob is in fact a physical embodiment of Luke's words: coiled like a spring of pent-up anger and frustration, his only means of release is a violent act against either himself or another.

Ashby saves his most effective use of cross-cutting for the film's final sequence. The last fourteen scenes are skillfully intercut. In order to see how Ashby has constructed the sequence, we must examine both the number of shots and the total length of each scene.

1. Bob receiving a medal (one shot, 33 seconds)
2. Introduction of Luke at the high school (one shot, 49 seconds)
3. Bob standing in full dress uniform while Sally tells him she is going to the store and suggests he light the barbecue (six shots, 45 seconds)
4. Luke beginning his speech to the high school (three shots, 30 seconds)
5. Bob walking down to the beach (one shot, 33 seconds)
6. Luke continuing his speech (three shots, 30 seconds)
7. Bob removing his clothes (one shot, 8 seconds)
8. Sally and Vi driving (one shot, 14 seconds)
9. Bob continuing to undress (one shot, 3 seconds)
10. Luke speaking (one shot, 17 seconds)
11. Bob taking off his wedding ring (two shots, 15 seconds)
12. Luke speaking (three shots, 73 seconds)
13. Shot of the ocean with Bob swimming out (one shot, 11 seconds)
14. Sally and Vi going into the supermarket (one shot, 18 seconds)

In this final sequence, Ashby displays his considerable talents as an editor, varying both the length of individual shots and the overall length of scenes in order to create a strongly syncopated rhythm that prevents the ending from becoming either maudlin or tendentious.[32] With an average shot length of 15.4 seconds, considerably longer than that of the film as a whole, the sequence attains an elegiac quality that is further accentuated by Tim Buckley's song "Once I Was."[33]

Except for the brief shot of Sally and Vi driving and the final shot of the two women entering the supermarket, the entire sequence is divided between the two male protagonists. The intercutting of the sequence emphasizes the stark differences between Luke and Bob at this point in the film. Luke is at the high point of his narrative of psychic recovery: he has achieved an emotional stability that allows him to express his feelings about the war in a public forum. Bob, on the other hand, is portrayed as nearly catatonic: his silence, stiff demeanor, and lack of facial expression are a striking physical representation of his inability to express his inner pain.

The sense of impotence Bob experiences during the war, his feelings of dislocation on his return from the war, and his feelings of betrayal when he discovers that his wife has had an affair with a paraplegic vet add up to a kind of symbolic castration. This symbolism is most clearly indicated in the scene in which Bob confronts Luke, and Luke is not only able to disarm Bob through his use of language but also manages to remove Bob's source of male power by unloading his rifle and retracting his bayonet. For the remaining scenes of the film, the only signifier of Bob's former male status is his marine uniform, which points less to his masculine authority than to its absence.

The question of what happens to the third of the film's major narratives—Sally's emerging political consciousness—is an important one, and one that has been raised by some of the film's critics. Michael Selig, for example, has argued that the film ultimately sublimates Sally's political consciousness in order to emphasize Luke's growing political commitment.[34] As Tania Modleski has argued, however, *Coming Home* is a film that succeeds in making an important feminist statement. With its emphasis on women's "sexual rights," and in particular on the right to choose a non-phallic sexuality over phallic intercourse, *Coming Home* has a "significant place in the ongoing struggles over sex-

CHAPTER 4

ual politics."[35] Further, *Coming Home* differs from the other two most significant Vietnam films of the late 1970s—Cimino's *The Deer Hunter* and Francis Ford Coppola's *Apocalypse Now*—in presenting a strong female character whose development, both political and sexual, is seen as equally important as that of the male protagonists. While it is true that Sally's growth is shown primarily during the first two-thirds of the film, the fact that Sally has more total screen time than either Luke or Bob makes it difficult to support the argument that her narrative is ever eclipsed by Luke's.

If we compare the character of Sally Hyde with Linda, the character played by Meryl Streep in *The Deer Hunter*, we can see the fundamental difference in the role women are allowed in the two films. Where Fonda's Sally is a strongly independent and psychologically complex woman, Streep's Linda is a relatively passive character. In fact, Linda's main function in the film is to act as the stereotypical feminine foil to the male characters. Unlike *Coming Home*, which uses the disintegrating marriage as a metaphor for the devastating effects of the war on homeland communities, *The Deer Hunter* is far more focused on the male bonding between Michael (Robert de Niro) and Nicky (Christopher Walken) than on their relationships with women.[36]

Coming Home closes with a shot of its two strong female characters, Sally and Vi, who will now be united by their shared experience of having lost a loved one to the war. Despite the fact that their last action in the film is a trip to the supermarket to buy steaks for a barbecue—a less dramatic gesture, to be sure, than either Bob's swim into the ocean or Luke's speech to the high school—the final moments of *Coming Home* represent not so much a return to domesticity as a movement toward a female solidarity that attempts to redress the almost obsessive preoccupation with male bonding in so many American war films.

Coming Home is unique in the canon of Vietnam films in its willingness to take seriously not only the intense bonds between male soldiers that result from the shared travails of war, but also the relationships between the women who are left to pick up the pieces when their men fall apart. This characterization is a notable difference from most Vietnam films, in which women are depicted either as background to the male-oriented action of the film (*The Deer Hunter*), or as figures who service the sexual desires of men—prostitutes (Stanley Kubrick's *Full*

Visions of the Military in *The Last Detail* and *Coming Home*

Metal Jacket), objects of male fantasy (*Apocalypse Now*), and victims of rape (Brian De Palma's *Casualties of War*).

Like many of Ashby's films, *Coming Home* ends with an ambiguous image that suggests closure but refuses to resolve completely the underlying tensions of the narrative. As Sally and Vi move toward the entrance to the Lucky supermarket, the camera pans across the glass doors of the automatic exit, where a sign reads "Out" in large letters, with "Lucky" in smaller letters above it. On the voiceover commentary accompanying the DVD release of the film, Bruce Dern suggests that the word "Out" is a reference to the United States getting out of Vietnam: "It's over, the war's over . . . Vietnam's over. We're out." The more obvious reference of the sign, however, is Sally's marriage. Bob's death, witnessed in the previous shot, has given Sally a way out of a painful and unsustainable marriage. Whether Bob's suicide can be seen as a "lucky out" for Sally, or even for Bob, remains an open question, and one that the film will not answer. Ashby, feeling that such a formulaic resolution would have been unrealistic and insulting to veterans, rejected earlier drafts of the screenplay that attempted to envision a romantic future for Sally and Luke. Despite the possibility of a happy ending, *Coming Home* leaves the future ambiguous, challenging the viewer with a narrative that complicates rather than simplifies the relationships between its central characters.

FIVE

I Like to Watch
Shampoo and *Being There*

> In this new era Chauncey Gardiner is ahead of us, since he is already the complete product of what is in store for us in the imminent future. . . . He's the first in the Videot's Paradise. He doesn't need to communicate with anyone—he has nothing to tell others that they don't already know (visual culture being the source of knowledge and experience) and therefore is adaptable. People around him, all of us, who should be able to decipher him, who should be able to disengage ourselves from his vacuum . . . are already unable to do so. We have been disarmed by the medium which daily feeds all of us.
> —Jerzy Kosinski

Toward the middle of *Coming Home*, Sally Hyde asks her husband Bob to describe his experience in Vietnam. "Why don't you tell me about it?" she asks. "I want to know what it's like." Bob's reply marks a striking departure from the typical dialogue of Hollywood war films: rather than elucidating his experience of the war for Sally so that she can come to a better understanding of his situation, Bob explains that it is impossible to communicate the experience at all. "I don't know what it's *like*. I only know what it *is*. TV shows what it's like. It sure as hell doesn't show what it is."

I Like to Watch: *Shampoo* and *Being There*

The dialogue in this scene is significant not only for what it reveals about Bob Hyde—whose shock at the reality of the war has made him virtually incapable of communicating his experiences—but also for what it tells us about Ashby's attitude toward the medium of television, and more generally toward the mass media. In Ashby's films, television is most often a conveyer of words and images that fail to communicate a meaningful sense of reality.

Television is a significant motif in several of Ashby's films of the 1970s. The presence of television in these films can be placed within the context of the growing mass media and the explosion of information that took place in the 1960s and 1970s. For Ashby, television represents in its most concrete and inescapable form the media's increasing intrusion on contemporary life. The two films in which Ashby makes most effective use of television are *Shampoo* and *Being There*.[1]

Both films are highly critical of the role of the mass media in the American political process. If *Shampoo* engages in a more conventional critique of American political life—focusing its satiric gaze on a presidential election that reflected the shift from the progressive political atmosphere of the 1960s to the conservative ideology of the early 1970s—*Being There* engages in a more radical critique of the American political system. In a postmodern allegory that suggests Jean Baudrillard's analysis of contemporary culture, *Being There* presents a vision of a world that resembles television programming, a world in which the endless recirculation of signs and images has resulted in a reality that is in fact a "hyperreality," a state in which it is no longer possible to distinguish the imaginary from the real. For Baudrillard, television is the technology that best exemplifies the condition of hyperreality: "With the television image—the television being the ultimate and perfect object for this new era—our own body and the whole surrounding universe becomes a control screen."[2]

In *Hollywood Films of the Seventies*, Seth Cagin and Philip Dray compare two of the most influential New Hollywood films of the mid-1970s: Ashby's *Shampoo* and Robert Altman's *Nashville*. Both films are "critical portraits of emblematic American communities," displaying the hypocrisy, complacency, and self-destructive lifestyles of contemporary Americans, who are portrayed as "an oblivious and benumbed populace."[3] The number of parallels between these two films is indeed

CHAPTER 5

striking. Both films were shot in 1974 (*Shampoo* in the spring, *Nashville* in the summer) and both were released in 1975. Both films contain frame narratives that place the actions of the characters within a larger political context: the events of *Nashville* unfold around a rally for a shady political candidate, Hal Phillip Walker, while the narrative of *Shampoo* is set within the days surrounding the 1968 election of Richard Nixon. Both films also feature characters who are political operatives: in *Nashville*, Walker's public-relations manager John Triplette (Michael Murphy) manipulates the other characters into doing what he wants, while in *Shampoo*, Republican fundraiser Lester Carp (Jack Warden) organizes an election-night party attended by all the principal characters.

The two films portray communities that would appear on the surface to be quite different—the country-music entertainment industry in *Nashville* and a cross-section of Beverly Hills society in *Shampoo*—but they actually present a vision of America that is fundamentally similar. Each film is governed by a central metaphor: In *Nashville*, show business stands for a society in which people are either performers or passive consumers of performance. In *Shampoo*, the Beverly Hills hairdressing salon is a metaphor for a fundamentally narcissistic society, while the sexual farce on which much of the film's plot is based and which takes place against a political backdrop provides a trenchant commentary on American political life. *Shampoo* also provides a chilling commentary on communication and the media.

The film's primary plot concerns Beverly Hills hairdresser George Roundy (Warren Beatty), who sleeps with practically all of his female customers but who is incapable of taking control of his life or establishing any lasting human connection. Torn between the financial backing of a corrupt businessman with ties to the Republican Party and the prospect of a lifetime working under the thumb of a querulous and demanding boss, George is in the unenviable position of many workers in the new economy. Unable to secure a bank loan that would allow him to start his own business and unwilling to refrain from his philandering in order to hold onto his girlfriend, Jill (Goldie Hawn), George is emblematic of the duplicity, self-absorption, and lack of introspection endemic in contemporary urban society. He is also, perhaps, the most

I Like to Watch: *Shampoo* and *Being There*

complex character in any of Ashby's films, one who is by turns vulnerable, unscrupulous, charming, dishonest, and insightful.

Although it is Beatty, rather than Ashby, who is generally credited as the principle auteur of the film, and commentators have drawn parallels between Beatty and George Roundy, *Shampoo* can also be read as an allegory of Ashby's professional and biographical situation at the time. Ashby's increasing desire for greater freedom from studio control is analogous to George's growing need for the financial and personal independence that would result from having his own hair salon.[4] Ashby also resembles George in his difficulty maintaining long-term relationships. By the time he began work on *Shampoo*, the director had ended his fifth and last marriage, to actress Joan Marshall, and had vowed never to marry again.[5] Finally, an analogy can be suggested between cutting film and cutting hair. George's talent with the scissors has made him a kind of "star" of the hairdressing world, just as Ashby's prodigious abilities in the cutting room had brought him to the top of his profession as an editor before he made the transition to directing.

In keeping with Ashby's own difficulties communicating verbally, one of the major themes of *Shampoo* is the breakdown of communication in American society. The scene that perhaps most clearly illustrates this theme is the scene at the bank in which George attempts to secure a loan to open his own salon. In his meeting with the loan officer, George seems hopelessly out of place: his clothes seem suddenly much too casual, and the language he uses—he mentions "doing the heads" of Hollywood celebrities—has little in common with the loan officer's technical vocabulary. The encounter ends with George feeling frustrated and alienated from the world of business and finance, a world that is clearly related within the context of the film, to the ascendency of Republican Richard Nixon to the presidency.

The breakdown of communication is symptomatic of a political and social culture in which the superficial nature of media-talk has eroded the quality of human interaction. The following dialogue between George and Jill is typical:

Jill: Where were you?
George: I'm great, honey. Fantastic. Couldn't be better. I'm really incred—

CHAPTER 5

> Jill: No, where were you?
>
> George: I'm getting it together. I'm going to open up a shop. You know, right now, I'm at the epitome of my life.
>
> Jill: Yeah? Well, what happened tonight?
>
> George: I don't want to talk about it. You know, I've been disgusted with my life.
>
> Jill: You just said you were at the epitome of your life.
>
> George: I am, I am.

In his interactions with Jill, George—who is in this scene hiding the fact that he has been with another woman all evening—cannot get past a level of meaningless pseudo-revelation: his claims to be "getting it together" and to be at the "epitome of [his] life" sound like the sort of affirmative "I'm OK, you're OK" language of late-sixties pop psychology. Jill, more interested in what George has actually been doing all evening than in his vague attempts to assess his life situation, tries unsuccessfully to pin him down. By the end of the film, in part because of George's inability to communicate with her in a meaningful way, Jill will leave him for the film director Johnny Pope (Tony Bill).

The inability of the characters in *Shampoo* to communicate clearly or directly with each other mirrors America's inability to address the serious social and political issues that confronted it at the end of the 1960s. In an interview conducted shortly after the film's release, Ashby suggested that the political context of the 1968 presidential election provides a larger frame within which to understand the behavior of the film's central characters: "When Nixon was elected in 1968 it meant more than many people thought at the time. There was a gigantic change during that election. In the film we've got a lot of people running around talking about [the election], some ignoring it, but no one goes and votes. There's a party with big contributors where no one pays attention to anything."[6] By placing the film's narrative within the context of the election, Ashby and his collaborators create an implicit link between the hypocrisy, self-absorption, and moral corruption of the principal characters and the values exemplified by the Nixon administration.

As in the film *Nashville*, the omnipresence of the media in *Sham-*

I Like to Watch: *Shampoo* and *Being There*

George (Warren Beatty) arrives at the Bistro with Jill (Goldie Hawn) and Jackie (Julie Christie), for the first of two election-night parties in Shampoo.

poo functions as a reminder that the story occurs within the frame of broader historical events and that the individual stories of the characters cannot be understood except within that larger context. In *Nashville*, Altman's treatment of the media has both comic and tragic resonances. The comic embodiment of the media is the character Opal (Geraldine Chapman), a correspondent for the BBC who is making a documentary about the city of Nashville and the country-music scene. On a more serious level, the media are represented by the city of Nashville itself, the capital of country music, a mass-media industry. Altman's film views the media as not only invasive but destructive: the country-music singer Barbara Jean is literally destroyed by her own fame when she is shot by a young man claiming to be a fan of her music.[7]

In *Shampoo*, on the other hand, the media function as an ironic commentary on the superficiality of the characters' lives. During sev-

CHAPTER 5

eral scenes, characters are unaware of the various media that surround them. As Lester prepares for his rendezvous with Jackie (Julie Christie), for example, we hear the radio droning on with the financial news. Later, as he is driving to Jackie's house in his car, he listens to the stock market updates, but when a real news story comes on the radio—a discussion of the Paris peace talks—Lester switches stations, passing over a music station until he finds one with more financial reports. Similarly, Jill is unaware of a large and conspicuous poster of Nixon and Agnew in the window of a liquor store, and later she seems uninterested in a television news story involving the Vietnam War.

With the exception of Lester, the film is inhabited by characters who have no real interest in the outcome of the election or, for that matter, in the political process. None of the other characters even mention the election during the course of the film, and Lester's own interest in the Republican Party seems motivated by self-interest rather than political idealism. When Lester tells his wife, Felicia, "Some of us are trying to make this country a better place to live in," she pokes a hole in his phony sincerity, saying, "You're not helping anybody. You're just twisting arms here to raise money for a lot of sons of bitches who are all out for themselves." The next morning, Lester admits to George that even he is unsure of his political convictions: "Maybe Nixon will be better. What's the difference? They're all a bunch of jerks."

The film satirizes the media most pointedly during the election-night party at the Bistro, when the central characters move, apparently oblivious, through a landscape of television sets, campaign posters and overblown photos, as the voices on the television news act as an ironic commentary. At times, this background commentary is used for comic effect. As Felicia leads George into the ladies' room, we hear Spiro Agnew in the background saying, "Exactly what can a president do to affect the moral tone of the country? The president can end the permissive attitudes." Then, as Johnny asks Jill why George went into the ladies' room, we hear Nixon's voice saying, "We'll restore respect for the United States of America, and in our administration, the American flag will not be a doormat for anybody." The juxtaposition of these television speeches and the behavior of the characters highlights the flaws in both: while the moralistic tone of the Republican candidates is characterized as phony and insincere, the lifestyles of the charac-

I Like to Watch: *Shampoo* and *Being There*

ters—who are presumably at the dinner to support the Republican candidates—are indeed decadent and shallow, a mockery of the very attitudes the candidates seem to be promoting.

As George leads a drunken Jackie down the stairs and out the door of the Bistro, we hear the televised voice of reporter David Brinkley saying, "I don't think we're going to get a winner tonight." Brinkley is commenting on the close election, of course, but his words also foreshadow the remaining events of the film. In fact, there will be no real winners on this night, either in the political sense—the American people will elect a leader whose presidency will end in scandal, impeachment, and resignation—or in the personal lives of the characters. Like *Nashville*—which concludes with an ironic comment on the possibilities of American democratic politics ("You may say that I ain't free / But it don't worry me")—*Shampoo* ends on a note of political cynicism. Lester's side may have won the election, but the future does not look particularly bright, either for him or for the American electorate.

The film's cynical take on the outcome of the election is emphasized by the mise-en-scène, which includes the use of television. As George pulls up to his apartment on his motorcycle, the morning after election day, we hear the sound of Nixon's voice in the background, presumably delivering his victory speech. As George enters the apartment, we cut to a medium frontal shot of him coming through the door. It is a carefully composed shot. George is located in the center of the frame. Lester sits on George's couch, slightly to the left of center, with his back to the camera. Two of Lester's henchmen stand on either side of the frame, and at the far right of the frame, we see the television set showing Nixon speaking. A bottle of scotch lies just below the center of the frame, a visual clue that Lester has been drinking as he awaits George's arrival. After Lester tells his goons to wait outside, we hear Nixon joking that "having lost a close one eight years ago and having won a close one this year, I can say that winning is a lot more fun." At this point, Lester turns off the sound on the TV and orders George to sit down.

The interaction between the television broadcast of Nixon's speech and the narrative can be read on several levels. Most obviously, perhaps, the scene foregrounds the theme of winning and losing. Lester perceives George as a loser whose bohemian lifestyle (Lester tells him he

CHAPTER 5

lives "like a pig") and anti-establishment attitudes are incomprehensible to him. Yet Lester himself does not seem to have come out a "winner," based on the revelations of the previous day: both his wife and mistress (not to mention his daughter) have been having sex with George, a hairdresser whom Lester had assumed was gay; his wife has threatened him with a costly divorce; and he seems far less elated about the election results than one might expect, given his political connections.

During the remainder of the scene, the television continues to play an important role. As Lester helps himself to another scotch, his attention shifts once again to the silent television set—temporarily forgotten in the heat of his conversation with George—and he turns the sound back on. Nixon's face, now in close-up on the screen, is framed between the two men. Read semiotically, the scene suggests a link between Lester's drinking and the election of Nixon: each is an attempt (whether on a personal or a national scale) to escape an imperfect reality, yet each will only lead to a greater demoralization. As Nixon speaks about his desire to "bring the American people together" in an "open administration," Lester at first appears to nod appreciatively, though he hardly seems to register the content of the speech. Instead, he comments to George that "the market went down ten points yesterday. Goddamn Lyndon Johnson!" The discrepancy between Nixon's vague idealistic speech and Lester's concern with the pragmatic details of his investments is emphasized when Lester, apparently bored by Nixon's speech, turns the television off, interrupting a repetition of his promise to "bring America together." Lester cares little for such empty political rhetoric; his gesture of turning off Nixon's speech represents, perhaps, his recognition that the conservative values promoted by the Republican Party do not provide all the answers. "I don't know what's right or wrong anymore," he tells George, shaking his nearly empty glass.

In *Shampoo*, television is a background presence that provides revealing commentary on the films' characters and their behavior within their political context, but it is in *Being There* that television becomes a central thematic focus. Made at a time when television had achieved a privileged status as both the dominant form of mass entertainment and the primary source of news and information, *Being There* explores an American psyche that has been so thoroughly bombarded with mes-

I Like to Watch: *Shampoo* and *Being There*

sages and images that it is no longer able to maintain a clear sense of its own identity.

Being There is the story of a feeble-minded gardener, Chance (Peter Sellers), who becomes a trusted advisor to American industrialists and politicians. Chance has lived in the same house his entire life and has seen the world only through the filter of television, but he is nonetheless able to rise to the highest level of American politics. A brilliant satire on the American political system and the influence of television on contemporary American life, *Being There* is a cautionary tale about the power of the media to manufacture reality and thus control the political process.

Being There can be compared with other political films of the 1970s that deal with the power of television, such as Michael Ritchie's *The Candidate* (1972), James Bridges's *The China Syndrome* (1979), and Sidney Lumet's *Network* (1976). Among these films, *Network* provides the most telling comparison with *Being There*. Lumet and screenwriter Paddy Chayefsky use television as a metaphor for the growth of a corporate state that progressively dehumanizes individuals, rendering them increasingly passive consumers of the programming they are fed. But where *Network* satirizes the inner workings of the television networks—which will do nearly anything to improve their ratings so they might profit from the product they sell to the public—*Being There* is concerned with the long-term effects of television upon an entire nation of viewers. Further, as film critic Frank Rich put it, television in Ashby's film "does not make audiences 'mad as hell' but instead reduces them to docile, passive children."[8] Viewed today, *Being There* seems a more subtle film than *Network*—less strident, less politically smug, and less hyperbolic, *Being There* is an arguably more frightening commentary on the effects of the televised image.

When the "Old Man" in whose house Chance has lived his entire life suddenly dies, Chance is forced to vacate the premises. Accidentally hit by the limousine of Eve Rand (Shirley MacLaine), the wife of one of the wealthiest and most powerful men in America, Chance is taken home to the Rand mansion and soon develops a close friendship with Eve and her husband, Benjamin Rand (Melvyn Douglas). Eve hears the name "Chance the Gardener" as "Chauncey Gardiner" and assumes he

CHAPTER 5

is a privileged WASP like herself and her husband, and from that point on, the misunderstanding about Chance's identity continues to grow in proportion and absurdity.

When he is invited to attend a private meeting between Rand and the president of the United States, Chance is immediately transformed by the media into a political figure of national importance, consulted on talk shows and hailed as a pundit and advisor to the president. While the president and the media attempt to investigate Chance's past (for which there is, of course, no record), "Chauncey"'s political prestige continues to grow. By the end of the screenplay, Chance is being considered as a candidate for president. Ashby's film is a satire on the media-driven political culture of contemporary America, a satire made more biting by the fact that Chance is constantly watching television and repeating the words and gestures he sees on the screen.

The film is based on the novel *Being There* by Jerzy Kosinski, who also wrote the screenplay. According to Mary Lazar, Kosinski viewed television as a dangerous medium, one that "insulates people from direct encounters with others, deters self-reflection, and implies a false sense of control."[9] In a 1974 interview, Kosinski proclaimed that "groups of solitary individuals watching their private, remote-controlled TV sets [represent] the ultimate future terror: a nation of videots."[10] Kosinski elaborated this position, focusing on the effects of television on children who watch five or six hours a day: "I notice that when in groups they cannot interact with each other. They are terrified of each other; they develop secondary anxiety characteristics. They want to watch, they don't want to be spoken to. They want to watch, they don't want to talk. They want to watch, they don't want to be asked questions or singled out. . . . So they grow up essentially mute."

Kosinski's description of the socialization of children who spend several hours in front of the television echoes the phrase that appears in *Being There*—both the novel and the screenplay: "I like to watch." Chance is Kosinski's characterization of a "videot"—the passive television viewer who has lost all connection to the world other than the falsified vision presented on the TV screen—but he is also a grown man who has been allowed to remain in the mental and emotional state of a child. Despite his ability to mimic the discourse of others, Chance is virtually mute with respect to the articulation of his own ideas and

I Like to Watch: *Shampoo* and *Being There*

desires. The film's title is an ironic reflection of the fact that Chance is incapable of being there in any sense that is not mediated by television.

The film's satire is directed primarily at American political life and at the power of the media to determine the course of political events. The president (Jack Warden) is an emblematic figure of the puffed-up but rather empty, indecisive, easily flustered, and ultimately impotent politician. His political impotence is accompanied by sexual impotence. ("This never happened when you were a senator," his wife comments after he fails to perform in bed.) In one scene, the president listens to a report from his chief of staff about what little they have been able to learn about Chance. The president's response to his frustration is to pick up the phone and order poached eggs for his breakfast. In another scene, the president stands at his desk with the head of the FBI sitting on one side, and the head of the CIA on the other. When the president asks them if it would be possible for anyone to erase all records of himself, the FBI official says, "The only one capable of pulling this off would be an ex-FBI man." When the President asks the CIA director what the "boys around Intelligence" think, he lamely replies, "They don't quite know." In editing this scene, Ashby cut away to another scene mid-sentence, accentuating the official's failure to respond in any useful manner.

Being There also satirizes American race relations. As Chance leaves the Old Man's house to walk through the decaying urban neighborhood, he passes the graffiti inscription, "the white man has a god complex." Later, the African-American maid who took care of Chance while he lived at the Old Man's house, Louise (Ruth Attaway), comments, "It's for sure a white man's world in America." In fact, the film contains a subtle but sustained commentary on race and class. This commentary is implicit both in the action and dialogue of film itself and in the television footage Chance watches. Two moments are particularly significant. The first can be found in the scene near the beginning of the film in which we move from the well-appointed interior of the Old Man's house to the surrounding neighborhood, where we see African-American men in a vacant lot attempting to keep warm around a fire they have built in a trash barrel—the specter of homelessness. The second is in the montage sequence that follows the reactions of

CHAPTER 5

various people to Chance's appearance on the *Gary Burns Show.* In this sequence, we cut from a shot of Dr. Allenby (Richard Dysart) watching the show on a television in the Rand mansion to a shot of a group of older African-Americans sitting around a TV set in the lobby of a shabby urban hotel. One of the viewers is Louise, who looks disgusted at the very notion of Chance appearing as the featured guest on the show and complains to her friends: "It's for sure a white man's world in America! I raised that boy since he was the size of a piss-ant, and I'll say right now he never learned to read or write. No, sir! Had no brain at all. Was stuffed with rice pudding between the ears. Shortchanged by the Lord and dumb as a jackass. Look at him now! Yessir, all you gotta be is white in America to get whatever you want." Ironically, Louise is the only character in the film to see Chance for what he really is, but her position as a poor black woman prevents her from revealing the truth to those whose power and influence have created Chauncey Gardiner.

Throughout the film, the mass media exercises an inordinate influence on American society. Chance succeeds at the highest levels of society, and of government, merely by imitating what he has seen on television. Further, it is his appearance on television, as a celebrity guest on the *Gary Burns Show,* that catapults him toward the pinnacle of political influence. This connection between media appeal and political capital is clear in the final sequence of the film: as Rand's business associates carry his casket toward his mausoleum, one of them mentions that Chauncey would make a strong candidate for president because of the positive audience response to his appearance on the *Gary Burns Show.* Ironically, Chance benefits from his lack of a past in either politics or business. He is the ideal media candidate, because his image has been created entirely by television.

Both the media and Washington society encourage Chance's celebrity through their tendency to promote the latest story or personality to an absurd degree. A *New York Times* reporter, having failed to get an interview with Chauncey, becomes obsessed with finding out about his background. Similarly, in one of the most humorous exchanges in the film, a major New York publisher, Ron Stiegler (Richard McKenzie), will say whatever it takes to persuade Chance to accept the book contract he offers:

I Like to Watch: *Shampoo* and *Being There*

Stiegler: Mr. Gardiner, my editors and I have been wondering if you would consider writing a book for us: something about your political philosophy. What do you say?

Chance: I can't write.

Stiegler: Of course not. Who can nowadays? Listen, I have trouble writing a postcard to my children. Look, we can give you a six-figure advance; I'll provide you with the very best ghost writer, proofreaders . . .

Chance: I can't read.

Stiegler: Of course you can't. No one has the time. We glance at things, we watch television.

Chance: I like to watch TV.

Stiegler: Sure you do. No one reads.

The medium of television has produced Chance, a character who can neither read nor write and whose very behavior, speech, and thoughts are simulated versions of the programs and commercials he watches. The constant presence of television screens within the film reinforces this theme of media saturation. Televisions appear everywhere in the film, from the garden of the Old Man's house to the Rand limousine to the stores Chance passes on his walk through the city. Rand's secretary, Mrs. Aubrey, has three television sets in her office, each tuned to a different channel.

Where Kosinski's book *Being There* rarely describes the particular programs Chance watches, in the film version, Ashby presents a careful sampling of cartoons, game shows, situation comedies, news programs, talk shows, and commercials that provides a shallow and often absurd picture of American society. These clips help to develop the film's themes and also often function as an outlandish contrast to Chance's blank demeanor. Each clip comments either directly or obliquely on what is happening in the film. As Chance prepares to leave the Old Man's home, for example, he tunes into a program in which a widow grieves at a cemetery. The widow turns out to be the agent Maxwell Smart (from the television program *Get Smart*) in disguise. The scene can be read as both a comic foreshadowing of Chance's relationship with soon-to-be-widow Eve Rand and a suggestion of his own "disguise" as Chauncey Gardiner.

CHAPTER 5

In another early shot, Chance watches the president on TV shaking hands with Chinese dignitaries. When Chance later meets the president, he mimics the handshake he has seen him use, thus emphasizing the empty and mechanical nature of the gesture. As Chance arrives at the Rand mansion in Eve's limousine, he watches an animated version of the song "Basketball Jones" in which the lines spoken by the character Tyrone Shoelaces reflect Chance's own situation: "I need help, ladies and gentlemens; I need somebody to stand beside me; I need someone to set a pick for me at the freethrow line of life."

While Chance's programmed responses are often oddly appropriate in a given situation, just as often, his reaction to a television program is at cross-purposes to what is happening to him in real life. In one scene at the Rand home, while talking to the *New York Times* reporter on the telephone, Chance catches a glimpse of an exercise program and becomes more interested in flexing his muscles than in talking to the media. In the parodic love scenes between Chance and Eve, the television programming is again used to comic effect. When, for example, Eve first comes to Chance's bedroom and begins to kiss him passionately, we hear in the background the theme song of the children's program *Mr. Rogers' Neighborhood*. The lyrics of the song—"In the daytime, in the nighttime, any time that you feel is the right time for a friendship with me"—function both as a humorous commentary on Eve's desire for a "friendship" with Chance and on Chance's childlike innocence with regard to sex.

One of the most effective uses of television to parallel and comment on the on-screen action occurs in the scene in which Eve masturbates in Chance's room. As Eve enters the room, intent on seducing Chance, the latter is watching a late-night love story on television. Chance begins to mimic the action, grabbing Eve, kissing her, and spinning her around while romantic music from the television show plays in the background. But when the television image disappears, Chance has no idea of what to do next. He responds to Eve's resultant frustration by telling her he would rather "watch." Misunderstanding his words, Eve begins to masturbate on the floor while he continues to watch television. At first, the television dialogue is in sync with what is happening, as when we hear the line, "You're rather lit-up tonight." Chance, losing interest in Eve's gyrations and moans of pleasure, soon

I Like to Watch: *Shampoo* and *Being There*

Chance/Chauncey watching one of many television screens in Being There.

becomes engrossed in a program of yoga exercises. As Eve climaxes, he remains completely uninterested, imitating the television yoga teacher by standing on his head.

Like *Shampoo*, *Being There* is concerned with miscommunication and misunderstanding. Chance's verbal habits create a number of misunderstandings, most resulting from the willingness of other characters to hear what they want to hear in a given social or political situation. Chance has a habit of repeating what others have said, parroting their speech in a way that makes it appear more original or profound. For example, when Dr. Allenby says that lawyers will soon legislate the medical profession right out of existence, Chance appears to agree, adding weight to the doctor's cliché: "Yes, right out of existence."

Chance's words, delivered with deadpan seriousness, are often taken in their metaphorical rather than their literal sense. When Chance says that the lawyers have closed his house, Rand assumes that he means that legal complications have forced him out of business. When he adds that all he has left is "the room upstairs" (referring to his bedroom

CHAPTER 5

in the Rand mansion), Rand assumes he is making a metaphorical reference to his own death. Conversely, Chance reduces the metaphorical expressions of his interlocutors to their literal level. When talking to the Russian ambassador Vladimir Skrapinov (Richard Basehart), Chance interprets Skrapinov's statement that "We [our two countries] are not so far from each other" literally, replying, "Yes, we are not far from each other. Our chairs are almost touching." The ambassador, of course, takes Chance's innocent rejoinder as an example of his brilliant metaphorical wit. This tendency to read everything Chance says as both metaphor and profound truth is a clever satire that targets the ways in which media—with their focus on sound bites—reduce everything to metaphor and cliché. We need only remember the media attention awarded to such metaphoric conceits as Ronald Reagan's "trickle-down economics" and George Bush Sr.'s "drawing a line in the sand."

Chance's repeated remarks about gardening and the changing seasons are taken by Rand, the president, and later, the media and general public as profound pronouncements about the economy and the state of the nation. The pattern of gardening metaphors begins when Ben Rand, assuming that Chauncey's business has been shut down, asks him what he would like to do with his life. When Chance tells him, "I would like to work in your garden," Rand interprets his reply as a metaphorical expression of his desire to work for his corporation. Later, when the president asks Chance what he should say in his speech about the American economy, Chance pauses in a seemingly profound manner, and then proceeds to speak in very literal terms about the only subject he appears to understand: "As long as the roots are not severed, all is well, and all will be well, in the garden. In a garden, growth has its seasons. First come spring and summer, but then we have fall and winter, and then we get spring and summer again."

Chance's speech, his longest single utterance in the entire film, appears to be an amalgam of different discourses: the first sentence, with its more sophisticated vocabulary ("severed") and elegant phrasing ("all is well, and all will be well") might be the language of a gardening program; the final sentence, however, a simple recitation of the progression of seasons, is more in the style of a children's program like *Sesame Street* or *Mr. Rogers' Neighborhood*, both of which we see him watching during the course of the film. When the president fails to grasp what

I Like to Watch: *Shampoo* and *Being There*

Rand believes to the deep symbolism of Chauncey's words, Rand inevitably interprets them according to a metaphorical logic. "I think what our insightful young friend is saying," Rand informs the president, "is that we welcome the inevitable seasons of nature, but we're upset by the seasons of our economy." "Yes," Chance replies with solemn emphasis, "there will be growth in the spring." This statement is further amplified by the president in his televised speech: "As long as the roots of industry remain firmly planted in the national soil, the economic prospects are undoubtedly sound."

When Chance appears on the *Gary Burns Show*, the interview revolves around the gardening metaphor. Burns finally asks Chance if he believes the president is "a very good gardener." Both Burns and the studio audience ignore the fact that Chance's reply is a non-sequitur.[11] The slippery nature of language in this media-driven society allows even unintended or misinterpreted metaphors to take on a life of their own.

The most striking sequence in *Being There* occurs when Chance first leaves the Old Man's house. Ashby uses every device in his arsenal—mise-en-scene, editing, camera movement, and musical soundtrack—to heighten this sequence, which is not only pivotal to the film's plot but also serves as a narrative and tonal bridge between the section of the film set at the Old Man's house and the much longer section that takes place at the Rand mansion.

The sequence begins with a long shot of Chance coming into the garden. The music intensifies as we see a wide-angle shot of Chance on the top step of the mansion closing the door, and we also see for the first time the exterior world surrounding the house. We have assumed that the house is located in a wealthy community, but we now realize that it is in fact surrounded by a decaying urban neighborhood. As Chance begins to walk along the street, we realize we are hearing an electronic version of Richard Strauss's "Also sprach Zarathustra." There is an ironic counterpoint between the grandeur of the musical theme and the wasteland in which Chance finds himself. Passing the vacant lot, he salutes (imitating a gesture he has seen on television) the group of African-American men huddled around their trashcan fire. He then passes a group of black youths playing basketball and arrives at

CHAPTER 5

a crowded urban street, where he asks an elderly black woman (whom he associates with the Old Man's maid, Louise) to give him lunch. This part of the sequence ends when Chance approaches a group of gang members, who mock him and ask whether he has been sent by "that punk Raphael," presumably a member of a rival gang. When Chance fails to understand the question, the leader of the gang pulls a knife on him. Chance, who until now has witnessed such violent acts only on television, pulls out his remote control and clicks it, attempting to remove the disturbing image.

The scene can be read not only as an illustration of Chance's naive relationships to the world, but also as an indictment of the television medium. When combined with technology that allows the viewer to control content via a remote device, the television becomes an apparatus that lets the viewer "turn off" unpleasant or disturbing aspects of the world, sealing him- or herself within an existence that admits only comfortable images and messages.

The sequence ends with another reference to television. An extreme high-angle long shot shows Chance walking uphill, his back to the camera, along the divider between two sides of a highway. The upward tilt of the camera informs us that he is in fact ascending toward the Capitol building, which is framed dramatically in the background. In the next shot, we see what appears to be Chance's reflection in a storefront window. When the camera pulls back, however, we become aware that what we are seeing is Chance's image broadcast on the large screen of a television, filmed by a camera set up inside the store in order to capture the images and the attention of passersby. Chance, confused when he sees himself on the screen, moves his umbrella back and forth to make sure it corresponds to the image and then attempts to peer into the television itself to discover the source of the image. Even more confused, he steps backward, away from the disorienting screen, and attempts to use his remote control to turn the television off. As he steps off the curb onto the street, he is hit by Eve Rand's limousine, which is backing out of its parking space. In this scene, Chance's alienation from his own televised image and his simultaneous detachment from reality is a metaphor for the alienating effects of television on society at large. No version of this key scene appears in the novel, and while Kosinski

I Like to Watch: *Shampoo* and *Being There*

received sole credit for the screenplay, Robert Jones and Ashby revised it once Kosinski's involvement with the film had ended.

As is clear from my analysis of this pivotal sequence, *Being There* is a brilliantly crafted film. Ashby relies on unusually long takes throughout the film; the average shot length of 13.7 seconds is about double that of the average Hollywood film of the era. Another stylistic feature that distinguishes the film is Ashby's frequent use of tightly symmetrical compositions, or tableau shots. This device is reminiscent of *Harold and Maude,* but *Being There* contains an even greater number of such shots, including Chance and Ben Rand stretched perpendicularly on hospital beds in Rand's "oxygen room"; Chance and the butler in the elevator, both facing the camera; Rand and Chance sitting face to face in wheelchairs; Rand and Chance being slowly wheeled down the hallway by two attendants; the two men walking side by side toward the camera while the attendants push their wheelchairs; Rand, Chance, and the President in a triangular formation during their meeting in the library; Chance and Eve standing perfectly still on either side of the frame, separated by a long corridor; and the president and his wife on opposite sides of the bed. The very frequency of such shots leads us to ask what their purpose might be.

In order to understand the use of visual framing in the film, we need to look not simply at the careful composition of so many of the film's shots, but also at the use of various kinds of frames and screens. In early scenes of the film, we see the blurred silhouettes of people's heads through a glass panel in the door of the Old Man's house, as if they are more shadowy versions of televised images. Throughout the film, we see countless television screens, as well as the screen of Rand's dictating machine, upon which his lighted words appear as he dictates into a microphone. When Chance first rides in Eve's limousine (the first time he has ever been inside an automobile), he compares the windows of the car to a television screen. "This is just like television," he tells Eve, "but you can see much further." Chance feels most comfortable with the outside world framed by the windows of the car just as the world he sees on television is framed within the perimeters of the screen.

Chance's observation about the moving car being like television highlights another motif in the film: the confusion between television's

CHAPTER 5

simulated (framed) reality and everyday existence. On meeting the president, for example, Chance tells him, "You look smaller on television." While Chance intends his observation quite literally (the president's head and body do look smaller on the screen of a television set than they do in person), the president is disconcerted by the comment, taking it as a criticism of his televised image. The conflation of televised image with reality is further emphasized when Chance appears on the *Gary Burns Show*. We never see Chance live on the set or present at the actual taping of the show; instead, we see the broadcast as Chance and the other characters are watching it on television. This scene highlights the fact that the media is in control of what the audience does and does not see. Similarly, the film viewer is subject to Chance's control of the television on which we are watching his show: when he decides to change the channel and watch another program, we are left in the same passive position as television viewers dependent on the network's programming choices.

An analysis of the film's use of frames and screens might help us to understand the most controversial aspect of *Being There:* its ending. In the final version—which is different from the book's ending or from any of the drafts of Kosinski's screenplay—Chance wanders off during the president's funeral eulogy for Ben Rand and walks out onto the surface of a nearby pond, drawn by his desire to inspect a tree that has become partially submerged in the water. He then sticks his umbrella down into the water as we hear the president quoting Ben Rand's observation, "Life is a state of mind."

Most critics have read the ending as an allegorical reference to the story of Christ walking on water. Barbara Tepa Lupack, who calls the ending "a weak moment in an otherwise fine and sustained handling of Kosinski's fable," interprets it as pointing to Chance as "the new social messiah."[12] Mary Lazar concurs, noting that "the film's denouement suggests deification . . . adding a solemnity which contrasts with the comic tone of the piece."[13] The ending contains enough ambiguity, however, that it can be read a number of different ways. This view is supported by Ashby's own claim, in an interview published in *Millimeter*, that he chose the ending because it offered a wide range of interpretations: "I did it basically for that reason: that there could be a lot of answers to it."[14]

I Like to Watch: *Shampoo* and *Being There*

Viewed in terms of the visual, the scene parallels the earlier scene in which Chance sees his image projected on the large screen of a television in a store window. Just as that earlier scene marked the demarcation between Chance's life at the Old Man's house and his "rebirth" in the Rand mansion, this scene marks the divide between his "apprenticeship" with Ben Rand and his new life in a post-Rand world. As in the earlier scene, we find a surface, or screen, that is unreadable to Chance. Here, as in the previous scene, he uses his umbrella to test the reality of the situation, but this time, instead of moving the umbrella from side to side, he pokes under the surface of the water. The resemblance between the two scenes creates a resonance in the film that—whether developed consciously or unconsciously by Ashby and Sellers—suggests both transition and closure.

If we take at face value Ben Rand's statement, "Life is a state of mind," we might see Chance's actions as testing that hypothesis. For someone who lives within the world of television as completely as Chance does, life is in fact "a state of mind," a state of hyperreality quite apart from our everyday notions of reality. Read in these terms, Chance's walk on the pond might be seen more as a whimsical ending to a postmodern fairy tale than as the serious commentary on Chance's future that some critics assume it to be. Throughout the film, a dichotomy has been established between two very different orders of experience and perception: on the one hand the natural, vegetative world, as represented by Chance's intuitive grasp of plant life and by the constant references to gardens and gardening; and on the other hand, the opposite world of electronic communication and technology, as represented by televisions, remote controls, and the way in which mass media has invaded nearly every corner of everyday life. Chance is not a messiah or even a saint, but he may have reached a point of tranquility within the "garden" of his own mind in which the laws of the natural universe no longer apply. Ashby's inconclusive ending leaves sufficient space for the viewer to create his or her own interpretation of Chance's walk on the pond. Through such an act, we resist the "videot" mentality depicted on the screen. Ashby's film, with its open-ended conclusion, is a collaborative project in the largest sense: a collaboration between the filmmaker and his audience in making meaning.

SIX

There's Something Happening Here
Music in Ashby's Films

> Hal comes in one day and says, "I'd like to introduce you to somebody who has a sense of this movie," and he brings in Cat Stevens. Cat Stevens is not someone you would even want to be in the same room with: he looked like a homeless person. But the two of them in their articulate post-sixties way started pitching *Harold and Maude*, and they had a great sense of the movie. It wasn't until Hal met Cat and they had this idea to do it as a kind of mini-opera that the thing made sense.
> —Peter Bart, in *A Decade Under the Influence* (Directed by Ted Demme, 2003)

Watching *Harold and Maude*, one has the sense that Cat Stevens's songs were written with Ashby's film in mind. Like the film, Stevens's music is concerned with life's difficult questions, and it seems to reject a technological, class-based society in favor of a more holistic and spiritual worldview. Stylistically, Stevens's songs are built on folk and blues structures, with distinctive, haunting melodies and syncopated rhythms that create a complex aural structure for the film. The songs bridge shots and scenes, providing a rhythmic background to Ashby's sequences and adding a layer of atmospheric depth to John Alonzo's cinematography. Stevens's craggy, resonant voice, most often sparely accompanied by acoustic guitar and piano, intensifies the emotional effect of the film's visual images.

Ashby's discovery of Stevens's music during the shooting of *Harold and Maude* completed his aesthetic conception of the film. Ashby had known from the early stages of preproduction that he wanted to use the songs of a single musician to achieve a unified tone for the film, but it was only during the shooting that he settled on Stevens.[1] Though only two original songs were written for the film—"Don't Be Shy" and "If You Want to Sing Out"—Ashby would use a total of nine Stevens songs: the two new songs, four songs from *Tea for the Tillerman*—"Where Do the Children Play?" "Miles from Nowhere," "On the Road to Find Out," and "Tea for the Tillerman"—and three from *Mona Bone Jakon*—"Trouble," "I Think I See the Light," and "I Wish, I Wish."[2]

We understand the importance of music in *Harold and Maude* from the very first shot. As the credits begin, we watch the figure of a young man—dressed in a brown suit and viewed only from the waist down—as he descends a wooden staircase, walks across the floor to a phonograph cabinet, and puts a record on the turntable. As the young man, soon to be identified as protagonist Harold Chasen, places the needle on the record, we hear the gentle guitar and piano introduction to Stevens's song "Don't Be Shy." Harold then continues across the room, sits down, and writes something on a piece of paper, which he then attaches to his lapel.

As the scene proceeds, we hear the lyrics of Stevens's song:

Don't be shy, just let your feelings roll on by.
Don't wear fear, or nobody will know you're there . . .

After lighting several candles, Harold steps onto a chair and then off again, his swinging legs and limp body suggesting that he has hanged himself. The song cuts off abruptly the moment Harold steps from the chair. It is not immediately clear whether we are witnessing an actual suicide, in part because of the lighthearted mood set by the music, but a long shot of the room reveals that Harold's body is indeed hanging from a rope attached to the ceiling.

At that moment, Mrs. Chasen enters the room, glances at Harold,

CHAPTER 6

and begins to dial the telephone. "I suppose you think that's very funny, Harold," she admonishes him as she waits for her connection. Without missing a beat, she cancels her hairdressing appointment, claiming that she is too busy preparing for her dinner party that night. As Mrs. Chasen gets up to leave the room, Harold makes a series of choking noises and then, seeing that his act is having no effect on his mother, abruptly stops. Mrs. Chasen turns to face him: "Oh, dinner at eight, Harold. And do try to be a little more vivacious!"

As she leaves the room, we hear the sound of a harp playing the traditional air "Greensleeves," the reason for which will become clear only when we enter the next shot: a group of people at Mrs. Chasen's dinner party that evening. In the background, we see a woman playing the harp.

The initial scene illustrates Ashby's use of music to heighten the narrative, visual, and rhythmic aspects of the film. The scene is highly effective in narrative terms. While the camera first presents Harold as a faceless and truncated young man whose unhappiness and hostility toward his mother can be expressed only through the desperate act of a fake suicide, the soundtrack suggests the possibility of an alternate reality in which Harold might form meaningful relationships with others ("Just lift your head, and let your feelings out instead").

The scene also works symbolically, since it is Harold himself who, by putting on the record, initiates the film's soundtrack. Harold's act functions on two levels. As an action within the narrative, it suggests that he has the initiative to break the destructive emotional cycle he has established with his mother and to move from isolation and despair to love and self-realization. In a meta-narrative sense, the immediate presence of music in the movie signals Ashby's intention to make the soundtrack—and sound itself—an integral part of the film. Even ambient sounds are foregrounded in the scene. The sounds of Harold's shoes on the stairs and Mrs. Chasen dialing the telephone are heightened, as if to emphasize the gap between silence and noise.

Throughout the scene, Ashby also indicates his intention to use the musical score in a nontraditional way, blurring the line between the world within the film and the world outside it. The Cat Stevens song begins diegetically—as a record played by Harold—but it ends nondiegetically, its sudden termination as Harold steps off the chair establishing its extradiegetic status.³ Reversing that dynamic, "Greensleeves" begins nondiegetically and is only later revealed to be diegetic. In *Harold and Maude*, the boundary between the diegetic world of the film and the extradiegetic world is not clearly defined. This point is made most dramatically in the scene in which Harold, having sent his first computer date running from the house screaming in horror, directs his gaze straight at the camera and smiles conspiratorially at the viewer.

Harold is associated throughout the film with the nondiegetic score of Cat Stevens's songs, while Maude is associated not only with diegetic music, but with music as live performance. In their first encounter, Maude asks Harold if he sings and dances. Later, she gives him a banjo from her collection of musical instruments and teaches him how to play it. "Everyone should be able to make some music," she says. "That's the cosmic dance!" Maude's performance of Stevens's composition "If You Want to Sing Out" cleverly links Maude's diegetic music-making with the film's extradiegetic score.

It is also clear in the opening scene that music will have a formal function: to heighten the visual aspects of the film. The repetitive rhythms and lyrics of the first song accentuate Harold's deliberate actions in the scene—walking slowly down the stairs, putting on the record, lighting the candles. Ashby also tends to use music in the film as an overt structuring device, ending the song abruptly, for example, to mark Harold's suicide. Throughout the film, he matches musical rhythm with the rhythm of the camera movements; with the characters' movements, actions, and dialogue; and with his editing (for example, cutting to a new shot on the downbeat).

Ashby was certainly not the only New Hollywood director to create a score using previously recorded songs by popular musicians. The rock score, which Jeff Smith has more accurately labeled the "compilation score," was a staple of 1970s films. Unlike the classical Hollywood score, these scores helped to create a style of filmmaking geared toward younger, more progressive viewers.⁴ The two soundtracks most often cited as seminal examples of the compilation score are Mike Nichols's *The Graduate* (1967) and Dennis Hopper's *Easy Rider* (1969).

In *The Graduate*, Nichols used previously recorded songs by the pop-rock duo Simon and Garfunkel to reveal the inner conflicts of its central character, Benjamin Braddock, while also making an implicit comment on the cultural and ideological gap between Benjamin and his parents' generation. As David Ehrenstein and Bill Reed suggest, the film was a watershed in its use of popular songs both as "a form of interior monologue" and as a commentary on the film's characters and action.[5]

In *Easy Rider*, Hopper took Nichols's experiment with the rock score a step further. The film was originally intended to have a score written by the folk/rock group Crosby, Stills, Nash, and Young. Instead, Hopper convinced his collaborators to use a score of songs by a variety of rock bands. The resulting soundtrack contained a mix of very different performers and styles—including Steppenwolf, Jimi Hendrix, The Band, and The Byrds—which in their ensemble reflected the diverse musical energies of the period. As Lee Hill describes it, the soundtrack "is a vivid snapshot of the fusion of styles that typified American rock in the late 60s."[6] *Easy Rider*'s score, as innovative in its own time as imitated since, accomplished exactly what the film's loose, picaresque narrative required: while capturing the flavor of the youth rebellion that was the film's subject, it also "took full advantage of rock music's ability to fill in gaps where narrative imagination flagged."[7]

In the early 1970s, following the trend set by *Easy Rider* and *The Graduate*, a number of films made effective use of compilation scores. Stuart Hagmann's *The Strawberry Statement* (1970) represented the youth culture through songs by Joni Mitchell and Crosby, Stills, Nash, and Young; Michelangelo Antonioni's *Zabriskie Point* (1971) used songs by Pink Floyd, the Rolling Stones, and the Grateful Dead to construct a surreal epic of late 1960s America; finally, George Lucas's *American Graffiti* (1973), which featured forty-one songs that could have been heard on the radio during the summer of 1962, set a new standard for the "wall-to-wall" score.[8]

The compilation score functions differently from the classical film score, which was designed (with rare exceptions) to remain subordinated to the narrative and go virtually unnoticed by the audience. The compilation score serves two central functions, both of which relate to the presentation of nonvisual information. First, the compilation score helps to define characters and explore psychological states. Because popular songs contain not just music but lyrics, the compilation score functions not only as a musical analogue to the action but also as a verbal commentary on the action and characterizations.[9] When we hear the song "Sounds of Silence" in *The Graduate*, for example, both the music and the words influence our interpretation of the protagonist's actions and choices.

Second, the compilation score emphasizes the generic conventions and themes within the film. While the purpose of the composed score is certainly to contribute to the development of thematic material, the contemporary rock and pop score does so more directly, both because of its verbal content and because of the cultural connotations provided by the songs themselves, many of which the audience already knows. In the 1960s and 70s, compilation scores were often used to highlight themes of "generational disaffection, independence, and identity,"[10] themes particularly prevalent in the rock, folk, and pop songs of the period. Steppenwolf's "Born to Be Wild," for example, is perfect for the soundtrack of *Easy Rider*, since the song emphasizes the generational quest for freedom from society's laws and social strictures that is the film's primary subject.

The compilation soundtrack functions on three different levels in Ashby's films, which I will designate here as narrative commentary, historical placement, and aesthetic enhancement. Ashby uses it first to provide a commentary on the narrative action and the psychological states of his characters. This commentary can be ironic—as when there is a clear juxtaposition between the visual narrative and the accompanying music and lyrics—or it can function in a more affirmative way, reinforcing our sense of the characters' needs, motivations, and desires. For example, Ashby sets the opening scene of *Shampoo* to the Beach Boys' "Wouldn't it Be Nice," allowing the contrast between the action and the song's lyrics to introduce the film's satiric message. Ashby uses the rock score as an affirmation in *Harold and Maude*, for example when Cat Stevens's "I Think I See the Light" plays in the scene following Harold and Maude's night together.

Ashby also uses the musical score (along with cinematography, production design, costume, and dialogue) to help create a specific historical context, to place the film within a particular moment in history. Like other scores that include popular songs—from *Easy Rider* to *American Graffiti*—Ashby's scores for *Shampoo* and *Coming Home* help to establish the historical setting. As Jeff Smith suggests, the use of popu-

CHAPTER 6

lar music in a film score "is an especially effective means of denoting particular time periods or suggesting a particular social milieu."[11] Both *Shampoo* and *Coming Home* are set in 1968, a high point in the development of rock as a musical genre, and a moment at which popular music emerged as a vital expression of social and cultural change.

Finally, the music in Ashby's films functions as a formal element within the structure of the film itself. Ashby, whose training as an editor made him highly sensitive to the visual and rhythmic qualities of the filmic medium, used music in a number of formal ways: as a bridge between consecutive scenes, as a rhythmic counterpart to a scene or sequence, and as a means of increasing the emotional or aesthetic impact of a given shot. Ashby's films, like *The Graduate* and Martin Scorsese's *Mean Streets*, display a remarkable symbiosis between musical rhythm and visual image.

Music is an integral part of *Harold and Maude*, *Shampoo*, and *Coming Home*, but it functions in each film in very different ways. In *Harold and Maude*, Cat Stevens's songs serve as a lyric accompaniment to the film's visual rhythms, reinforcing the fable-like quality of the narrative. In *Shampoo*, the diegetic musical score helps to establish the film's historical period while providing an ironic commentary on its characters, themes, and narrative action. And in *Coming Home*, a nondiegetic score of rock music from the late 1960s recreates an historical moment, appropriating the emotional and mnemonic power of a wide range of late 1960s bands as a visceral reminder of a time when music was the primary expression of a counterculture.

Near the beginning of *Harold and Maude*, Ashby uses the song "On the Road to Find Out" as a transition between a scene in which Harold visits the psychiatrist and a sequence involving Harold buying and driving the hearse. The song introduces one of the principal themes of the film: Harold's search for the knowledge and experience that can break his cycle of despair. The psychiatrist has been asking Harold about his favorite activities.

> Psychiatrist: Tell me, Harold, what do you do for fun? What activity gives you a different sense of enjoyment from the others? What do you find fulfilling? What gives you that special satisfaction?
>
> Harold (flatly): I go to funerals.

Ashby then employs a device that is a trademark of his style in *Harold and Maude*: he cuts to a scene that is either a reversal on or a visual pun of the scene suggested by the dialogue. Here, he cuts to a long establishing shot of an automobile graveyard, thus playing with the viewer's expectation that the next scene will show a funeral. The song "On the Road to Find Out" begins to play. Ashby then cuts twice more: once to a medium-long shot of the same junkyard and then to a medium shot of Harold and a junk dealer inspecting a hearse. Each subsequent cut is made on the downbeat of the music:

[cut 1] Well I found myself alone, hoping someone would miss me.
[cut 2] *instrumental passage*
[cut 3] Thinking about my home, and the last woman to kiss me.

At this point we cut away to a close-up of Harold, shot from behind, driving the hearse through a car wash with one hand on the wheel, the other holding a bottle of soda to his lips. The next line of the song, "But sometimes you have to moan," is synched with the fourth cut, to a medium close-up shot from the side of Harold driving along the highway. Harold sways in time to the music, as though he were listening to it on the car radio. The final cut of the sequence introduces a shot of treetops framed against a blue sky, followed by the slow tilt of the camera down to an overhead shot of a cemetery where a funeral is in process. As the song begins to fade, we hear the sound of the priest's voice delivering the eulogy, the precise words becoming clear only when the song ends.

Here, Ashby matches the rhythms of his editing to the rhythms of the music, giving a greater density to what would otherwise be a series of fairly ordinary narrative shots. Though the sequence contains a total of only six shots and no dialogue, the combination of visual footage, music, and lyrics manage to create a vivid self-enclosed narrative depicting Harold's movement away from his mother's stultifying influence, a movement from confinement to freedom. This progression begins in the boxlike psychiatrist's office (where, in an inspired use of costume design, Harold and the psychiatrist wear identical clothes) and moves to the automobile graveyard, where Harold's decision to buy and restore the hearse suggests the cycle of death and resurrection that

CHAPTER 6

becomes one of the film's central motifs. The car wash represents an act of spiritual cleansing, but it also provides a visual analogue for the lyrics "you're locked toward the future." Harold's body movements as he drives the hearse, swaying to the music, suggest a greater freedom and assurance than we have seen in his actions up to this point.

Another strikingly effective fusion of music and visuals occurs near the middle of the film. As Harold and Maude walk through a field of flowers, the sounds of an acoustic guitar introduce the song "Where Do the Children Play?" On the downbeat of a guitar chord, we cut to a medium close-up of the two characters, accompanied by Maude's dialogue: "I feel that much of the world's sorrow comes from people who are *this* [pointing to one flower] yet allow themselves to be treated as *that*." Another cut reveals that Harold and Maude are standing in a cemetery, and at this point the song begins in earnest. The camera then pulls back to reveal an enormous cemetery with white gravestones in perfect rows as far as the eye can see.

As in the previous example, the song in this scene builds a bridge between a number of different but visually connected shots: the field of white flowers, the cemetery with its visually analogous white gravestones, a car speeding along a dirt road, and finally the same car driving into a city, where it circles around and comes to a stop. Tonally, the song enhances the lyricism of the scene, while also contributing to the narrative and thematic development of the film by posing questions about the state of contemporary society:

> Switch on summer from a slot machine.
> Get what you want to if you want 'cause you can get anything.

The lyrics are associated with Maude as well as with Harold, since it is Maude's statement that initiates the singing, and it is her ethos of ecological awareness that that is expressed in the lyrics, though the song's refrain "where do the children play?" also refers to Harold's transition from childhood to adulthood.

The final scene of the film displays the most effective interplay of sound and visuals, made all the more riveting by the contrast between the relatively fast editing rhythms and the slow rhythm of the music. The sequence consists of thirty-five shots in three minutes, meaning that the shots are, on average, half as long as the shots that make up the rest of the film. The rapid editing and frequent cross-cutting in the sequence are juxtaposed with the slow pace of the song "Trouble," a disparity reinforced by the absence of either dialogue or ambient sound during the entire sequence.

The song begins on a cut away from a dramatic dialogue scene between Harold and Maude in the ambulance to a shot of Harold driving his car along a wet road. This shot, as we soon discover, is being shown out of chronological sequence. This nonsequential cut initiates a montage of shots that includes admitting Maude to the hospital (13 shots), and Harold waiting in the hospital waiting room and being informed of Maude's death (7 shots). This chronological sequence is intercut with shots of Harold driving his car from the hospital to the ocean (15 shots). The song's simple, ballad-like structure, plaintive tone, and expressive lyrics convey Harold's emotional upheaval at Maude's impending death.

The final lyrics of the song express Harold's despair after he learns that Maude has in fact died:

> Trouble, oh trouble please be kind
> I don't want no fight, and I haven't got a lot of time.

On the word "time," the song ends abruptly, and the music is replaced on the soundtrack by the sound of the car engine straining as Harold drives up a dirt road to a cliff overhanging the ocean. We watch the car fly over the edge, plunging to the beach below. The action of the film's ending, including its delayed resolution, mirrors that of the opening sequence. In the opening, Harold apparently hangs himself; here, we see his car drive off the cliff, apparently with him inside it. We hear the crash of the car hitting the beach, followed by the sounds of the waves and the wind, and then the camera tilts to show Harold standing, alive, on the cliff above. Walking away from the cliff, he lifts his banjo and picks out the tune of "If You Want to Sing Out." The film ends, just as it began, with music. Here, however, rather than simply putting a record on the phonograph, Harold makes music, becomes an active performer. No longer "shy," he has learned to sing out and be free. He has joined Maude in the cosmic dance.

CHAPTER 6

In directing *Shampoo*, Ashby did not have the same free rein he had enjoyed while making *Harold and Maude*. While he favored using a compilation score of songs by a number of late 1960s bands—the Beach Boys, the Mamas and the Papas, the Beatles, Simon and Garfunkel, Jefferson Airplane, the Byrds, Bob Dylan, and Buffalo Springfield— his collaborator Warren Beatty did not share his vision. As Ashby explained, "We tried a lot of different things, and then that [music] started to be eliminated and . . . when we got Paul [Simon] and we listened to some different things Paul had done we liked that particular theme—it was just kind of a melody—it just evolved."[12] The theme composed by Paul Simon, which is repeated in different variations throughout the second half of the film, provides only the barest hint of a nondiegetic film score. In fact, the film cannot even be said to *have* a score in the traditional sense, since nearly all of the music heard in the film is diegetic. "All we wanted was a suggestion of a theme," Ashby noted. "In other words, what I think we were doing is going anti-score."

Despite the relatively limited use of music in the soundtrack, it is still crucial to both character development and to the film's depiction of a particular moment in the history of American society. The film's diegetic score begins immediately, before we hear any dialogue or even see an image on the screen. In a completely dark room, we hear the Beach Boys' song "Wouldn't It Be Nice" playing on the radio, along with the sounds of George and Felicia making love. As we are introduced to the characters, we realize that the song functions as an ironic counterpoint to their actions. The song celebrates a young man's desire to be with, perhaps even to marry, his girlfriend, whereas George's relationship with Felicia is a purely sexual liaison between a flagrant lothario, now approaching middle age, and an older married woman.

When we juxtapose the song lyrics and the dialogue of the opening scene, the contrast between the song's hopeful melody and naively romantic narrative and the more cynical perspective of the film becomes clear.

> Maybe if we think and wish and hope and pray it might come true.
> Baby then there wouldn't be a single thing we couldn't do.

While the song plays, we also hear Felicia Karp and George Roundy in the midst of a sexual encounter: moans of pleasure are followed by the sounds of a bed thumping against the wall, and, finally, Felicia's voice as she approaches orgasm, saying, "The headboard . . . it kind of makes me nervous. It really thumps. George, could you just put your hand up there and hold it. That's right . . . that's . . . oh, Jesus! Jesus Christ!" It is at this point that the phone rings. George rolls over, turns off the radio, and answers the phone. Learning that it is one of his female clients from the salon, he tells her to come by the shop. Almost immediately, the phone rings again, and this time it is George's girlfriend, Jill, demanding that he come over. George gets out of bed and dresses. His night with Felicia is over, ending with a bang that is more like a whimper.

The lyrics of the Beach Boys' song reflect on George's situation in a number of ways. The repeated line, "We could get married, and we could be happy" establishes the central fact of the film's narrative: George is incapable of settling down with any woman. The refrain "Wouldn't it be nice" seems to refer to George's prevailing state of dissatisfaction. George lives in a dream world in which, because of his considerable charm and his talent as a hairdresser, he has been allowed to remain self-involved and immature. George "hopes and prays" that his wishes will come true, without ever making the necessary effort to reach his goals. When he speaks to a loan officer at the bank about starting his own hairdressing business, he has neither references nor a financial plan; when he goes to Felicia's house to do her hair, he jumps into bed with her sixteen-year-old daughter Lorna, not stopping to consider the disastrous consequences such an act might have for his relationship with both Felicia and Lester Karp, whom he hopes might finance his beauty salon. Because George is only able to "talk about" his plans for a future without really acting on them, he will always have to "live without it."

Among the several other instances of diegetic music in the film, the most significant concern the music at the two election-night parties attended by the main characters. *Shampoo* is firmly located in time and place: three successive days in early November 1968 in Beverly Hills and Los Angeles, a crucial moment in American politics. The election of Richard Nixon over Hubert Humphrey marks the ascendancy of a more conservative political climate in America, and it is largely through

CHAPTER 6

the musical score that Ashby conveys the political and social divisions that are at the center of his film. Music is one of the markers of a dividing line that separates the two primary spheres depicted within the film: the older, more conservative America represented by Lester Karp and his Republican Party connections at the Bistro, and the younger, culturally progressive, politically liberal America represented by the party at Sammy's house.

Lester Karp has booked the upscale Los Angeles restaurant the Bistro for his Republican election-night party. As George and Jackie enter the bar, they are greeted by a kitschy jazz version of the Beatles' song "Yesterday." This musical reference works on several levels: First, the song's title makes a wry allusion to the fact that this political and social scene is stuck in the past; second, the song itself, a pop classic now reduced to pabulum, represents the stiffly artificial quality of everything associated with the setting—from Lester's canned stories to Jackie's chicken, which "tastes like rubber." At the second party, we will hear two Beatles songs in their original formats, suggesting that this party is more authentic than the party at the Bistro. Finally, the song's lyrics ("Yesterday all my troubles seemed so far away / Now it looks as though they're here to stay") seem to comment ironically both on the narrative situation as it concerns the main character, George, and on the situation of the country as a whole, which is about to enter the troubled era of the Nixon administration. Ashby's thematic use of "Yesterday" is made more pointed by the mise-en-scène: several shots display a large picture of Nixon's face on the wall, while other shots of the Bistro's interior show a Nixon/Agnew campaign poster and a portrait of Ronald Reagan.

The rendition of "Yesterday" is followed by a similarly jazzy arrangement of the movie theme song "Born Free," thus linking this political event with Lester, who we have heard humming the same tune. Again, the title of the song suggests a pun: the stifling environment provides little opportunity to be "as free as the wind blows." Finally, we hear a version of "Strangers in the Night," a song popularized by Frank Sinatra and associated with an older, pre-rock generation. The title may be read as yet another pun, an ironic comment on the attempts of certain characters—Lester and Jackie, Jackie and George, George and Felicia, George and Jill—to pretend they have never met or never been intimate. They act the part of "strangers in the night, exchanging glances" in a social charade that becomes increasingly uncomfortable and untenable.[13]

When we shift to the second party, a continuous medley of late 60s rock-and-roll songs characterizes the quintessentially "hip" scene and creates a sharp contrast with the socially regressive culture represented by the event at the Bistro. Here, too, the mise-en-scène coordinates with the music to create a vivid portrait of a subculture. When we first see George and Jackie at Sammy's, they move freely in the relaxed, mellow atmosphere, seeming much more comfortable than they did within the formal setting of the Bistro. As psychedelic strobe lights play on the walls, the partygoers either stand or sit in relaxed groups, smoking joints, drinking punch, and talking. Compared to the stiffly choreographed scenes at the Bistro, the scenes at Sammy's involve a much greater sense of fluidity in the movement and spatial orientation of characters, as they go in and out of doors and move about the extensive grounds from the house to the Jacuzzi or the tennis courts. While the Bistro scenes are filmed in strict sequence, creating feelings of stasis, constriction, and boredom, the scenes that take place at Sammy's party involve a great deal of action, largely generated by the extensive use of cross-cutting as characters leave one party and arrive at the other.

When George and Jackie arrive at Sammy's party, they are greeted by the Beatles' "Sgt. Pepper's Lonely Heart's Club Band." The music is apparently diegetic: although its exact source is never identified, it sounds louder inside the house than outside. Here, the song played at one party is used to comment on the action at the other: We cut away from Sammy's party back to the Bistro, where we hear the lyrics of the Beatles song—"I don't really want to stop the show"— right after the announcement that there has been a bomb scare. The bomb scare effectively stops the "show" being put on by the Republican senator (an out-of-tune rendition of an "old ancient" song), and more generally alludes to the national spectacle of the presidential election, a show no one at Sammy's party seems to notice.[14] The Beatles song celebrates a kind of participatory ethos ("I thought you might like to know that the singer's going to sing a song / And we want you all to sing along") associated with the liberal politics this party—as opposed to the party at the Bistro—represents.

CHAPTER 6

At this point we cut to a brief shot of Felicia driving away angrily from the Bistro, and then we cut back to Sammy's, where we hear the lyrics "We'd like to take you home with us / We'd love to take you home"—clearly a reference to George's feelings for Jackie, as well as Johnny's growing feelings for Jill. The shift to the next song, Neil Young's "My Soul," takes place as Johnny, Jill, and Lester arrive at the party. The song continues to play as Lester tries to talk to a bearded, hip-looking black man, who offers him a joint. When Lester declines, holding up his glass of punch to indicate that alcohol and not marijuana is his drug of choice, his evident discomfort is reflected in the soundtrack:

> In a while will the smile on my face turn to plaster.
> Stick around . . .
> [A scraping sound is heard as the record is changed]

Here the lyrics are interrupted by a scrape on the record, just as Lester's conversation with his interlocutor is cut off by his "uncool" behavior. Lester, whose "plaster smile" will not work on this crowd the way it did on the conservative businessmen and politicians at the Bistro, is clearly trying to "stick around" in a scene that rejects everything he represents. After wandering aimlessly through the crowd, he walks into a plate-glass door, a symbolic reminder of his inability to read the codes of this subculture.

We hear the opening strains of the Beatles' "Lucy in the Sky with Diamonds" as George and Jackie, who have now wandered out to the tennis cabana, begin to kiss. The psychedelic lyrics suggest that any relationship between them now is more imaginary than real:

> Picture yourself in a boat on a river
> With tangerine trees and marmalade skies.

At this point, we cut to a shot of Johnny and Jill walking across the tennis court and then to Lester taking off his tuxedo as he prepares to get into the Jacuzzi. As Lester goes to get a towel from outside the tennis cabana, we hear the opening bars of the next song, Jimi Hendrix's "Manic Depression." Lester, in the process of retrieving a towel, peers into the cabana, where he is captivated by the silhouette of a couple having sex. Jill and Johnny arrive at the cabana, where they find Lester. Lester suddenly recognizes the amorous couple as Jackie and George, and he walks quickly away as Jill and Johnny peer in. When Jill realizes who it is, she picks up a chair, throws it through a window of the cabana, and runs away. George follows Jill, telling Jackie he will return soon. In the first of what will be a series of journeys back and forth across the grounds, George runs to the house, passing through the crowd inside and arriving at the front driveway just in time to see Johnny and Jill pulling away in Johnny's Porsche. George runs back to the cabana, only to find that Jackie is also gone.

In this sequence, the action reflects the lyrics of the previous song—"Look for the girl with the sun in her eyes and she's gone"—while setting up the Hendrix song that follows. The music and lyrics of "Manic Depression" echo the agitated state of all the characters. The shots in this section of the film have an average length of 5.7 seconds, about half that of an average shot in the film, a stylistic choice that heightens the sense of agitation and speed established by the nervous rhythms of the music and the increasingly frenetic physical movement of the characters.

The song's lyrics seem to apply most specifically to George's situation and state of mind:

> Manic depression is touching my soul.
> I know what I want but I just don't know how to go about getting it.

These lyrics reflect George's inability to find fulfillment either in his work or in his relationships. The line "Really ain't no use in me hanging around in your kinda scene," heard later in the song as George pursues first Jill and then Jackie, indicates the fact that George cannot hope to hold onto either woman. The instrumental climax of the song matches the growing emotional urgency of the scene, culminating in the moment when George realizes that Jackie has left the party without him.

The score of *Coming Home* is at once Ashby's most ambitious use of music in a film and his most controversial adaptation of the compila-

CHAPTER 6

tion score format. The film, which features a wide range of late 1960s rock and pop songs, is positively saturated with music: more than three quarters of the film's scenes are backed up by some form of musical accompaniment. As David Ehrenstein and Bill Reed assert, *Coming Home* is "a unique interplay of image/sound" so radical in its approach to musical scoring that it has divided critics and commentators ever since its release.[15]

Having been thwarted in his attempt to include more music in *Shampoo*, Ashby was determined to put as much music as possible into *Coming Home*. "If we had [had] the money it would have been wall-to-wall music," he later claimed. "I would have started it right over the UA logo and maybe even put a good disc-jockey in there now and then, like it was on a big radio station playing. But I did the next best thing, which was to put in as many songs as I could."

The music of the Rolling Stones played a particularly important role in determining the direction of the score. In the months prior to shooting the film, Ashby had been spending time with Mick Jagger and listening to the Stones' music. As Ashby began watching the dailies of *Coming Home*, the rhythm and sound of the Stones' songs seemed to him to match the rhythms of the film, just as Cat Stevens's songs had so perfectly complemented the visual aspects of *Harold and Maude*. When the final cut was completed, the score contained six songs by the Stones: "Out of Time," "No Expectations," "Jumpin' Jack Flash," "My Girl," "Ruby Tuesday," and "Sympathy for the Devil." Songs by other rock, folk, and soul musicians included Simon and Garfunkel's "Bookends," The Beatles' "Hey Jude" and "Strawberry Fields," Jefferson Airplane's "White Rabbit," Richie Havens's "Follow," Bob Dylan's "Just Like a Woman," Steppenwolf's "Born to Be Wild," Jimi Hendrix's "Manic Depression," Aretha Franklin's "Save Me," Janis Joplin's "Call on Me," Buffalo Springfield's "For What It's Worth," the Chambers Brothers' "Time Has Come Today," and Tim Buckley's "Once I Was."

Unlike the score of *Shampoo*, in which nearly all of the music occurs diegetically, the score of *Coming Home* is primarily nondiegetic. The instances of diegetic music fall into two categories: those involving live performance (Bill Munson playing his song at the Fourth of July picnic, for example) and scenes in which music is heard diegetically from another source. The latter category includes the scene in which Luke turns on his car radio and we hear the Rolling Stones' song "Ruby Tuesday," and the later scene in which he turns down the sound on his stereo as the song "For What It's Worth" plays. Though music does occur diegetically in these two scenes, the same songs continue to play in the background of subsequent scenes. "Ruby Tuesday," for example, plays through the next three scenes, cutting from Luke at his apartment complex to Sally and Bob in Hong Kong and then back to Luke at the supermarket. This continuation of songs from diegetic settings into nondiegetic background suggests that, as in *Harold and Maude*, Ashby had little interest in the kind of sonic realism created by maintaining strict diegetic and nondiegetic boundaries.

According to producer Jerome Hellman, the music in *Coming Home* was an attempt "to get a visceral response, to recreate the feeling of that time as effectively as we could" in order to enhance "the emotional texture of the film." But as Hellman also acknowledged, "the scoring was a source of considerable controversy" among members of the cast and crew: "The fact, simply stated, was that the scoring divided us. If we ourselves had mixed points of view that we had to work out until we could refine the concept to the point where it satisfied all of us, then, clearly, we anticipated that it was going to have the same effect on the audience."[16]

Jeff Wexler, the sound recorder for the film, was one of those who felt that Ashby had overdone the music: "The amount of music was a problem," Wexler claimed, "particularly for the dialogue scenes, when the song lyrics distracted the audience from what the characters were saying." Several critics agreed with Wexler's assessment. Vincent Canby commented that "Mr. Ashby has poured music over the movie like a child with a fondness for maple syrup on his pancakes."[17] Gilbert Adair, in his book *Vietnam on Film*, unfairly dismisses the entire soundtrack, calling it "one of the most dispensable in the history of the cinema ... as if Ashby had had a huge jukebox placed on the set in which he remembered, from time to time, to insert a coin."[18]

In his essay on the use of rock music as a mode of representation in Vietnam films, David James provides a more nuanced reading of the film's score. While acknowledging that the music and lyrics of *Coming*

CHAPTER 6

Home contribute a "social meaning" that is beyond any "purely musical signification," James argues that Ashby excludes from the score songs that might supply opportunities for ironic musical counterpoint with the narrative or direct commentary on the film's antiwar themes. The musical score, James asserts, "only vaguely underlines the themes in the drama."[19]

However, James—along with earlier critics like Canby and Adair—understates the social and political resonance of Ashby's musical score. In the very first scenes of the film, for example, the Rolling Stones' "Out of Time" is used to reveal the irony associated with Bob's character and his eagerness to go to war. Later, both the Rolling Stones' "Sympathy for the Devil" and Buffalo Springfield's "For What It's Worth" are used to fortify the film's antiwar message.

Moreover, the musical score plays a crucial role in establishing the film's historical context (the period immediately following the Tet Offensive of 1968), while also commenting on the characters' actions, life choices, and mental states. Ron Elwood has called the musical score "the dominant narrative element in the film," an only mildly hyperbolic evaluation.[20] The soundtrack is a constant presence throughout the film, with many of the songs overlapping several scenes. With the exception of the Rolling Stones' "Jumpin' Jack Flash," which accompanies images of a game of wheelchair football, nearly all the music is played behind dialogue scenes. The song "Time Has Come Today" alone spans fourteen different scenes, its "reverberating crescendos and clock-like ticking"[21] helping to build the tension toward the moment when Bob moves into the house for the final confrontation scene. In fact, the song's final chord is synched with a shot of Bob angrily closing the garage door after loading his M-16 and affixing its bayonet.

The Stones' "Out of Time" is the first song we hear in the film, and it serves as a transition from the pseudo-documentary opening scene of the paraplegic veterans playing pool to the first shots of Bob Hyde running through the military base. As the song's instrumental introduction begins, Ashby provides a medium shot of Luke Martin lying on a gurney, followed by a slow zoom in to a close-up of Luke's face. From here, we cut to a close-up of a jogger's knees and feet, gradually panning up to Bob Hyde's face. In this opening sequence, Luke and Bob are connected by parallel shots, just as they will be in the final sequence as Bob prepares to commit suicide while Luke speaks at the high school.

During the shot of Bob, the lyrics of the song begin: "You don't know what's going on, you've been away for far too long.... You're out of touch my baby, my poor discarded baby." We move to an extreme long shot of Bob jogging, the length of the shot emphasizing the ironic message of the lyrics. Bob is healthy, his strong legs contrasted through parallel editing with the wasted legs of the paraplegics receiving physical therapy in the hospital swimming pool, but he is "out of touch" with the reality of the war. Though he is not yet aware of the fact, soon enough he will be a "poor discarded baby," like the paraplegic veterans who have been abandoned by their government. Rather than fulfilling his ambitions of a glorious military career, he will instead disgrace himself by shooting himself accidentally, returning to the home front in a state of psychological turmoil that will ultimately lead him to end his own life. The repeated phrase "You're out of time," then, works on two levels. It foreshadows Bob's suicide at the end of the film (just as the lyrics "You can't come back and think you are still mine" anticipate the problems Bob will have in his marriage with Sally), and it suggests that Bob's brand of macho soldiering is outdated: according to the lyrics, he has become "obsolete."

During the scene, the visuals interact with the music and lyrics to ironic effect: Shots of Bob running down the yellow line in the center of the road emphasize his conformist mentality and his inability to adjust to change. The song is cut off abruptly in the middle of the last chorus by the sound of gunshots, accompanied on the visual track by a close-up of a gun-barrel pointed directly at the camera. It is a jarring transition on both the visual and aural planes, a stark reminder of the inherent violence of war.

The second song of the film, Simon and Garfunkel's "Bookends," connects three different scenes: the scene of Bob and Sally having a last drink with their friends at the Officer's Club before Bob's departure for Vietnam, a transitional scene showing the base barracks where Sally and Bob live, and finally a brief scene of Sally packing Bob's bags. The music begins as the colonel's wife informs Bob that the colonel won't be coming to say goodbye because of his "chess night." The song plays against the dialogue and action of the scene:

CHAPTER 6

> Time it was and what a time it was.
> It was a time of innocence, a time of confidences.

The song is elegiac, its ironic application to the characters in the film lyrics just beneath the surface. The colonel's priorities are distorted, his chess night taking precedence over the departure of his troops and officers. Once again, the music hints that Bob is a "poor discarded baby," though this time he is discarded not simply by American society as a whole, but by a superior officer whose obligation it should be to show his solidarity with the men under his command. This same hypocrisy will surface again in a later scene when the colonel's wife refuses to consider running an article about wounded veterans in the base newspaper.

The lyrics of "Bookends," rather than calling attention in any direct way to this hypocrisy, emphasize that it is a "time of innocence" for Bob and Sally; more generally, it is a time of naiveté for the American people, bolstered by the postwar prosperity of the 1950s and early 1960s and not yet jaded by the effects of political scandal and a drawn-out and costly war. We hear the line "I have a photograph, preserve your memories" as we watch Sally pack Bob's suitcase for his trip to Vietnam. It is a potentially tender scene of married life, but this image too will be shattered in the course of the film as Sally discovers levels of experience beyond that of her self-described position as "cheery Sally, the captain's wife."

"For What It's Worth" is another song that makes an important contribution to the narrative and thematic development of *Coming Home*. The Buffalo Springfield song, which became a classic of the late 1960s protest movement, was written in response to a confrontation between Los Angeles police and a crowd of hippies who were arrested for loitering in the streets. Here, Ashby takes the protest rhetoric of the song and turns it into a powerful statement about the Vietnam War. "For What It's Worth" functions as a narrative link between scenes involving Sally and Luke in their everyday lives and the pivotal scene in which Bob returns from Vietnam. The song begins as Sally looks wistfully at her empty garage, perhaps thinking about the prospect of Bob's return and what it will mean for her new lifestyle and her relationship with Luke. The song continues through a scene of Luke working on his wheelchair and speaking on the phone. Narratively, the song juxtaposes Luke responding to a request to speak at a local high school with Sally waiting for Bob on the tarmac of the airbase. On a thematic level, the song establishes a connection between Luke's growing commitment to the antiwar cause and Bob's unheroic return from a war he can no longer fully condone.

During these scenes, Ashby creates a complex relationship between the song lyrics, the visual track, and the ongoing dialogue:

> There's something happening here.
> [Shot of Sally in her bathrobe, walking away from the camera]
> What it is ain't exactly clear.
> [Cut to parallel shot of Luke fixing his wheelchair]
> There's a man with a gun over there,
> A-tellin' me I've got to beware.
> [The phone rings, and Luke answers]
> I think it's time we stop, children, what's that sound?
> Everybody look what's going down.
> [Luke turns the music down on his stereo in order to talk]
> There's battle lines being drawn.
> Nobody's right if everybody's wrong.
> [Luke: "Hey, what I have to say to high school kids, they're not ready for."]
> Young people speakin' their minds,
> A-gettin' so much resistance from behind.
> It's time we stop, hey, what's that sound?
> Everybody look what's going down.
> [Cut to shot of wounded soldiers lying on the tarmac]
> What a field day for the heat.
> [More shots of wounded soldiers getting off the plane and being loaded into ambulances]
> A thousand people in the street,
> Singin' songs and carryin' signs,
> Mostly say, "Hooray for our side."
> [Shot of flag-draped coffins being unloaded from a plane]
> We better stop, hey, what's that sound?
> Everybody look what's going down.

CHAPTER 6

> Paranoia strikes deep.
> [Shot of Bob walking with a limp toward Sally]
> Into your life it will creep.
> [Bob looks up and sees Sally]
> It starts when you're always afraid.
> [Bob waves to Sally]
> You step out of line, the man come and take you away.
> We better stop . . .

As the song continues, Bob walks toward Sally, staring fixedly at her through the chain-link fence separating the tarmac from the waiting area. When he addresses her, his first words are accusatory:

Bob: What the hell did you do to your hair?

Sally: I stopped straightening it.

Bob: Where's all the demonstrators? Some asshole on the plane said there was going to be a bunch of flower-heads out here.

Sally: There's some kids out there, but they can't come onto the base. Does your leg hurt?

Bob: No.

    The song interacts with the film's visuals and dialogue on several levels. Two of the most striking examples are the ironic use of the line "Mostly say, 'Hooray for our side,'" while we watch coffins draped with American flags being unloaded from the airplane, and the lines "Paranoia strikes deep / Into your life it will creep," as we catch our first glimpse of Bob returning from the war. Bob's "paranoia," which will become more pronounced in later scenes, is initially evident in his treatment of Sally. Bob's immediate response to Sally is to interrogate her, as if in an attempt to put her in a defensive posture; further, Bob is convinced that there will be antiwar protestors on the air-base, a fact that, as Sally quickly reminds him, is impossible given the degree of security on military bases.[22] Underlying his question about her hair may be a fear that she has gone over to the "other side," a fear that is to some measure justified, given her association with Luke. Bob's paranoid feelings have apparently been prompted both by his fear of being abandoned by Sally and by his fears of being shot by his own men in Vietnam. He is shattered by the experience of being "always afraid" and he has, in a sense, "stepped out of line" by shooting himself in the leg and thus becoming a source of embarrassment to the military.

The final song in the film's soundtrack is Tim Buckley's "Once I Was," which begins during Luke's speech at the high school and ends on the last shot of the film, after Bob has swum out to his death. As in the case of "For What It's Worth," the song links the three central characters, though here the focus remains almost entirely fixed on the two men and their opposite trajectories. As in *Harold and Maude*, Ashby uses the ballad-like form of the film's final song to create a sustained emotional intensity. The song's simple yet evocative lyrics and haunting melody interact with the rhythms of the cross-cutting between Luke's and Bob's scenes, creating a kind of visceral layering the sequence might otherwise have lacked. The instrumental introduction begins as Ashby cuts from Luke's speech to a medium-long shot of Bob walking out onto the beach in his dress uniform. As Bob begins to take off his uniform, the lyrics speak eloquently about his need to be recognized for his attempt to be a good husband and provider as well as a good soldier:

> Once I was a soldier, and I fought on foreign sands for you.
> Once I was a hunter, and I brought home fresh meat for you.

Ashby cuts back to a medium shot of Luke speaking into a microphone and then cuts again to Bob, who is now removing his shoes. The song continues with the line, "And soon there'll be another to tell you I was just a lie." The commentary is obvious: Bob feels he is "just a lie," both as a husband and as a soldier. As if to emphasize this point, Ashby cuts away to an extreme long shot of Sally and Vi driving in the speedster with the top down. Sally's apparent sense of freedom here contrasts sharply with Bob's evident pain as he prepares to enter the water. We hear the line "Will you ever remember me?" as Ashby intercuts shots of Luke speaking to the audience at the high school with a shot of Bob taking off his ring and running into the ocean. As the music swells to a crescendo, and Bob swims out to sea, waves breaking over and around him, we once again hear the refrain, "Will you ever

CHAPTER 6

remember me?" The final shot, of Sally and Vi walking toward the entrance of the supermarket, is accompanied by the last fading notes of the song.

As a result of the song, the film itself ends with a question: "Will you ever remember me?" In fact, the film's narrative does not reveal how Bob will be remembered, either by Sally or by his friends and fellow soldiers. In a larger sense, the question relates to the general situation of veterans wounded both physically and psychologically by the war: how will they be remembered, if at all, by the American people? *Coming Home* is an act of memory, an insistence on remembering certain unpleasant facts about the war and its aftermath. More than any other film about the Vietnam experience, *Coming Home* pushes us to remember not only the violent *acts* of war (the invasion of Indochina, the burning of villages, the bombing), but also the *effects* of the war on an entire generation of American men and women. The musical score of *Coming Home* functions as a facilitator of both individual and collective memory, rendering more tangible the social conscience that is at the heart of Ashby's film.

SEVEN

A Director under the Influence
Ashby's Final Decade

Toward the end of his career, Hal started to make a lot of enemies in the studio system. He became obsessed with the work and with the films, to the point where he really started to lock out the studio. There was an arrogance: I think his hubris got in the way. I would tell him, "Listen, Hal, you can't isolate yourself from everybody. You can't go up to your house and lock up the film. You can't become that obsessive. All directors are paranoid, but you've gone over the limit here."
—Norman Jewison

If you wanted to see Hal, you had to go to his house and hang out: that was the way he got things together. He would just say, "I read this great book: maybe it would make a good movie." But by the eighties, that's not the way the business worked anymore.
—Jeff Wexler

The release of Ashby's eighth film, *Second-Hand Hearts*, was practically a nonevent. After sitting on the shelf for nearly two years while Ashby fiddled with the editing, the film had a disastrous screening in front of the New York Film Festival committee in May 1981. Released to the public a month later, *Second-Hand Hearts* played for less than two weeks and in only six cities. The reviews ranged from bad to atrocious. Vincent Canby wrote that the screenplay "treats its characters as if they were wastebaskets to be filled with prose that any self-respecting writer would hide from his best friend," while David Denby proclaimed that Ashby's direction showed "astonishingly little feeling for what holds an audience," and Andrew Sarris called the film "one of the most excruciating tortures ever inflicted on an audience."[1] Marketed as a "recession romance," *Second-Hand Hearts* provided little comfort to viewers expecting a light summer comedy.

The film's plot involves two of society's rejects—Loyal Muke and Dinette Dusty—who become romantically involved and decide to drive from Texas to California, accompanied by Dinette's two children, in search of their "Bluebird of Happiness." (The pre-release title, *The Hamster of Happiness,* refers to a pet hamster they buy at a roadside market.) The action of the film is confusing on first viewing. One especially disturbing scene involves the molestation of one of Dinette's children by a young man, an incident that is never alluded to again and has no obvious function in the film's plot. In both artistic and commercial terms, *Second-Hand Hearts* was Ashby's first failure as a director. Despite a naturalistic visual appeal—attributable in large part to Haskell Wexler's cinematography—the film suffers from the performances of the lead actors, from a weak plot, and from a lack of tonal consistency.

Ashby encouraged improvisation from his actors, but Robert Blake and Barbara Harris do not seem up to the task; they are much less convincing in their performances than Jon Voight and Jane Fonda in *Coming Home,* where Ashby's unstructured method of directing had worked to his advantage. While Blake brought a kind of manic energy to his portrayal of Loyal Muke, his performance in many scenes is marred by overacting, as if he is attempting to play up the broadly comic elements of the script rather than adjust his performance to the more lyrical tone of the film as a whole. Harris's performance as Dinette Dusty is equally problematic. An appealing and versatile actress who had worked with Robert Altman and had trained with various improv groups, Harris and Ashby seemed a perfect match. Unfortunately, the chemistry between the two actors was not good: Blake would lose his temper when

Harris missed her lines or failed to hit her marks, causing friction on the already overheated set.[2]

From the start of shooting, there were serious problems. Half the crew members were chosen by Ashby and the other half by Blake, and the two groups did not always work well together. As the film critic Charles Champlin put it after visiting the set in southwest Texas, "[T]he first weeks of shooting . . . suggested a road company of *Who's Afraid of Virginia Woolf.*"[3] Champlin's allusion refers specifically to off-screen tensions between Blake and Harris, which were making the shoot difficult for everyone involved. Additionally, the physical conditions were almost unbearable: for six straight weeks, the temperature soared to over ninety degrees every day and often to over 100 degrees in the shade.

Haskell Wexler saw other problems with the project: "Charlie Eastman had written a cute, interesting cult script, but even when we were shooting it didn't seem to work. Robert Blake seemed somewhat out of control: watching him while shooting, I didn't know if his performance was going to be funny or not funny. It was a picture that when you're working on it you think, 'Well, I sure *hope* it's going to be good.'"[4]

Though no one involved in the making of *Second-Hand Hearts* felt it was a great film, the intensity of the negative response came as a shock. "We just kept thinking that Hal was going to do his thing and make the movie work," said stunt director Buddy Joe Hooker. "But it never happened. And that, it seems to me, was the beginning of things going downhill."[5] James Foley, a young filmmaker who had gotten to know Ashby in the late 1970s, observed the effect of the film's failure on the director:

> Up to the time of *Second-Hand Hearts*, Hal had experienced only success, certainly not any kind of crushing failure. And the experience of *Second-Hand Hearts* was so negative. For some reason it was very damaging to him personally. I couldn't help thinking: "So you make a bunch of films, and one of them doesn't work. So what?" But the destructiveness of that film was out of proportion to how bad it was. My memory of personal interactions with him was that at that point something dramatically changed, and he began to stumble and seem less fun. Before that,

CHAPTER 7

he had had a real sense of self-assurance, not arrogance but also not self-doubt. And then after *Second-Hand Hearts,* he became self-doubting. He seemed to be much more burdened by what was going on, and in retrospect I had the sense he did not have a taste for the fight that goes on with every movie. The free ride he had been given from a distance by studio executives ended, and he was totally unprepared to deal with that. It was as if he'd had a blissfully naive experience, and then reality hit.[6]

Ashby's spirits were not lifted by the experience of making his next film, *Lookin' to Get Out.* Ashby had received the screenplay in January 1980, around the time of the release of *Being There.* Written by Jon Voight and Al Schwartz, the project was a caper comedy based on two ne'er-do-wells who flee New York for Las Vegas in order to escape a pair of thugs who want to collect on a gambling debt. The screenplay may have appealed to Ashby's penchant for offbeat humor, but his decision to make the film was primarily influenced by his friendship with Voight. Unfortunately, it was a fundamentally weak script, and neither Voight's energetic acting performance nor Haskell Wexler's cinematography could save the movie from failure. Voight had not originally intended to play the lead role of Alex Kovak himself, and the fact that several actors—including Burt Reynolds, James Caan, Bruce Dern, Alan Arkin, and Peter Falk—had turned the part down should have been an indication that the script needed substantial work. Wexler, who agreed only reluctantly to shoot the picture, knew from the beginning it was a problematic film:

> *Lookin' to Get Out* was a lousy script. Everyone reading that script knew that it was lousy! And as we were making the film, Hal started to doubt that he could do it. One of the reasons Hal made the film with a lousy script was that he was very arrogant about what he could fix in the editing. There was one weakness Hal had: Hal was confident that he could weave gold out of flax. He was confident that if he had enough of that stuff in his mitt there was something magical or Hal-Ashbyal that he could do to make it work. Rather than try and rewrite it, he would say, "We'll shoot this, and I'll cut to the reaction of this guy, and it'll be fine."[7]

By the time principal photography was completed, *Lookin' to Get Out* was vastly over its $10 million budget, and Ashby's relationship with Lorimar had soured. Rumors were circulating that Ashby had a worsening drug habit and that he had done his preparation for the film on the drive from Los Angeles to Las Vegas. "In many ways," Ashby later explained in a memo he sent to several friends and associates, "*Lookin* was jinxed. It was a semi-high budget [film] that ended up high at a time when interest rates were at all-time highs. There was an actor strike in the middle of shooting and I had managed to hire a totally inept editorial crew."[8]

But others tell a different story, one that had more to do with Ashby's arrogant nonchalance than with the incompetence of his technicians. After the shooting, Ashby disappeared for two months, leaving the film in the hands of a team of relatively inexperienced editors. According to Janice Hampton, one of the editors, Ashby's disappearance left the editing crew completely unsupervised. According to Ashby, however, when he returned to the editing room, he was appalled by the cut his editors had made, and he spent months trying desperately to salvage the film. But Hampton claims Ashby spent much of that time cutting complex montages of Las Vegas nightclub acts set to The Police's "Message in a Bottle," none of which were ultimately used in the picture.[9]

Ashby brought in Robert Jones to help with the editing, after which point he began carrying the reels of the film around with him in his car in an attempt to prevent the studio from seizing them. He did not finish his cut until October 1981, and when he and Jones had finished, the film was two hours and forty-five minutes long, far longer than its rather flimsy plot and weak dialogue could sustain. Voight asked Ashby if Jones could reedit the film, and Ashby reluctantly agreed. In the final cut, nearly an hour of footage was removed, and as a result, the film feels choppy and badly edited. When the cost of delays and additional editing expenses were added up, the film would cost Lorimar $17 million. Given the fact that that it would earn only $500,000 in domestic box office, it was a financial disaster of monumental proportions.

Lookin' to Get Out was a critical as well as a commercial failure. Although the film did manage to get a handful of positive reviews—from Gene Siskel and Jack Kroll among others—the vast majority of review-

CHAPTER 7

ers panned the film. Peter Rainer set the tone for most critics, noting that the film's "buddy-buddy badinage and rompy psychodrama" were simply camouflage for an empty core, while Richard Corliss called *Lookin'* "a sloppy mess that stumbles toward oblivion like a drunk on a losing streak," and Sheila Benson noted the film's "strident charmlessness," adding that the performances, especially Voight's "blowhard" Alex, would "set improvisational acting back a decade."[10]

In the summer of 1981, Ashby was given a chance to regain his credibility as an A-list director. *Tootsie*, a Dustin Hoffman project about an out-of-work actor who pretends to be a woman in order to land a part on a soap opera, was in need of a director. Hoffman, who had wanted to work with Ashby for several years, convinced both producer Charles Evans and executives at Columbia to let Ashby direct the picture, despite what were now growing rumors about his drug habit and conflicts with studios. As Ashby completed work on his cut of *Lookin' to Get Out* in September 1981, *Tootsie* entered preproduction, with Ashby and Haskell Wexler doing makeup tests on Hoffman. Unfortunately, Ashby would never have the opportunity to make *Tootsie*. Claiming that Ashby's continuing postproduction commitments on *Lookin' to Get Out* were interfering with preproduction on *Tootsie*, Columbia announced in October that Ashby was being taken off the film. What exactly happened between Lorimar and Columbia may forever remain a mystery, but it appears that Lorimar played a decisive role in preventing Ashby from directing the film for Columbia. Ashby was incensed, feeling that Lorimar had no right to block him from directing a film for a different studio.[11]

Losing *Tootsie* was a severe blow to what remained of Ashby's already damaged reputation, leaving him with a dwindling range of opportunities in Hollywood. He directed no feature films between 1981 and 1984, though he did make a concert film, *Let's Spend the Night Together*, based on the Rolling Stones' 1981 United States tour. Several projects Ashby had hoped to direct during these years fell through. One of them was *The Hawkline Monster*, a movie based on a Richard Brautigan novella in which two early-twentieth-century gunmen are hired by a pair of identical twins, the Hawkline sisters, to exorcise a monster created by their father's experiments and now living in an ice-cave under their mansion. Other unrealized projects included *Kalki*, a film based on Gore Vidal's satirical novel about a man who claims to be the last incarnation of the Hindu god Vishnu, with Mick Jagger playing the title role, and *Hand Carved Coffins,* based on Truman Capote's nonfiction novella, with Jack Nicholson playing a detective on the trail of a serial killer. Ashby remained attached to the *Hand Carved Coffins* project until his death, with Lester Persky as producer.

Ashby's tenth feature film, *The Slugger's Wife,* was a disaster on nearly every level, making even *Lookin' to Get Out* seem, by comparison, like an inspired piece of directing. The script was one of Neil Simon's least promising efforts, and Ashby's style of New Hollywood filmmaking was in almost direct opposition to Simon's highly conventional approach to comedy. One manifestation of this creative divide was a running disagreement about lighting: Simon and producer Ray Stark wanted to shoot the film using bright lighting throughout, while Ashby and his cinematographer Caleb Deschanel intended to take a more creative approach to lighting certain scenes. To make matters worse, there were problems with the performance of Rebecca de Mornay, who was cast opposite Michael O'Keefe as the female lead. By late June, with shooting completed, relations between Ashby and Stark had deteriorated to the point where they were barely communicating. Columbia finally fired Ashby from the film, accusing him of unprofessional conduct and material breeches of contract, and released the film in a version re-edited by Margaret Booth.

Ashby's next film, *8 Million Ways to Die,* was entirely different from any film he had made before. A crime thriller about an alcoholic ex-cop who solves the murder of a prostitute, the film seemed ill-suited to Ashby's directorial talents. Nonetheless, *8 Million Ways to Die* intrigued him as a project that he might transform from a standard thriller into a character-based film about addiction and recovery. Based on two novels by Lawrence Block, *8 Million Ways to Die* and *A Shot in the Dark,* Oliver Stone's original screenplay involved an alcoholic New York detective investigating the murder of a young prostitute who turns out to be involved in an emerald-smuggling ring.

In its first incarnation, the film was to be directed by Walter Hill, with Nick Nolte playing the lead role. When that deal fell through, Stone tried to make a deal to direct the film himself. Stone was at the beginning of a directorial career that would soon include films like *Pla-*

CHAPTER 7

toon and *Wall Street*, but at this point he lacked the profile that would allow him to get financing for a relatively big-budget action film. The producer, Steve Roth, suggested Ashby as the director, and approached PSO Productions, a relatively new independent production company run by former MGM head Frank Yablans along with his partners Mike Moder and Mark Damon. Damon was interested in executive producing the project, but he first needed to be convinced that the director was drug-free and ready to be more accommodating in his dealings with PSO than he had been with Lorimar and Columbia. In two meetings, one at the PSO offices and one at Damon's home, Ashby was able to convince Damon to give him the job.

Perhaps Ashby saw *8 Million Ways to Die* as his comeback film, a vehicle that could prove to his detractors that he was still capable of making good movies. In a letter to Chuck Mulvehill, Ashby expressed his concern that the rumors of his drug problems would prevent him from getting a fair treatment from the studio in making the film:

> I've had a lot of crud thrown my way the last couple of years. My, my, the things that have been said about me. You are also one of the only people who really know I've never been addicted to anything but work. So most everything said about me is totally false. . . . I guess if they were really fearful because of all they had heard, and this made them believe I was some burnt out being just pretending to be me, then they would be suspicious of every move I make. But, my god, if that's what's going on please try to make them understand that it would really be the wisest thing to replace me as quietly as possible. They wouldn't be able to go through a whole picture with those kinds of fears nagging at them.[12]

It is also likely that Ashby saw in the story of Matt Scudder, a recovering alcoholic who succeeds in pulling his damaged life back together, a metaphor for his own battle to resurrect his career after accusations of drug addiction. Ashby asked Jeff Bridges to play the lead role of Matt Scudder. While Bridges was not particularly impressed by the script, Ashby's vision of the film, along with the opportunity to work with the legendary director, convinced him to give it a try. As Bridges recalled:

> I remember feeling so excited that Hal had a project he wanted me to be

involved in. He was such a great director, one of the master filmmakers of his time. Hal came to me with the script, and I didn't really see much in it, but Hal said this was just the basic structure of the film and that he wanted it to be really different from the script. He wanted it to be more about a recovering alcoholic. I remember asking Hal why he wanted to make the film, and he said, "I don't know why. That's why I want to make the film: to find out why I want to make it." This was typical of Hal: so much of Hal's work had to do with improvisation.[13]

Ashby knew that he would not be able to work with Stone's first-draft screenplay, which involved Scudder in three graphic sex scenes. "Hal wanted it totally changed," said Stone. "He was on a completely different wavelength than I was." Still uncomfortable with the revised script Stone gave him in early April, Ashby began his own rewrite, spending the next three weeks working on the script and getting as far as page fifty-two. Ashby, however, was not a writer. After Roth showed the pages to Damon and other executives at PSO, they decided to hire another writer, Lance Hill, to do yet another draft.

At the end of June, still unhappy with the script, Ashby gave it to his friend Robert Towne to rework yet again. Towne made extensive notes and held discussions with a crew of four writers, as well as a former police detective he brought with him as a consultant. As it stood, Towne realized, the script had serious problems: it read like two different films, one a crime story about a murdered prostitute who had been involved in a drug ring, and the other a character-based love story about an alcoholic ex-cop who becomes involved with the druglord's girlfriend. Towne hoped to rewrite the script to emphasize the theme of addiction and to tie together the different parts of the plot.

Unfortunately, even Towne's considerable skills as a script doctor were unequal to the task of making the mangled screenplay more coherent. Towne worked on the script for only about five weeks before he left the picture. The incident that precipitated Towne's departure involved a disagreement with Ashby over one of the film's early scenes, part of a crucial sequence that establishes the reason for Scudder's dismissal from the police force. In Towne's script, Scudder shoots a suspect during a drug bust, overreacting when the man hits a policeman with a rocking chair. But when Ashby filmed the scene, he had the suspect hit

CHAPTER 7

the cop with a baseball bat instead. When Towne heard that Ashby had changed the scene without consulting him or the film's producers, he was livid, telling Ashby that the bat was too lethal a weapon to make sense in the plot and that the scene would have to be reshot using a chair. Ashby replied that the scene had already been shot and he would not consider shooting it again. Though Towne was cordial afterward, his relationship with Ashby would never be the same.

When Towne left the film in mid-August, Ashby and his actors were reduced to improvisation. They began writing their own dialogue based on the existing screenplays, doing improvisations in Bridges's trailer with the help of an ex-vice cop named Art Fransen. It was hardly the method of filmmaking that made producers and studios comfortable, and PSO was becoming increasingly impatient with the slow progress of the film, as well as what they saw as Ashby's uncooperative behavior. According to Jeff Bridges, Damon had little respect for Ashby or his filmmaking methods: "Even though Hal's methods were unorthodox, he was a master who had made some of the greatest films ever. Yet Mark was on Hal's back the whole time, and he even sent one of his assistants as a henchman to be on the set."

Ashby's job was made more difficult by the fact that the postproduction schedule had gotten squeezed by PSO. Although the start date of the film had been set back, the studio refused to move the release date, thus giving Ashby less time to prepare an acceptable cut. Knowing that Ashby was a meticulous editor, PSO was worried that he would take so long on the editing that they would not have time to make their own cut before release. Two weeks after the last day of shooting, Ashby was fired from the picture and the negative was taken by PSO to another editing facility. To make sure Ashby would have nothing more to do with the picture, PSO replaced the editor Robert Lawrence with another editor, Stuart Pappé. Since Pappé never spoke to Ashby during the editing, Ashby had no idea what was happening to his film; indeed, he would never see *8 Million Ways to Die* in any edited form.[14]

Ashby took the case to arbitration by the Director's Guild, claiming that he was contractually entitled to at least ten weeks to edit the film. But despite a favorable ruling by the DGA, PSO and the film's distributor, Tri-Star, made the case that because of the April release date they would need an "expedited arbitration," allowing Ashby only five weeks to edit the picture. Ashby declined. As he later told Michael Dare, "It would have been silly to go for expedited arbitration and end up having to hand the film over unfinished. It would have been too frustrating. And there would have been nothing to stop them from releasing *their* version in the meantime."[15]

If the situation was galling to Ashby, once more deprived of the opportunity to oversee the editing of his own picture, it was equally frustrating to the actors, who had agreed to do the film only because they knew Ashby was directing and assembling the final cut. According to Bridges,

> This was a man who was one of the best editors in the business, who had won an Academy Award for best editor. And they really cut the film against the grain of what he wanted to do. I remember asking Hal if we were going to be doing a lot of looping, and he said, "I've never done looping in my life." He said he always could find a way in the editing to make the dialogue work. But after the film was taken away from Hal, there were long looping sessions, as if they were trying to make the film more like the original script, more of a traditional cops-and-robbers story.[16]

The resulting film is maddeningly uneven. The clumsiness of certain scenes is not entirely attributable to Ashby's direction. Since Ashby was not permitted to edit the film, we can only assume that the film Ashby had envisioned would have been radically different from the one PSO ultimately released. Rosanna Arquette, who played the role of Sarah, explained to Michael Dare that Ashby's improvisational method of working with actors sometimes resulted in takes that were not intended to be used in the final cut: "We'd purposely do takes where we'd overact, then calm down and do a take right after that which was perfect. One example is [the scene] when Jeff and I were riding down on the tram the first time. The way it is now, I say, 'Prick' and he says, 'Fucking cunt,' and I say, 'Fuck you.' That was just us on the first take, warming up to get into it. Hal would never have put that [take] in the movie."

Still, there are a handful of moments in the film in which we glimpse Ashby's ability, even at the end of his career, to put together

CHAPTER 7

effective scenes involving raw, energetic performances from his actors. In an online review of the film, Jack Sommersby notes that while *8 Million Ways* is clearly flawed by its weak script and confusing plot, it is ultimately salvaged by "an aliveness, a pulsating sense of sleaze and profaneness."[17]

It is the quality of the acting that most clearly identifies the film as one of Ashby's productions. Jeff Bridges, as Matt Scudder, can be seen as a New Hollywood descendent of the troubled private detective of film noir. Though Bridges's performance is not as dark as those of Gene Hackman in Arthur Penn's *Night Moves* (1975), Elliott Gould in Robert Altman's *The Long Goodbye* (1973), or Jack Nicholson in Roman Polanski's *Chinatown* (1974), it clearly owes something to the New Hollywood turn on the noir tradition. Andy Garcia's performance as Angel Maldonado, a version of the gangster figure immortalized by Al Pacino in Brian de Palma's *Scarface* (1983), is equally impressive. Garcia was near the beginning of his career at the time he made the film, and like Bud Cort and Randy Quaid—two other actors Ashby directed to outstanding performances early in their careers—Garcia credits Ashby with allowing him the space to do his best work.

The most memorable scene in the film is the climactic shootout that takes place in an empty hangar in San Pedro. Scudder has found Maldonado's cocaine hidden in the loading dock of a Poor Boy supermarket, and he calls the drug lord to arrange for a meeting in which he will trade the cocaine for Sarah. While Scudder stands over an enormous pile of cocaine that is rigged to explode and a police swat team hides in the rafters above, Angel enters the hangar from the far end with Sarah, whose neck is bound with electrical tape to the barrel of a shotgun held by one of his goons. It is an extremely tense scene that runs for nearly nine minutes. Garcia recalled making this scene:

> The dialogue in this scene was completely improvised. On the day of the shooting, Hal was coming from his trailer to the hangar, and I said to him, "I was thinking about what I should say to Jeff." And he said, "What you have to do is haggle with him, but at some point you have to cut Sarah loose: otherwise the movie is over." And I said, "OK, but what I was thinking of saying was—" And he cut me off, saying "Just do it in the scene. Don't waste it on me; just do it." He didn't want me

pre-editing the scene in my head and deciding beforehand what I was going to do.[18]

The scene is powerfully staged, the immensity of the hangar lending an epic theatricality to the action. The dramatic setting, the unstructured acting performances, and the extremely violent nature of the scene all anticipate the work of Quentin Tarantino. In *Reservoir Dogs*, filmed five years after the release of *8 Million Ways to Die*, the longest, most violent, and most famous sequence occurs in a downtown Los Angeles warehouse. Despite the parallels between the two films, the underlying sensibility of Tarantino's work is diametrically opposed to Ashby's.[19] In Tarantino's films, brutal acts of violence are an integral part of a filmmaking aesthetic. For Ashby, violence is a last resort; moments of violence are never gratuitous, and they never go beyond what the narrative requires. It is striking, for example, how many of Ashby's films pull back from a potentially violent act: Copee does not kill Elgar with an axe when he corners him at the top of stairs (*The Landlord*); Lester does not order his henchmen to rough up George (*Shampoo*); in the climactic scene of *Coming Home*, Bob does not shoot Sally or Luke; in *Being There*, members of the urban gang threaten Chance with a knife but do not harm him.

It is not that Ashby shies away from violence out of an excessive squeamishness. We see Bad-Ass beat Meadows into submission at the end of *The Last Detail*, and we witness an equally brutal beating of Woody Guthrie by antiunion thugs in *Bound for Glory*. But unlike many American directors—Tarantino and Oliver Stone among them—Ashby does not exploit the spectacle of violence or revel in the depiction of violent acts. If it is true, as Robert Kolker suggests, that since the late 1960s violence has been "sutured . . . into the very structure of cinema," and that acts of on-screen violence have evolved "from convention into display,"[20] Ashby's reticent treatment of violence can be said to go against the grain of most recent American filmmaking. In the climactic scene of *The Last Detail*, after a brief series of handheld shots of Buddusky hitting Meadows with his revolver, Ashby pulls back to an extreme long shot, less interested in emphasizing the violent nature of Buddusky's act than in underlining its futility. In *Coming Home*, Ashby rejected Waldo Salt's violent ending not only because it would have

CHAPTER 7

sensationalized violence in a film that was opposed to the politically sanctioned violence of the war, but also because, by presenting a returning veteran as a violent "psycho," it would have turned the experience of psychologically wounded veterans into a Hollywood cliché.

Among all of Ashby's films, *8 Million Ways to Die* is the only film in which Ashby depicts acts of extreme and even lethal violence. While the scene in the hangar is effective—primarily because of the riveting interaction between Bridges and Garcia—the film's final scenes are anticlimactic, and as a result, the film fails to offer the payoff it might have delivered in the hands of directors like Stone, Tarantino, or William Friedkin, whose stylish thriller *To Live and Die in L.A.* had been released the year before.

Sadly, *8 Million Ways to Die* has yet to be released in DVD format, an unusual fate for an action film with major stars and a world-class director. A provocative study of a filmmaker's effort to transform a genre film into a more original project, *8 Million Ways to Die* is a film that exemplifies, once again, Ashby's desire to resist generic categories and to attempt a more personal statement within the structure of a standard Hollywood film.

In 1976, at what was arguably the height of Ashby's directorial career, the film critic Joseph McBride wrote that Ashby "deserves to be ranked with Coppola and Altman in the forefront of Hollywood directors who have emerged in the Seventies."[21] By the end of the decade, however, the careers of a number of the most promising New Hollywood filmmakers, including Ashby, had fallen onto hard times. As Marshall Fine suggests in his biography of Ashby's contemporary John Cassavetes, the final years of the 1970s saw the emergence of a blockbuster mentality that subsumed the "personal, provocative, idiosyncratic cinema that had flourished for the first half of the decade."[22]

Several theories have been voiced about Ashby's rapid decline as a filmmaker after 1980, though no single theory can adequately explain what must be counted as one of the saddest and most surprising reversals in the history of Hollywood directors. The most frequently cited explanation for Ashby's problems in the industry is his use of drugs. In an article that appeared in October 1982 in the *Los Angeles Times*, Dale Pollock alluded to "ugly rumors" of a drug problem, suggesting that

Ashby's Final Decade

Ashby's disappearance from the A-list of Hollywood directors may in fact have been drug-related. It is important to remember, however, that Ashby was not the only successful Hollywood director of the 1970s to suffer a decline in the 1980s. As Peter Biskind suggests, "[T]he American directors of the '70s, with few exceptions, burned out like Roman candles after an all-too-brief flash of brilliance."[23] Among the high-profile New Hollywood filmmakers, only Martin Scorsese and, to a lesser degree, Robert Altman and Francis Ford Coppola were able to maintain successful directorial careers in the 1980s, while the rest of their peers suffered significant downturns.

In the relatively short time that he was directing Hollywood movies, Ashby left an indelible imprint on American filmmaking. As a director of film comedy, Ashby is in a select company that includes Charlie Chaplin, George Cukor, Preston Sturges, Woody Allen, and Mel Brooks.[24] Ashby's films articulate a prescient analysis of American life that has been a source of inspiration for a new generation of American filmmakers. Sean Penn dedicated his first film, *The Indian Runner* (1991), to Ashby and Cassavetes. More recently, directors such as Wes Anderson (*Rushmore*, 1998), Alexander Payne (*Sideways*, 2004), Zach Braff (*Garden State*, 2004), and Mike Mills (*Thumbsucker*, 2005) continue to exhibit the influence of Ashby's style and themes on their work. The Ashby touch, a unique combination of serious social commentary and a playful, surreal observation of the human condition, lives on in some of today's best filmmaking.

NOTES

Chapter 1

1. Biskind, *Easy Riders, Raging Bulls*.
2. Jacobs, Hollywood Renaissance, 216.
3. Sarris, *The American Cinema*, 31.
4. Lehman, "The American Cinema and the Critic Who Guided Me through It," in *Citizen Sarris*, ed. Emanuel Levy, 75.
5. Thomson, *A Biographical Dictionary of Film*, 27.
6. There have been at least eight critical monographs on Altman's work, as well as a full-length biography and a collection of interviews.
7. Kolker, *A Cinema of Loneliness*, 331.
8. University Press of Kentucky, forthcoming.
9. Kolker, *A Cinema of Loneliness*, 331.
10. For a delineation of auteur theory and its origins in Romantic theories of the individual creative artist, see Edward Buscombe, "Ideas of Authorship," 75–85.
11. See Robert Carringer's discussion of such theories in "Collaboration and Concepts of Authorship," 370–79. Probably the best account of collaborative filmmaking in action is Carringer's own *The Making of Citizen Kane*. See also Bruce Kawin's discussion of collaborative filmmaking in *How Movies Work*. Kawin provides a number of illustrative examples of "collaborative decision-making" in the making of both European and American movies.
12. Caughie, *Theories of Authorship*, 9.
13. Elsaesser, *Fassbinder's Germany*, 237.
14. Stillinger, *Multiple Authorship and the Myth of the Solitary Genius*, 179.
15. Carringer, *The Making of Citizen Kane*, 72–73.
16. Schatz, "Anatomy of a House Director: Capra, Cohn, and Columbia in the 1930s," in *Frank Capra: Authorship and the Studio System*, ed. Robert Sklar and Vito Zagarrio, 13.

NOTES TO CHAPTER 2

17. See my discussion in chapter 2 of the arguably difficult collaboration between Ashby and Beatty on *Shampoo*.

18. Kawin, *How Movies Work*, 300.

19. Deschanel, interview with author.

20. Hamburger, interview with author.

21. Cynthia Baron, Frank Tomasulo, and Diane Carson, *More Than a Method*, 7. Nearly all of the performances in Ashby's films can be described as what Baron, Tomasulo, and Carson call a "neonaturalist" style of performance, one in which the character belongs "to a clearly delineated social environment," and in which the character's actions can be read as "a consequence of personal history and environmental determinants."

22. Cox, interview with author.

23. Peter Wollen, *Signs and Meaning in the Cinema*, 81. While it could be argued that a director who makes movies on very different subjects develops the kind of broad range one would expect of an auteur, such an argument has not been borne out in the way auteurism has been defined. Directors acknowledged as auteurs are generally identified with a given genre—Alfred Hitchcock, Chaplin, Scorsese—or with two or three defining genres, as in the case of Ford or Hawks. Peter Wollen, for example, argues that even though Hawks made films in ostensibly disparate genres, he exhibits "the same thematic preoccupations, the same recurring motifs and incidents, the same visual style and tempo" in nearly all his films. Hawks was able to achieve such consistency, according to Wollen, "by reducing the genres to two basic types: the adventure drama and the crazy comedy." Ashby's films, on the other hand, are radically different from one another not only in terms of genres and themes, but also in their visual style, pacing, and mood.

24. It is clear, however, that Ashby worked closely on the scripts of all of his films, and he was instrumental in rewriting the endings of at least two films—*Coming Home* and *Being There*.

25. Hellman, interview with author.

26. For the purposes of this discussion, I include *Second-Hand Hearts* among Ashby films of the 1980s rather than his films of the 1970s. Although he completed principal photography on the film in the fall of 1978, the postproduction was not completed until May 1981, when the film received its first public screening.

Chapter 2

1. Ashby, Interview by Paul Frizler in *Close-Up: The Contemporary Director*, Jon Tuska, ed. Frizler gets other facts wrong as well, such as the date of Ashby's arrival in Los Angeles, which he places in 1953. Diane Jacobs, in *Hol-

lywood Renaissance, also writes that "Ashby was a non-Mormon born among Mormons in Ogden, Utah."

2. The promotional bio released by Paramount Pictures (1971) states that "after being graduated from Utah State University, [Ashby] joined one little theatre group after another."

3. Hellman, interview with author.

4. Hamburger, interview with author.

5. Jack Ashby, interview with author.

6. Ashby, Interview by Paul Frizler, 225. According to Hal's brother, Jack Ashby, their father's death was never officially reported as a suicide, but absent any evidence to the contrary, I accept Hal Ashby's account of his father's death.

7. Ashby was married a total of five times: in 1947, again in 1949, a third time in 1956, a fourth in 1963, and a fifth in 1969. Ashby's fifth and last marriage, which ended in a divorce in 1971, was to the film and television actress Joan Marshall.

8. In his interview with Frizler, Ashby claimed to have had fifty or sixty jobs between the time he arrived in Los Angeles and when he began working for Republic Studios.

9. Ashby, Interview by Frizler, 226.

10. Haskell Wexler, interview with author.

11. Jewison, *This Terrible Business*, 98.

12. Jewison, interview with author.

13. Ashby received a best director nomination for *Coming Home* but lost to Michael Cimino for *The Deer Hunter*.

14. Elsaesser, "American Auteur Cinema," in *The Last Great American Picture Show*, ed. Thomas Elsaesser, Alexander Horwath, and Noel King, 37.

15. Jewison, interview with author.

16. Mahoney, *Hollywood Reporter*, 3.

17. Harmet, Review of *The Landlord*; Riley, "When the All-American Boy Meets Miss Sepia of 1957."

18. Gordon, *My Side*, 395.

19. See the interview with Alonzo by Dennis Schaefer and Larry Salvato in *Masters of Light*, 24–25. See also my more detailed discussion of the film's visual style in chapter 3.

20. Geer, interview with author.

21. Peter Bart and Peter Guber, *Shoot Out*, 185.

22. December 16, 1971. Reviews in academic or scholarly film journals tended to be more appreciative of the film than the popular media. Michael Shedlin's review in *Film Quarterly*, for example, praised *Harold and Maude* as "one of the best movies to come out of Hollywood in years . . . a love story,

a sentimental black comedy, a ludicrous tear-jerker [and] a grisly social satire," 51.

23. Quoted in Biskind, *Easy Riders*, 174.
24. Ibid.
25. McGilligan, *Jack's Life: A Biography of Jack Nicholson.*
26. Towne, Transcript of American Film Institute Seminar, January 22, 1975.
27. Canby, "There's No Doubt—Jack Nicholson is a Major Star," 2.1.
28. Walling, *Society*, 77.
29. Kesey to Hal Ashby, Hal Ashby Papers.
30. Towne, in contrast, claimed that Beatty hired Ashby because he was seen as a director who "would be willing to 'collaborate,'" which was a euphemism for ceding control of the film to Beatty. See Suzanne Finstad, *Warren Beatty: A Private Man*, 414.
31. Quoted in Finstad, 414.
32. Ashby, Transcript of American Film Institute Seminar, March 18, 1975.
33. Biskind, *Easy Riders*, 193.
34. Canby, "Shampoo Could Be the Year's Best Comedy," 2.15.
35. Kael, "Beverly Hills as a Big Bed," 86.
36. Ashby and Wexler experimented with other photographic techniques as well: for one sequence, Wexler put a small camera in a suitcase and had one of his cameramen walk around the migrant camp, shooting impromptu footage.
37. McBride, "Song for Woody," 26.
38. Jacobs, *Hollywood Renaissance*, 231
39. Canby, "In Films, Acting is Behavior," 2.13.
40. Kauffman, "Poor Folk," 18.
41. Kael, "The Current Cinema: Affirmation," 148–52.
42. Wexler also won awards for cinematography from the National Society of Film Critics and the Los Angeles Film Critics.
43. Ashby, "The Five-Year Struggle to Make *Coming Home*," Interview by Rick Honeycutt, B13.
44. Ashby quoted in Richard Turner, "The Worst Year of Our Lives," 64.
45. Champlin, "'Coming Home': A Reminder of the Costs of War," Cal. 1; Kroll, "Vietnam Hero Worship," 89–90.
46. No actor had won both the Oscar and the top prize at Cannes since Ray Milland in *The Lost Weekend* over thirty years earlier.
47. See my detailed discussion of the film in chapter 7.

Chapter 3

1. Ashby, Transcript of American Film Institute Seminar Seminar, January 11, 1972.

2. As Dan Harries suggests, the boundary between satire and parody is often difficult to articulate. Since both satire and parody are forms of critique intended to "jar the spectator into questioning norms [and] taking a more critical stance toward 'everyday' normative assumptions," all parody "can be subsumed under a more general mode of satire" (*Film Parody*, 32). In the case of Ashby's first two films, I would argue that while the primary mode is satire, we find in certain scenes the parody of a particular genre or character type. The use of parody, pushed further in *Harold and Maude* than in *The Landlord*, virtually disappears from Ashby's later, more serious films.

3. Another humorous scene involves the impromptu lunch of ham hocks and collard greens shared by Marge and Elgar's mother in Marge's apartment. During the course of the lunch, Mrs. Enders gets drunk on Marge's carbonated wine and becomes increasingly less inhibited.

4. *The Landlord*, like Ashby's last film, *8 Million Ways to Die*, has unfortunately not yet been released in DVD format and is therefore difficult to view under ideal conditions.

5. I am not including Ashby's last three films, *Lookin' to Get Out*, *The Slugger's Wife*, and *8 Million Ways to Die*, in this analysis. Since Ashby did not oversee the final editing of these films, the average shot length does not reflect his editing choices, which in many cases would have differed from those made in postproduction.

6. See Barry Salt, *Film Style and Technology: History and Analysis*. According to Salt, the typical ASL for American films made during the period 1964–1969 was 7.5 seconds.

7. Ashby's other films of the 1970s all fall within this range: *Shampoo* has an ASL of 11.3, *Bound for Glory* 13.2, *Coming Home* 12.0, and *Being There* 13.7. *Being There* is often considered to be Ashby's slowest-paced film, even though *The Last Detail* actually has a longer ASL. Barry Salt, for example, remarks that *Being There* is an example of a long average shot length that is "associated with high artistic ambition."

8. Another filmic reference that may be less obvious to the average viewer occurs in the scene when Mrs. Chasen comes into the bathroom to find Harold apparently slashed to death in the bathtub. Here, there is an implied reference to Hitchcock's *Psycho*, in which the central male character, Norman Bates, is also dominated by a distant and forbidding mother. Of course Harold, unlike Norman, is no murderer. While there are moments when his rage takes the form of a murderous impulse (as when he points the gun at his mother during her monologue about the dating service form), Harold's psychic anger

NOTES TO CHAPTER 4

is primarily turned on himself. Nevertheless, the allusion to Hitchcock and the horror genre foregrounds both Harold's borderline psychotic personality and the grotesque humor that pulls *Harold and Maude* beyond the normative genre boundaries of comedy and even traditional satire.

9. Ruth Gordon gives a remarkable performance as Maude, a performance that would almost certainly have received an Academy Award nomination if the film had been better received by audiences and critics. Though Gordon has far less time on screen than Bud Cort, her energetic, funny, and moving performance is integral to the success of the film.

10. Hughes, "Hal Ashby," *Senses of Cinema* 30.

11. Alonzo, Interview by Dennis Schaefer and Larry Salvato in *Masters of Light*, 25.

12. I am defining the tableau shot as a formal, carefully composed shot in which a single character or group of characters is framed within a well-defined visual space.

Chapter 4

1. The "Vietnam Western" was an early-1970s genre represented by such films as *Soldier Blue*, Arthur Penn's *Little Big Man* (1970), and Tom Laughlin's *Billy Jack* (1971).

2. Keathley, "Trapped in the Affection Image: Hollywood's Post-Traumatic Cycle (1970–1979)," in *The Last Great American Picture Show*, ed. Thomas Elsaesser, Alexander Horwath, and Noel King, 293.

3. Ibid., 296.

4. Jacobs, *Hollywood Renaissance*, 225.

5. Suid, *Guts and Glory*, 296.

6. Ibid.

7. Towne, Transcript of American Film Institute Seminar, January 22, 1975.

8. Quoted in Robert David Crane and Christopher Fryer, *Jack Nicholson: Face to Face*, 115.

9. Buddusky, on the other hand, tries to capitalize on his military experience as a means of seducing a sophisticated young woman. Bad-Ass makes himself increasingly ridiculous with his talk of "doin' a man's job" in the navy, and completely misses the sarcasm of his interlocutor's comment: "I can see what it's done for *you!*" To make matters worse, Buddusky informs the young woman—with a line apparently ad-libbed by Nicholson himself—that what he likes best about his navy uniform is "how it makes my dick look."

10. Hughes, "Hal Ashby," *Senses of Cinema* 30.

11. Suid, *Guts and Glory*, 296–98.

12. Gilbert, interview with author.

NOTES TO CHAPTER 4

13. The complicated genesis of *Coming Home* is misrepresented in several published discussions of the film, including that of Frank McAdams in *The American War Film: History and Hollywood*. Presumably basing his version of events on an interview with Dowd, McAdams identifies Dowd as the sole author of *Buffalo Ghosts*. However, Gilbert and Dowd were in fact co-authors of the screenplay, after which Dowd resigned from the project and Waldo Salt was brought in to write a new script. When Gilbert, Fonda, and Jerome Hellman made their deal to produce *Coming Home* for United Artists, Dowd asked to be paid for the rights to the *Buffalo Ghosts* screenplay and demanded that Gilbert's name be removed as screenwriter. Gilbert was given the title of associate producer on the film, but he received no screenwriting credit and no part of the film's Academy Award for best screenplay, which went to Dowd, Salt, and Robert Jones. The omission of Gilbert's name from published histories of the project has been rectified in Jane Fonda's recently published autobiography, *My Life So Far* (New York: Random House, 2005). See Fonda's discussion of the genesis of the film on pages 244–45.

14. See Jerry Lembcke, "From Oral History to Movie Script: The Vietnam Veteran Interviews for *Coming Home*." According to Lembcke, the character of Luke was a composite figure, based both on Kovic and another paraplegic veteran, Bob Muller. Kovic, who was interviewed by Salt in November 1974, was the basis for the portrayal of Luke in Salt's first-draft screenplay. In November 1976, Salt conducted an extensive interview with Muller, who helped him round out the character of Luke.

15. See William Crane, "Creative Conflict: Bruce Dern and the Making of *Coming Home*," 30: Dern told Crane, "I would not have played the role if I hadn't known they were going to change [the ending]."

16. Ashby, "The Five-Year Struggle to Make *Coming Home*," Interview by Honeycutt, 13.

17. Suid, *Guts and Glory*, 328–29.

18. Arlen, *The Camera Age*, 101; Arnett, "Vietnam's Last Atrocity"; Rich, "The Dark End of the Tunnel."

19. James, "Rock and Roll in Representations of the Invasion of Vietnam," 91.

20. Anderegg, "Hollywood and Vietnam: John Wayne and Jane Fonda as Discourse," in *Inventing Vietnam*, ed. Michael Anderegg, 21–22.

21. Quoted in Maslin, "For Jon Voight: A Coming Home."

22. Quoted in Robert Blair Kaiser, "A Believable Movie about Vietnam."

23. Hellman, "Dialogue on Film: Jerome Hellman," Interview by James Powers, 34.

24. Haskell Wexler, interview with author.

25. Kotkin, "Fonda: I Am Not More Respectable."

NOTES TO CHAPTER 5

26. Turner, "The Worst Years of Our Lives," 65.

27. Martin, "Vietnam and Melodramatic Representation," 60.

28. Conlon, "Making Love, Not War: The Soldier Male in *Top Gun* and *Coming Home*," 24.

29. Devine, *Vietnam at 24 Frames a Second*, 156.

30. In the previous scene at the bar, Ashby uses dialogue to underscore the same point about the dissolution of Sally and Bob's marriage. When Sally says, "Let's just be alone for a few minutes," Bob replies, "We *are* alone."

31. This idea will become literal at the end of the film when Bob swims out to his death in the Pacific Ocean. As in *Harold and Maude*, the beginning and the ending of *Coming Home* have parallel structures. *Coming Home* begins with Bob jogging on the marine base while the paralyzed veterans receive physical therapy in the swimming pool. In the final scene, Bob is once again seen running, but this time it is toward his own death in the Pacific Ocean.

32. Ashby's editing, in collaboration with his editor, Don Zimmerman, was instrumental to the success of the film. Ironically, *Coming Home* won the Academy Award for best screenplay (despite a script that had been patched together and largely improvised by the actors) and failed to win the award for best editing, which went to the more conventionally edited *The Deer Hunter*.

33. See my more detailed discussion of the use of this song in chapter 6.

34. Selig, "Boys Will Be Men: Oedipal Drama in *Coming Home*," in *From Hanoi to Hollywood: The Vietnam War in American Film*, ed. Linda Ditmar and Gene Michaud: 199. According to Selig, the film's "displacement of the narrative's early emphasis on Sally's independence and developing political consciousness" in the final scenes of the film represents a "return to domesticity" and "a rather conventional melodramatic conclusion." I disagree strongly with this reading of the film, as my discussion in this chapter indicates.

35. Modleski, "Do We Get to Lose This Time? Revising the Vietnam War Film," ed. Robert Eberwein, *The War Film*, 157.

36. Several critics have noted this fact. Susan Jeffords has argued that the true subject of *The Deer Hunter* is "the primacy of the bonds between men," while Albert Auster and Leonard Quart suggest that the film's women characters are generally seen as "giggling or supportive adjuncts to the men." See Jeffords, *The Remasculinization of Gender and the Vietnam War*, 99; and Auster and Quart, *How the War Was Remembered*, 62.

Chapter 5

1. Ashby also makes effective use of television in several scenes of *Coming Home*, though the overall importance of television and the media is less apparent than in *Shampoo* or *Being There*.

2. Baudrillard, "The Ecstasy of Communication," in *The Anti-Aesthetic: Essays on Postmodern Culture*, ed. Hal Foster, 127–28.

3. Seth Cagin and Philip Dray, *Hollywood Films of the Seventies*, 237–38.

4. Ashby did, in fact, attempt to establish his own production company on two occasions. In the early 1970s, he founded DF Films with Chuck Mulvehill, a venture that faded after the disappointing reception of *Harold and Maude*. In the early 1980s, he founded Northstar International with Andrew Braunsberg. Northstar was involved in the production of only one film, *Lookin' to Get Out*, before it was dissolved.

5. See the discussion of Ashby's relationships with women in Biskind, 174: "He liked tall, thin, athletic girls built like boys. . . . When he was bored with a girl, he would ignore her, spend all day watching TV and then tell her to get out. According to his close friend Robert Downey, Sr., he used to say, 'When one's gone, you just open the window, there's another one climbing right in.'"

6. Ashby, Interview in the *UCLA Daily Bruin*, 3 March 1975.

7. For an insightful discussion of *Nashville*, see Robert Self, *Robert Altman's Subliminal Reality* (Minneapolis: University of Minnesota Press, 2002).

8. Rich, "Gravity Defied." Barbara Tepa Lupack makes much the same point, noting that *Being There* presents television viewers as "passive empty victims" in contrast to *Network*'s "mad-as-hell audiences who refused to take it anymore." See Lupack, "Chance Encounters: Bringing *Being There* to the Screen," in *Critical Essays on Jerzy Kosinski*, ed. Barbara Tepa Lupack, 213–14.

9. Lazar, "Jerzy Kosinski's *Being There*," 102.

10. David Sohn, "A Nation of Videots," in *Conversations with Jerzy Kosinski*, ed. Tom Teicholz, 98.

11. In his 1971 interview with Brandon Tartikoff, Kosinski argued that the talk-show medium encourages a kind of vapidity of expression: "A one-liner, a joke, a three-minute story, and of course anything gestural is its ideal format. That is why every statement Chauncey Gardiner makes seems to be tailored to fit this format." See Teicholz, 17.

12. Lupack, 219.

13. Lazar, 108. In a 1980 interview with Roger Copeland, Kosinski took credit for writing the ending, although by the time the ending was written, Kosinski was no longer actively involved with the screenplay, and Ashby had been working with Robert Jones revising Kosinski's script. Kosinski claimed that it was he who had "transformed the image of Chance floating into the world, buoyed up by a mysterious force, from the beginning of the book to the end of the film where it's more feasible that someone like this might one

NOTES TO CHAPTER 6

day become a saint and walk upon the water." However, no such ending exists in any of Kosinski's drafts of the script.

According to Melvyn Douglas, it was Ashby who arrived at the idea of having Chance walk on water after watching the interaction between Douglas and Peter Sellers during their scenes together: "As the shooting of the final scene approached, a writer friend of the director's asked him how the film was progressing. 'It's wonderful,' was the response. 'Peter Sellers and Melvyn Douglas are achieving such clarity, such simplicity, it looks like they're walking on water,' Ashby heard himself saying, even as he mentally started laying out revamped plans for the scene" (Douglas, *See You at the Movies*). Ashby decided to shoot the new ending without changing the screenplay or discussing the idea with the studio. See also Michael Dare, "How the Last Shot in *Being There* Actually Got Made."

14. Ashby, "Satisfaction in Being There," interview by Mike Bruns and Mike R. Young.

Chapter 6

1. In fact, Ashby had wanted to use a compilation score for *The Landlord* as well, and had discussed the possibility of such a score with Neil Young. Unfortunately, because Young did not own a majority of the rights to his own music, United Artists was unable to negotiate a satisfactory deal for the use of his songs. After considering a number of other musicians to provide the score, Ashby decided to use a far more limited score by Al Kooper.

2. Stevens visited the set to play the two new songs for Ashby, and he agreed to let Ashby use any songs from his recorded albums in the soundtrack. Once the shooting was finished, Ashby flew to Paris to discuss with Stevens what tracks he would use in the film. In postproduction, he had Stevens's albums transferred to tape and set the tracks to different pieces of film in order to find the ideal fit between visuals and music.

3. This is not the only moment in the film when a song from the extradiegetic score ends in conjunction with a diegetic cue. In the scene in which Harold goes to Maude's house and finds her posing in the nude for Glaucus, the song "I Think I See the Light" ends abruptly as Harold opens the door to Glaucus's studio.

4. See Jeff Smith, *The Sounds of Commerce*. The fact that the classical score had been the preferred form of musical soundtrack for Hollywood films throughout the studio era can be attributed primarily to two factors. First, traditional Hollywood producers and directors felt a responsibility to uphold certain production values associated with Hollywood films of the studio era (a product marketed to a public interested in a "quality" experience). These

values, they felt, were more accurately reflected in the classical score, with its pretensions to high art.

Second, as Rick Altman has observed, classical music is more readily adaptable to the filmic medium than popular songs, because it is relatively unobtrusive by nature and can more easily serve as accompaniment to a narrative rather than presenting what might be interpreted as an opinion about the narrative. As compared with popular songs, classical music "more easily convinces us that it is authored not by a composer, but by the image." See Altman, "Cinema and Popular Song," 26.

5. Ehrenstein and Reed, *Rock on Film*, 66.

6. Hill, *Easy Rider*, 22.

7. Ehrenstein and Reed, *Rock on Film*, 67.

8. For a more skeptical perspective on the early 1970s compilation score, see Howard Hampton, "Everybody Knows This Is Nowhere: The Uneasy Ride of Hollywood and Rock," in Thomas Elsaesser, Alexander Horwath, and Noel King, eds., *The Last Great American Picture Show*. Hampton comments that *Easy Rider* led to a "sure-fire studio formula that would promptly bring forth disasters like *The Strawberry Statement* and *Zabriskie Point*." According to Hampton, mainstream films like *Midnight Cowboy* (1969) and *Butch Cassidy and the Sundance Kid* (1969) exploited the use of popular songs made possible by *Easy Rider*: "This is the prism of middle-of-the-road hegemony through which pop music was still seen in Hollywood, which viewed *Easy Rider* as a wedge into the youth market more than a subversion of any 'Establishment'" (260).

9. See Jeff Smith, *Sounds of Commerce*, 169.

10. Ibid., 170.

11. Jeff Smith, "Popular Songs and Comic Allusion in Contemporary Cinema," in *Soundtrack Available*, ed. Pamela Robertson Wojcik and Arthur Knight, 415.

12. Ashby, Transcript of American Film Institute Seminar, January 22, 1975.

13. In his essay "Popular Songs and Comic Allusion," Jeff Smith analyzes the musical pun as it occurs in contemporary cinema. According to Smith, the popular song is an effective form of humorous allusion in many films, functioning as an ironic commentary either through its lyrics or through an "extramusical system of pop culture references" (In *Soundtrack Available*, ed. Pamela Robertson Wojcik and Arthur Knight, 408). We find the technique of the musical pun employed more frequently in *Shampoo* than in any of Ashby's other films.

14. One could argue that the two parties represent equally dysfunctional reactions to the election: on the one hand, an obsessive preoccupation with the outcome, and on the other hand a disturbing lack of interest.

NOTES TO CHAPTER 7

15. Ehrenstein and Reed, *Rock on Film*, 71.
16. Hellman, "Dialogue on Film: Hal Ashby," Interview by James Powers, 46.
17. Canby, "The Detritus of War."
18. Adair, *Vietnam on Film*, 105.
19. David James, "Rock and Roll in Representations of the Invasion of Vietnam," 91–92.
20. Elwood, *How We Live*, 162.
21. Ibid., 167.
22. Bob's interrogation of Sally might also suggest to viewers the kind of interrogations American soldiers were obliged to conduct on Vietcong prisoners.

Chapter 7

1. Canby, "Barbara Harris in *Second-Hand Hearts*"; Denby, "Movies: From the Waist Up" 67–68; Sarris, "Films in Focus: What Are the Alternatives?"
2. The strongest performances in the film are those of the supporting players, especially Bert Remsen and Shirley Stoler.
3. Champlin, "Robert Blake Shifts Gears for 'Hamster.'"
4. Wexler, interview with author.
5. Hooker, interview with author.
6. Foley, interview with author.
7. Haskell Wexler, interview with author.
8. Ashby memo in Hal Ashby Papers, Margaret Herrick Library of the Academy of Motion Picture Arts and Sciences.
9. For Hampton's comments, see Peter Biskind's discussion of the film in *Easy Riders, Raging Bulls*, 353–54.
10. Rainer, *Los Angeles Herald-Examiner*, October 8, 1982; Corliss, *Time*, October 18, 1982; Benson, *Los Angeles Times*, October 8, 1982.
11. Ashby's legal wrangling with Lorimar over the issue would continue almost to the end of his life. In February 1987, Lorimar finally settled, paying Ashby $40,000 in damages and making a $20,000 payment to Camp Ronald McDonald in his name.
12. Ashby, Memo to Charles Mulvehill, July 19, 1985, in Hal Ashby Papers, Margaret Herrick Library of the Academy of Motion Picture Arts and Sciences.
13. Jeff Bridges, interview with author.
14. PSO also fired the film's producer, Steve Roth, clearly intending to keep Ashby as far away from the film as possible.
15. Ashby, Interview with Michael Dare.

NOTES TO CHAPTER 7

16. Ibid.

17. Sommersby, Review of *8 Million Ways to Die.*

18. Garcia, interview with author.

19. I have not seen any mention of Ashby's film in discussions of *Reservoir Dogs* or in published interviews with Tarantino, so the resemblance between the two films may be coincidental rather than a case of imitation or homage.

20. Kolker, *A Cinema of Loneliness,* 50.

21. McBride, "Song for Woody," 26.

22. Fine, *Accidental Genius,* 355. Like Ashby, Cassavetes was born in 1929; Cassavetes died from cirrhosis of the liver in February 1989, only two months after Ashby's own death from pancreatic cancer. This remarkable coincidence in the life spans of Ashby and Cassavetes was not the only similarity between the two directors. Both were independently minded filmmakers who challenged, and at times infuriated, those within the Hollywood system. Each of them did his best work during the period from 1968 to 1979, and each of them directed a total of a dozen feature films. Cassavetes directed twelve films; Ashby also directed twelve features, including one concert documentary.

23. Biskind, *Easy Riders,* 409.

24. Three of Ashby's films are ranked within the top fifty on the American Film Institute's "Funniest American Movies of All Time": *Being There* is #26, *Harold and Maude* #45, and *Shampoo* #47. See the *American Film Institute Desk Reference.*

FILMOGRAPHY

As Assistant Editor

Friendly Persuasion (Allied Artists, 1956)
Director: William Wyler
Editor: Robert Swink

The Big Country (United Artists, 1958)
Director: William Wyler
Editor: Robert Swink

The Diary of Anne Frank (Twentieth Century-Fox, 1959)
Director: George Stevens
Editors: Dave Bretherton, Robert Swink, and William Mace

The Young Doctors (United Artists, 1961)
Director: Phil Karlson
Editor: Robert Swink

The Children's Hour (United Artists, 1961)
Director: William Wyler
Editor: Robert Swink

Captain Sindbad (MGM, 1963)
Director: Byron Haskin
Editor: Robert Swink

The Best Man (United Artists, 1964)
Director: Franklin Schaffner
Editor: Robert Swink

FILMOGRAPHY

The Greatest Story Ever Told (United Artists, 1965)
Director: George Stevens
Editor: Harold Kress

As Editor

The Loved One (MGM/Filmways, 1965)
Director: Tony Richardson
Editors: Hal Ashby, Anthony Gibbs, and Brian Smedley-Aston

The Cincinnati Kid (MGM, 1965)
Director: Norman Jewison
Editor: Hal Ashby

The Russians are Coming, the Russians are Coming (United Artists, 1966)
Director: Norman Jewison
Editors: Hal Ashby and J. Terry Williams

In the Heat of the Night (United Artists, 1967)
Director: Norman Jewison
Editor: Hal Ashby

As Associate Producer and Supervising Editor

The Thomas Crown Affair (United Artists, 1968)
Director: Norman Jewison
Editors: Hal Ashby, Byron Brandt, and Ralph Winters

Gaily, Gaily (United Artists, 1969)
Director: Norman Jewison
Editors: Byron Brandt and Ralph Winters

As Director

The Landlord (1970)
Produced by Norman Jewison for Mirisch Corporation.
Associate producer: Pat Palmer
Screenplay: William Gunn, based on the novel by Kristin Hunter
Photography: Gordon Willis
Editors: William Sawyer and Edward Warshilka
Production designer: Robert Boyle
Sound: Christopher Newman

Music: Al Kooper
Assistant director: Terence Nelson
Cast: Beau Bridges (Elgar Enders), Diana Sands (Fanny Copee), Lee Grant (Joyce Enders), Marki Bey (Lanie), Pearl Bailey (Marge), Louis Gossett Jr. (Copee), Melvin Stewart (Professor Duboise), Susan Anspach (Susan Enders), Walter Brooke (William Enders Sr.), Robert Klein (Peter Cootes), Will MacKenzie (William Enders Jr.), Stanley Greene (Heywood)
Distributed by United Artists. 110 min.
Release date: 12 May 1970
Budget: $1.95 million

Harold and Maude (1971)
Produced by Colin Higgins and Charles Mulvehill for Paramount.
Screenplay: Colin Higgins
Photography: John Alonzo
Editors: William Sawyer and Edward Warshilka
Production designer: Michael Haller
Sound: William Randall
Music: Cat Stevens
Assistant director: Michael Dmytryk
Cast: Bud Cort (Harold Chasen), Ruth Gordon (Maude), Vivian Pickles (Mrs. Chasen), Cyril Cusack (Glaucus), Charles Tyner (Uncle Victor), Ellen Geer (Sunshine Dore), Eric Christmas (Priest), G. Wood (Psychiatrist), Judy Engles (Candy Gulf), Shari Summers (Edith Phern), Tom Skerritt— as M. Borman (Motorcycle Cop)
Distributed by Paramount. 91 min.
Release date: 15 December 1971
Budget: $1.5 million

The Last Detail (1973)
Produced by Gerald Ayres (Acrobat Productions) for Columbia.
Associate producer: Charles Mulvehill
Screenplay: Robert Towne, based on the novel by Darryl Ponicsan
Photography: Michael Chapman
Editor: Robert Jones
Production designer: Michael Haller
Sound: Tom Overton
Music: John Mandel
Assistant director: Wesley McAfee
Cast: Jack Nicholson (Billy "Bad-Ass" Buddusky), Otis Young ("Mule" Mulhall), Randy Quaid (Larry Meadows), Clifton James (M.A.A.), Carol Kane (Young Whore), Michael Moriarty (Marine O.D.), Luana Anders

FILMOGRAPHY

(Donna)
Distributed by Columbia. 105 min.
Release date: 12 December 1973
Budget: $2.3 million

Shampoo (1975)
Produced by Warren Beatty for Columbia.
Associate producer: Charles Maguire
Screenplay: Warren Beatty and Robert Towne
Photography: László Kovács (as Laszlo Kovacs)
Editor: Robert Jones
Production designer: Richard Sylbert
Art director: W. Stewart Campbell
Sound: Tom Overton
Music: Original theme by Paul Simon and songs by various artists
Assistant director: Art Levinson
Cast: Warren Beatty (George Roundy), Julie Christie (Jackie Shawn), Goldie Hawn (Jill), Lee Grant (Felicia Karp), Jack Warden (Lester Karp), Tony Bill (Johnny Pope), Carrie Fisher (Lorna Karp), Jay Robinson (Norman)
Distributed by Columbia. 112 min.
Release date: 12 February 1975
Budget: $4 million

Bound for Glory (1976)
Produced by Robert Blumofe and Harold Leventhal for United Artists.
Associate producer: Charles Mulvehill
Screenplay: Robert Getchell, based on the book by Woody Guthrie
Photography: Haskell Wexler
Editors: Robert Jones and Pembroke Herring
Production designer: Michael Haller
Art directors: James Spencer and William Sully
Sound: Jeff Wexler (uncredited)
Music: Leonard Rosenman arrangements of songs by Woody Guthrie
Assistant director: Charles Myers
Cast: David Carradine (Woody Guthrie), Melinda Dillon (Mary Guthrie, Memphis Sue), Ronny Cox (Ozark Bule), Gail Strickland (Pauline), Randy Quaid (Luther Johnson), John Lehne (Locke), Ji-Tu Cumbuka (Slim Snedeger), Elizabeth Macey (Liz Johnson)
Distributed by United Artists. 147 min.
Release date: 27 October 1976
Budget: $10 million

FILMOGRAPHY

Coming Home (1978)
Produced by Jane Fonda (Jayne Productions) and Jerome Hellman for United Artists.
Associate producer: Bruce Gilbert
Screenplay: Waldo Salt and Robert Jones, based on a screenplay by Nancy Dowd and Bruce Gilbert
Photography: Haskell Wexler
Editor: Don Zimmerman
Production designer: Michael Haller
Art director: James Schoppe
Sound: Jeff Wexler
Music: Compilation of songs by various artists
Assistant director: Charles Myers
Cast: Jane Fonda (Sally Hyde), Jon Voight (Luke Martin), Bruce Dern (Capt. Robert Hyde), Penelope Milford (Viola Munson), Robert Ginty (Sgt. Dink Mobley), Robert Carradine (Bill Munson), Mary Gregory (Martha Vickery), Beeson Carroll (Capt. Earl Delise), Kathleen Miller (Kathy Delise), Willie Tyler (Virgil), Louis Carello (Bozo), Charles Cyphers (Pee Wee), Arthur Rosenberg (Bruce), David Clennon (Tim)
Distributed by United Artists. 127 min.
Release date: 15 February 1978
Budget: $5.28 million

Being There (1979)
Produced by Andrew Braunsberg (Northstar International) for Lorimar.
Associate producer: Charles Mulvehill
Screenplay: Jerzy Kosinski and Robert Jones (uncredited), based on the novel by Kosinski
Photography: Caleb Deschanel
Editor: Don Zimmerman
Production designer: Michael Haller
Art director: James Schoppe
Sound: Jeff Wexler
Music: John Mandel
Assistant director: David Hamburger
Cast: Peter Sellers (Chance), Shirley MacLaine (Eve Rand), Melvyn Douglas (Benjamin Rand), Jack Warden (President), Richard Dysart (Dr. Robert Allenby), David Clennon (Thomas Franklin), Fran Brill (Sally Hayes), Ruth Attaway (Louise), Richard Basehart (Vladimir Skrapinov)
Distributed by United Artists. 130 min.
Release date: 13 December 1979
Budget: $7 million

FILMOGRAPHY

Second-Hand Hearts (1981)
Produced by James Guercio for Lorimar.
Associate producer: Charles Mulvehill
Screenplay: Charles Eastman
Photography: Haskell Wexler
Editor: Amy Holden Jones
Production designer: Peter Wooley
Art director: Richard Carter
Sound: Art Rochester
Music: Willis Alan Ramsey
Assistant director: David Hamburger
Cast: Robert Blake (Loyal Muke), Barbara Harris (Dinette Dusty), Bert Remsen (Voyd Dusty), Sondra Blake (Ermy), Shirley Stoler (Maxy)
Distributed by Paramount. 102 min.
Release date: 8 June 1981
Budget: $6.7 million

Lookin' to Get Out (1982)
Produced by Robert Schaffel and Andrew Braunsberg (Northstar International) for Lorimar.
Screenplay: Jon Voight and Al Schwartz
Photography: Haskell Wexler
Editors: Robert Jones, Eva Gardos, Janice Hampton, Walton Dornisch, and Wayne Wahrman
Production designer: Robert Boyle
Art director: James Schoppe
Sound: Jeff Wexler
Music: John Mandel
Assistant director: Charles Myers
Cast: Jon Voight (Alex Kovac), Burt Young (Jerry Feldman), Ann-Margret (Patti Warner), Bert Remsen (Smitty Carpenter), Richard Bradford (Bernie Gold), Jude Farese (Harry), Allen Keller (Joey)
Distributed by Paramount. 105 min.
Release date: 8 October 1982
Budget: $17 million

Let's Spend the Night Together (1983; alternate title *Time Is On Our Side*)
Produced by Ron Schwary.
Co-director: Pablo Ferro (credited as "creative associate")
Photography: Caleb Deschanel and Gerald Feil
Editor: Lisa Day
Music editor: Michael Tronick

Sound: Jeff Wexler
Assistant director: Charles Myers
Cast: Mick Jagger, Keith Richards, Ron Wood, Charlie Watts, Bill Wyman, Ian Stewart, Ian McLagan, Ernie Watts, Bobby Keys
Distributed by Embassy Pictures. 90 min.
Release date: 11 February 1983

The Slugger's Wife (1985)
Produced by Ray Stark (Rastar Films) for Columbia.
Screenplay: Neil Simon
Photography: Caleb Deschanel
Editors: Don Brochu and George Villaseñor
Production designer: Michael Riva
Art director: Richard Carter
Sound: Jeff Wexler
Music: Quincy Troupe (arrangements of songs by various artists)
Assistant director: Frank Bueno
Cast: Michael O'Keefe (Darryl Palmer), Rebecca De Mornay (Debby Palmer), Martin Ritt (Burly DeVito), Randy Quaid (Moose Granger), Cleavant Derricks (Manny Alvarado), Lisa Langlois (Aline Cooper), Loudon Wainwright III (Gary)
Distributed by Columbia. 105 min.
Release date: 29 March 1985
Budget: $15 million

8 Million Ways to Die (1986)
Produced by Steve Roth (SFR Productions) for PSO Productions.
Screenplay: Oliver Stone, Lance Hill, and Robert Towne (uncredited), based on the novel by Lawrence Block
Photography: Steve Burum
Editors: Robert Lawrence and Stuart Pappé
Production designer: Michael Haller
Art director: Mark Mansbridge
Sound: Jeff Wexler
Music: James Newton Howard
Assistant director: Andy Stone
Cast: Jeff Bridges (Matt Scudder), Rosanna Arquette (Sarah Armstrong), Andy Garcia (Angel Maldonado), Alexandra Paul (Sunny Hendryx), Randy Brooks (Willie "Chance" Walker)
Distributed by Tri-Star. 115 min.
Release date: 25 April 1986
Budget: $12.8 million

BIBLIOGRAPHY

In writing this book, I have relied on three types of sources: published materials, personal interviews, and unpublished archival materials. I have correspondingly divided this bibliography into three sections.

Published Sources

INTERVIEWS

Alonzo, John. "John Alonzo." Interview by Dennis Schaefer and Larry Salvato. In *Masters of Light: Conversations with Contemporary Cinematographers*, edited by Dennis Schaefer and Larry Salvato, 23–46. Berkeley and Los Angeles: University of California Press, 1984.

Ashby, Hal. "Gambling on a Film about the Depression." Interview by Aljean Harmetz. *New York Times* 5 December 1976: B1+.

———. "Hal Ashby." Interview by Robert David Crane and Christopher Fryer. In *Jack Nicholson: Face to Face*, edited by Robert David Crane and Christopher Fryer, 110–16. New York: M. Evans, 1975.

———. "Hal Ashby." Interview by Paul Frizler. In *Close-Up: The Contemporary Director*, edited by Jon Tuska, 223–50. Metuchen, NJ, and London: Scarecrow Press, 1981.

———. "Hal Ashby Getting the Right Drift." Interview by William Avery. *Soho Weekly News*, 23 February 1978: 18–19.

———. "Hal Ashby Interview." By Larry Salvato and Dennis Schaefer. *Millimeter* 4 (October 1976): 36+.

———. Interview of Hal Ashby by Michael Dare. *LA Weekly*, May 16, 1986.

———. "Positive Thinking." Interview with Hal Ashby by Ralph Appelbaum. *Films and Filming* 24 (July 1978): 1–7.

———. "Satisfaction in Being There." Interview with Hal Ashby by Mike Bruns and Jordon R. Young. *Millimeter* 8 (May 1980): 91–97.

Hellman, Jerome. "Dialogue on Film: Jerome Hellman." Interview with Jerome Hellman by James Powers. *American Film* 5.7 (1980): 53–60.

Kosinski, Jerzy. "An Interview with Jerzy Kosinski." By Roger Copeland. *New York Art Journal* 21 (1980): 10–12.

BIBLIOGRAPHY

REVIEWS AND ARTICLES

Arnett, Peter. "Vietnam's Last Atrocity." *Los Angeles Times* 8 Apr. 1979: F1.

Ashby, Hal. "Breaking Out of the Cutting Room." *Action* Sept.–Oct. 1970: 7–10.

Benson, Sheila. Review of *Lookin' to Get Out*. *Los Angeles Times* 8 Oct. 1982: Cal. 1.

Buscombe, Edward. "Ideas of Authorship." *Screen* 14.3 (1974): 75–85.

Canby, Vincent. "Barbara Harris in *Second-Hand Hearts*." *New York Times* 8 May 1981: C11.

———. "The Detritus of War." *New York Times* 16 Feb. 1978: C20.

———. "In Films, Acting is Behavior." *New York Times* 12 Dec. 1976: B13.

———. "Post-Vietnam Romantic Triangle." Review of *Coming Home*. *New York Times* 16 Feb. 1978.

———. "*Shampoo* Could Be the Year's Best Comedy." *New York Times* 13 April 1975: B15.

———. "There's No Doubt: Jack Nicholson is a Major Star." Review of *The Last Detail*. *New York Times* 24 Feb. 1974: B1+.

Carringer, Robert. "Collaboration and Concepts of Authorship." *PMLA* 116.2 (2001): 370–79.

Cassavetes, John. "What's Wrong with Hollywood." *Film Culture* (April 1959).

Champlin, Charles. "'Coming Home': A Reminder of the Costs of War." *Los Angeles Times* 12 Feb. 1978: Cal. 1.

———. "Robert Blake Shifts Gears for 'Hamster.'" *Los Angeles Times* 8 Oct. 1978: Cal. 1+.

Conlon, James. "Making Love, Not War: The Soldier Male in *Top Gun* and *Coming Home*." *Journal of Popular Film and Television* 18.1 (1990): 18–27.

Corliss, Richard. Review of *Lookin' to Get Out*. *Time* 18 Oct. 1982: 96.

Crane, William. "Creative Conflict: Bruce Dern and the Making of *Coming Home*." *Post Script: Essays in Film and the Humanities* 1.2 (1982): 27–45.

Crist, Judith. "Of Heads and Heels." Review of *Shampoo*. *New York* 17 February 1975: 72.

Dare, Michael. "How the Last Shot in *Being There* Actually Got Made." http://www.dareland.com/lastshot/htm.

———. "How to Kill a Movie." Review of *8 Million Ways to Die*. *LA Weekly* 16 May 1986: 31–33.

Denby, David. "Movies: From the Waist Up." Review of *Second-Hand Hearts*. *New York* 18 May 1981: 67–68.

Harmet, Richard. Review of *The Landlord*. *Los Angeles Free Press* 5 June 1970.

"Harold and Maude." *Variety* 16 December 1971: 18.

Honeycutt, Rick. "The Five-Year Struggle to Make *Coming Home*." *New York Times* 19 Feb. 1978: B13+.

Hughes, Darren. "Hal Ashby." *Senses of Cinema* 30 (January 2004). http://

www.sensesofcinema.com/contents/directors/04/ashby.html.

James, David. "Rock and Roll in Representations of the Invasion of Vietnam." *Representations* 29 (Winter 1990): 78–98.

Kael, Pauline. "Beverly Hills as a Big Bed." Review of *Shampoo*. *New Yorker* 17 Feb. 1975: 86–90.

———. "The Current Cinema: Affirmation." Review of *Bound for Glory*. *New Yorker* 13 Dec. 1976: 148–52.

Kaiser, Robert Blair. "A Believable Movie about Vietnam." *Horizon* 21 (1978): 19+.

Kauffman, Stanley. "Poor Folk." Review of *Bound for Glory*. *New Republic* 27 Nov. 1976: 18.

Kotkin, Joel. "Fonda: I Am Not More Respectable." *New Times* 10 (1978): 58.

Kroll, Jack. "Vietnam Hero Worship." *Newsweek* 20 Feb. 1978: 89–90.

Lazar, Mary. "Jerzy Kosinski's *Being There*, Novel and Film: Changes Not by Chance." *College Literature* 31.2 (2004): 99–116.

Lembcke, Jerry. "From Oral History to Movie Script: The Vietnam Veteran Interviews for *Coming Home*." *Oral History Review* 26.2 (1999): 65–86.

Mahoney, John. Review of *The Landlord*. *Hollywood Reporter* 21 May 1970: 3.

Martin, Andrew. "Vietnam and Melodramatic Representation." *East-West Film Journal* 4.2 (1990): 54–67.

Maslin, Janet. "For Jon Voight: A Coming Home." *New York Times* 13 Feb. 1978: C15.

McBride, Joseph. "Song for Woody: On the Set of *Bound for Glory*." *Film Comment* 12.6 (1976): 26–28.

Pollock, Dale. "Whatever Happened to Hal Ashby?" *Los Angeles Times* 17 October 1982: Cal. 1+.

Rainer, Peter. Review of *Lookin' to Get Out*. *Los Angeles Herald-Examiner* 8 Oct. 1982: D4.

Rebello, Stephen. "A Mild and Wild Maverick." *Variety* Dec.–Jan. 2005: Supp. 94+.

Rich, Frank. "The Dark End of the Tunnel." Review of *Coming Home*. *Time* 20 Feb. 1978: 68.

———. "Gravity Defied." Review of *Being There*. *Time* 14 Jan. 1980: 70.

Riley, Clayton. "When the All-American Boy Meets Miss Sepia of 1957." Review of *The Landlord*. *New York Times* 2 Aug. 1970: B9.

Sarris, Andrew. "Film in Focus: What Are the Alternatives?" *Village Voice* 6–12 May 1981: 53.

Shedlin, Michael. Review of *Harold and Maude*. *Film Quarterly* 26.1 (1972): 51–53.

Sommersby, Jack. Review of *8 Million Ways to Die*. *EFilmCritic* 17 Dec. 2002. http://efilmcritic.com/review.php?movie=6524.

Turner, Richard. "The Worst Year of Our Lives." *New Times* 10 (1978): 55+.

Walling, William. Review of *The Last Detail*. *Society* 11 (Sept./ Oct. 1974): 77–80.

Willson, Robert F. "Being There at the End." *Literature/ Film Quarterly* 9.1 (1981): 59–65.

BOOKS, ESSAYS, AND DISSERTATIONS

Adair, Gilbert. *Vietnam on Film: From the Green Berets to Apocalypse Now*. New York: Proteus, 1981.

Altman, Rick. "Cinema and Popular Song: The Lost Tradition." In *Soundtrack Available: Essays on Film and Popular Music*, ed. Pamela Robertson Wojcik and Arthur Knight, 19–30. Durham: Duke University Press, 2001.

American Film Institute Desk Reference. New York: Stonesong Press, 2002.

Anderegg, Michael, ed. *Inventing Vietnam: The War in Film and Television*. Philadelphia: Temple University Press, 1992.

Arlen, Michael. *The Camera Age: Essays on Television*. New York: Farrar, Strauss, and Giroux, 1981.

Auster, Albert and Leonard Quart. *How the War Was Remembered: Hollywood and Vietnam*. New York: Praeger, 1988.

Baron, Cynthia, Diane Carson, and Frank Tamasulo, eds. *More Than a Method: Trends and Traditions in Contemporary Film Performance*. Detroit: Wayne State University Press, 2003.

Bart, Peter, and Peter Guber. *Shoot Out: Surviving Fame and (Mis)Fortune in Hollywood*. New York: Putnam, 2002.

Biskind, Peter. *Easy Riders, Raging Bulls: How the Sex-Drugs- and-Rock'n'Roll Generation Saved Hollywood*. New York: Simon and Schuster, 1998.

Cagin, Seth, and Philip Dray. *Hollywood Films of the Seventies: Sex, Drugs, Violence, Rock 'n' Roll and Politics*. New York: Harper and Row, 1984.

Carringer, Robert. *The Making of Citizen Kane*. Berkeley: University of California Press, 1985.

Caughie, John, ed. *Theories of Authorship: A Reader*. London: Routledge, 1981.

Cook, David. *Lost Illusions: American Cinema in the Shadow of Watergate and Vietnam, 1970–1979*. New York: Charles Scribner's Sons, 2000.

Devine, Jeremy. *Hollywood at 24 Frames a Second: A Critical and Thematic Analysis of over 400 Films about the Vietnam War*. Jefferson, NC: McFarland and Company, 1995.

Ditmar, Linda, and Gene Michaud, eds. *From Hanoi to Hollywood: the Vietnam War in American Film*. New Brunswick: Rutgers University Press, 1990.

Douglas, Melvyn and Tom Arthur. *See You at the Movies: The Autobiography of Melvyn Douglas*. Lanham, MD: University Press of America, 1986.

Eberwein, Robert, ed. *The War Film*. New Brunswick: Rutgers University Press, 2005.

Ehrenstein, David, and Bill Reed. *Rock on Film*. New York: Delilah Books,

1982.

Elsaesser, Thomas. *Fassbinder's Germany: History, Identity, Subject*. Amsterdam: Amsterdam University Press, 1996.

Elsaesser, Thomas, Alexander Horwath, and Noel King, eds. *The Last Great American Picture Show: New Hollywood Cinema in the 1970s*. Amsterdam: Amsterdam University Press, 2005.

Elwood, Ron. *How We Live: An Analysis of the Films Directed by Hal Ashby from 1970 to 1980*. PhD Dissertation, 1988.

Fine, Marshall. *Accidental Genius: How John Cassavetes Invented the American Independent Film*. New York: Miramax Books, 2006.

Finstad, Susan. *Warren Beatty: A Private Man*. New York: Harmony Books, 2005.

Fonda, Jane. *My Life So Far*. New York: Random House, 2005.

Foster, Hal, ed. *The Anti-Aesthetic: Essays on Postmodern Culture*. Port Townsend: Washington Bay Press, 1983.

Gerstner, David and Janet Staiger, eds. *Authorship and Film*. New York and London: Routledge, 2003.

Gordon, Ruth. *My Side: The Autobiography of Ruth Gordon*. New York: Harper and Row, 1976.

Harries, Dan. *Film Parody*. London: BFI, 2000.

Hill, Lee. *Easy Rider*. London: BFI, 1996.

Jacobs, Diane. *Hollywood Renaissance*. 2nd ed. New York: Dell, 1980.

Jeffords, Susan. *The Remasculinization of Gender and the Vietnam War*. Bloomington: Indiana University Press, 1989.

Jewison, Norman. *This Terrible Business Has Been Good to Me*. New York: St. Martin's, 2005.

Kawin, Bruce. *How Movies Work*. Berkeley and Los Angeles: University of California Press, 1992.

Kolker, Robert. *A Cinema of Loneliness: Penn, Stone, Kubrick, Scorcese, Spielberg, Altman*. 3rd edition. New York: Oxford University Press, 2000.

Lev, Peter. *American Films of the 70s: Conflicting Visions*. Austin: University of Texas Press, 2000.

Levy, Emanuel, ed. *Citizen Sarris, American Film Critic: Essays in Honor of Andrew Sarris*. Lanham, MD: Scarecrow Press, 2001.

Lupack, Barbara Tepa, ed. *Critical Essays on Jerzy Kosinski*. New York: G. K. Hall, 1998.

Man, Glenn. *Radical Visions: American Film Renaissance, 1967–1976*. Westport, CT: Greenwood, 1994.

McAdams, Frank. *The American War Film: History and Hollywood*. Westport, CT: Praeger, 2002.

McGilligan, Patrick. *Jack's Life: A Biography of Jack Nicholson*. New York: Norton, 1994.

Salt, Barry. *Film Style and Technology: History and Analysis*. London: Starword, 1983.

Samuels, Stewart. *Midnight Movies*. New York: Collier, 1983.

Sarris, Andrew. *The American Cinema: Directors and Direction 1929–1968*. New York: Dutton, 1968.

Self, Robert. *Robert Altman's Subliminal Reality*. Minneapolis: University of Minnesota Press, 2002.

Sikov, Ed. *Mr. Strangelove: A Biography of Peter Sellers*. London: Sidgwick and Jackson, 2002.

Sklar, Robert and Vito Zagarrio, eds. *Frank Capra: Authorship and the Studio System*. Philadelphia: Temple University Press, 1998.

Smith, Jeff. "Popular Songs and Comic Allusion in Contemporary Cinema." In *Soundtrack Available: Essays on Film and Popular Music*, ed. Pamela Robertson Wojcik and Arthur Knight, 407–30. Durham: Duke University Press, 2001.

———. *The Sounds of Commerce: Marketing Popular Film Music*. New York: Columbia University Press, 1998.

Stillinger, Jack. *Multiple Authorship and the Myth of Solitary Genius*. New York: Oxford University Press, 1991.

Suid, Lawrence. *Guts and Glory: The Making of the American Military Image in Film*. Revised ed. Lexington: University Press of Kentucky, 2002.

Teicholz, Tom, ed. *Conversations with Jerzy Kosinski*. Jackson: University of Mississippi Press, 1993.

Thomson, David. *A Biographical Dictionary of Film*. Revised ed. London: Andre Deutsch, 1994.

———. *Warren Beatty and Desert Eyes: A Life and a Story*. New York: Doubleday, 1987.

Wexman, Virginia Wright, ed. *Film and Authorship*. New Brunswick: Rutgers University Press, 2003.

Wollen, Peter. *Signs and Meanings in the Cinema*. Revised ed. Bloomington: Indiana University Press, 1972.

Author Interviews

For each interview, I have indicated the month in which the interview was conducted, except in those cases where there was a series of conversations that took place over the course of more than one month, in which case I have listed the interview by year only. "T" indicates a telephone interview, and "E" indicates an e-mail interview.

Susan Anspach (May 2003)
Jack Ashby (January 2005 T)
Tony Bill (November 2003)
Beau Bridges (August 2003 T)

Jeff Bridges (June 2003 T)
Garrett Brown (June 2003)
David Carradine (August 2003 E)
Robert Carradine (October 2003)
Michael Chapman (April 2003)
Julie Christie (October 2003 T)
David Clennon (August 2003 T)
Ronnie Cox (September 2003)
Caleb Deschanel (May 2003)
James Foley (September 2003)
Jane Fonda (November 2003 T)
Andy Garcia (October 2003)
Ellen Geer (October 2002)
Bruce Gilbert (November 2003)
Robert Ginty (August 2003)
David Hamburger (June 2003)
Jerome Hellman (October 2003)
Buddy Joe Hooker (July 2003)
Norman Jewison (February 2003)
Amy Holden Jones (May 2003)
Robert Jones (February 2003)
Art Levinson (March 2003)
Toby Lovallo (April 2003 T)
Michael O'Keefe (July 2003 T)
Alexandra Paul (October 2003 T)
James Schoppe (March 2003)
Dianne Schroeder (2003 T)
Ed Warschilka (January 2003)
Haskell Wexler (June 2003)
Jeff Wexler (June 2003)
Gordon Willis (April 2003 E)
Peter Wooley (March 2003 T)
Don Zimmerman (March 2003 T)

Unpublished Research Materials

Transcripts of American Film Institute Seminars. American Film Institute Louis B. Mayer Library (Los Angeles, California).

Hal Ashby Papers, Special Collections Department, Margaret Herrick Library of the Academy of Motion Picture Arts and Sciences (Beverly Hills, California).

This extensive collection, donated by Larry Reynolds and Rick Pedilla, contains production files on all the films directed by Ashby, as well as files on many of his uncompleted projects. The collection also contains business, legal, and financial files, as well as files pertaining to Ashby's personal and family life.

INDEX

Academy Award (Oscar), 9, 15, 25, 28, 32, 34
Allen, Woody, 6, 45, 157
Alonzo, John, 21, 45, 61
Altman, Robert, viii, 1, 2, 3–5, 16, 20, 23, 27, 28, 67, 97, 154, 156, 157
American Graffiti (Lucas), 22–23
Anchors Aweigh (Sidney), 73
Anderson, Wes, 157
Andrews, Dana, 81
Anspach, Susan, 17, 50
Antonioni, Michelangelo, 122
Apocalypse Now (Coppola), 94–95
Arkin, Alan, 146
Arquette, Rosanna, 153
Arzner, Dorothy, 13
Ashby, Eileen (mother), 11
Ashby, Hal: and actors, 3, 7, 19–20, 23–24, 29, 32, 144, 154–55; as auteur, 2–6, 8; awards won by, 9, 15 (*see also awards for individual films*); childhood, 11–12; collaborative approach to filmmaking, 3, 6–8, 45; comic sensibility, 8, 19, 35, 42; comparison with Altman, 3–4; countercultural persona of, 15, 21, 23, 25; critical neglect of, viii, 3–4; decline of filmmaking career, ix, 37, 145–46, 156–57; difficulties with studios and producers, 9, 18–19, 21, 26–28, 147; drug use, 4, 150, 156–57; as editor, 13–17, 25, 28, 45, 47–48, 91–93, 147, 152–53; illness, 37; improvisational style of, 7, 23–25, 33; marriages, 12, 99; and Mormonism, 11–12; music in films of, viii-ix, 123–24 (*see also musical scores of individual films*); openness to innovation, 31, 46; personality, 4, 11–12, 15; reticence about personal life, 9, 11; tableau shots, 49, 62, 115; uncompleted film projects, 22–26, 148–49; violence in films of, 155–56; visual style of, 8, 18–19, 21, 24–25, 27, 31, 45, 61–63, 68–69, 115
Ashby, Jack (brother), 11–12, 161n. 6
Ashby, James (father), 11
Attaway, Ruth, 107
auteurism, 2–6
Ayres, Gerald, 23, 77

Bailey, Pearl, 17, 19, 40
Bart, Peter, 21, 34, 65, 118
Basehart, Richard, 112
Baudrillard, Jean, 97
Beach Boys, the: "Wouldn't It Be Nice," 123, 128–29
Beatles, the: "Lucy in the Sky with Diamonds," 132–33; "Yesterday," 130
Beatty, Warren, 7, 26–29, 98, 99, 162n. 30
Bedig, Sass, 30
Being There (Ashby), ix, 6, 7, 8, 42, 48, 59, 63, 155, 171n. 24; adaptation of novel, 109; awards, 36–37; commercial success of,

INDEX

Being There (Ashby) (*continued*)
36; compared with *Network*, 105; critique of media and television, viii, 2, 35, 97. 104–17 passim; critique of race relations, 107–8; ending, 115–17, 167n. 13; miscommunication as theme, 111–13; as postmodern allegory, 97; satire in, 35, 107–8; screenplay, 35, 160n. 24, 167n. 13; screens as visual motif, 115–17

Best Years of Our Lives, The (Wyler), 80–81, 83

Bey, Marki, 17, 40

Bergman, Ingmar, 27

Bill, Tony, 100

Biskind, Peter, 4

Blake, Robert, 34–35, 144–45

Block, Lawrence, 149

Blumofe, Robert, 29

Bogdanovitch, Peter, 1, 16, 27

Boorman, John, 67

Booth, Margaret, 149

Bound for Glory (Ashby), viii, 7, 8, 47, 48, 58, 155; awards, 32; cinematography, 31, 162n. 36; cost, 31; locations, 29–30; reception of, 32

Braff, Zach, 157

Brando, Marlon, 81

Braunsberg, Andrew, 35, 167n. 4

Brautigan, Richard: *Hawkline Monster, The* (novel) 148

Bridges, Beau, 16, 17–18, 19, 38, 39

Bridges, James, 105

Bridges, Jeff, 150–54, 156

Brooke, Walter, 40

Brooks, Mel, 157

Brown, Garrett, 31

Buckley, Tim: "Once I Was," 141–42

Buffalo Springfield: "For What It's Worth," 138–41

Caan, James, 146

Calley, John, 14

Capote, Truman: *Hand Carved Coffins* (novel), 149

Capra, Frank, 5–6

Carradine, David, 7–10, 29–32

Cassavetes, John, viii, 1, 2, 3, 7, 10, 16, 25, 156, 157, 171n. 22

Casualties of War (De Palma), 95

Chaplin, Charlie, 6, 157, 160n. 23

Chaplin, Geraldine, 101

Chapman, Michael, 7, 24, 45, 68, 78

Chayefsky, Paddy, 105

Christie, Julie, 26–28, 102

Cimino, Michael, 34, 66, 94

Cincinnati Kid, The (Jewison), 14–15

Columbia Pictures, 24, 28, 148–49, 150

Coming Home (Ashby), ix, 7, 11, 58, 59, 63, 68, 96, 155; awards, 33–34; casting, 33; compared with *The Deer Hunter*, 66–67; critique of military, viii, 2, 81–84, 135–42; editing, 85, 91–93, 166n. 32; ending, 93, 95, 166n. 31; as "homecoming" film, 80–83; irony in, 85, 87, 137, 140; mise-en-scène, 85, 88–89, 90–91; musical score, 123–24. 133–42; opening sequence, 86; political viewpoint of, 84–86; reception of, 33–34, 83; screenplay, 33, 78–80, 160n. 24, 165n. 13; treatment of women, 82–83, 88–89, 93–95, 166n. 34

"compilation score" of 1970s films, 121–24, 169n. 8

Compton, La Von, 12

Coppola, Francis Ford, 1, 2, 3, 5, 6, 45, 67, 94, 156, 157

Corman, Roger, 21

Cort, Bud, 20, 22, 154

Cotton, Joseph, 5

Cox, Ronny, 7

Crosse, Rupert, 23

Cukor, George, 6, 157

Damon, Mark, 150–51

Daves, Delmer, 80

Deer Hunter, The (Cimino), 65–66, 94, 166n. 34, 166n. 36

De Mornay, Rebecca, 149

INDEX

De Niro, Robert, 29, 94
De Palma, Brian, 1, 16, 95, 154
Dern, Bruce, 33, 80, 82, 90, 95, 146, 165n. 15
Deschanel, Caleb, 6, 36, 45, 149
Douglas, Melvyn, 36, 105, 167n. 13
Douglas, Michael, 25–26
Dowd, Nancy, 78–79, 165n. 13
Downey, Robert, 16, 167n. 5
Dylan, Bob, 128, 134
Dysart, Richard, 108

Eastman, Charles, 34–35, 145
Eastwood, Clint, 21
Easy Rider (Hopper), 121–23, 169n. 8
8 Million Ways to Die (Ashby), viii, ix, 37, 149–56, 163n. 5, 163n. 8, 164n. 9
Evans, Charles, 148
Evans, Robert, 19

Falk, Peter, 146
Ferguson, Perry, 5
Foley, James, 145–46
Fonda, Jane, 7, 33–34, 78–79, 81, 83–84, 90, 94, 144, 165n. 13
Ford, John 6, 160n. 23
Franzen, Art, 152
Friedkin, William, 1, 156
Full Metal Jacket (Kubrick), 94–95

Gaily, Gaily (Jewison), 17
Geer, Ellen, 21
Getchell, Robert, 29
Gilbert, Bruce, 78–79, 165n. 3
Ginty, Robert, 66
Godard, Jean-Luc, 17
Gordon, Ruth, 20, 164n. 9
Gossett, Louis Jr., 40, 41
Gould, Elliott, 154
Graduate, The (Nichols), 121–23
Grant, Lee, 7, 19, 26–28
Greene, Stanley, 44
Gunn, Bill, 43
Guthrie, Woody, 29–32, 48, 155

Hackman, Gene, 154

Hagmann, Stuart, 17, 22, 122
Hall, Conrad, 12
Haller, Michael, 20, 29–30, 61
Hamburger, David, 7, 11–12
Hampton, Janice, 147
Harold and Maude (Ashby), 3, 6, 8, 23, 31, 34, 35, 38–39, 42, 47, 68, 115, 171n. 24; acting, 57; allusions to other films, 56; awards, 22; character of Harold, 51–52; cinematography, 21, 61; comedy in, 54–55; compared with *The Landlord*, 60–61; critique of middle-class values, viii, 2; critique of military, 73–76, 85; editing, 64–65, 125–26; ending, 65, 126–27, 166n. 31; locations, 19–21, mise-en-scène, 53, 64; musical score, 118–21, 123–28, 168n. 2; parody in, 55–56, 163n. 2; performance styles in, 57–59; production design, 61–62; reception of, 21–22, 161n. 22, 167n. 4; as satire, 52–54; screenplay, 19, 52; shot selection, 62–64; symbolic structure, 59–60
Harris, Barbara, 34–35
Hawks, Howard, 6, 160n. 23
Hawn, Goldie, 26–28
Hellman, Jerome, 8–9, 11, 83–84, 135, 165n. 13
Higgins, Colin, 3, 19, 35, 52
Hill, Walter, 149
Hitchcock, Alfred, 160n. 23
Hoffman, Dustin, 29, 56, 148
Hooker, Buddy Joe, 145
Hopper, Dennis, 16, 121–22

In the Heat of the Night (Jewison), 16–17
Indochina Peace Campaign (IPC), 78
Jagger, Mick, 134, 149
Jewison, Norman, vii, 1, 14, 15–18, 22, 45, 144
Jones, Amy Holden, 9
Jones, Robert, 7–8, 27–28, 33, 37, 147, 165n. 13, 167n. 13
Joplin, Janis, 134

191

INDEX

Karlson, Phil, 14
Kelly, Gene, 73
Kesey, Ken: *One Flew Over the Cuckoo's Nest* (screenplay) 25–26
Klein, Robert, 44
Kooper, Al, 168n. 1
Kovacs, Laszlo, 27
Kovic, Ron, 79, 165n. 14
Kozinski, Jerzy: *Being There* (novel) 35, 106, 116; *Being There* (screenplay) 35, 106
Kubrick, Stanley, 94

Landlord, The (Ashby), 14, 17–19, 20, 52, 55, 58, 60, 62–64, 155, 163n. 4; budget, 19; character of Elgar, 38–40; cinematography, 18–19, 46; comic tone of, 42–43; critique of middle-class values, viii, 51; critique of race relations, 2, 41–45; editing, 45–50; location shooting, 18; mise-en-scène, 50–51; musical score, 168n. 1; reception of, 19; satire in, 2, 17, 42; screenplay, 43
Last Detail, The (Ashby), 3, 7, 8, 11, 27, 38, 47, 59, 63, 82, 155, 164n. 9; awards, 25; critique of military, viii, 2, 68, 73, 75–78; critique of race relations, 76; mise-en-scène, 70; profanity in, 24; reception of, 24–25; screenplay, 23–24, 72, 75–76; shot selection, 70; soundtrack, 73, 168n. 1
Lawrence, Robert, 152
Lean, David, 13
Lemmon, Jack, 25
Let's Spend the Night Together (Ashby), 148
Leventhal, Harold, 29
Levinson, Art, 28
Lookin' to Get Out (Ashby), viii, 37, 146–49, 167n. 4; reception of, 147–48
Lorimar Productions, 34, 147–48, 150, 170n. 11
Loved One, The (Richardson), 14
Lucas, George, 20, 122
Lumet, Sidney 27, 35, 67, 105

MacLaine, Shirley, 105
Malick, Terence, 1
Mankiewicz, Herman, 5
March, Fredric, 81
Marshall, Joan 99, 160n. 7
M*A*S*H (Altman), 67
Mazursky, Paul ,1, 2, 16, 28
McKenzie, Richard, 108
Mean Streets (Scorsese), 124
Men, The (Zinneman), 80–82
Metro-Goldwyn-Mayer Studio (MGM), 22
Milius, John, 5
Mirisch, Harold, 16
Mirisch, Walter, 16, 17–19
Mitchell, Joni, 122
Moder, Mike, 150
Mulvehill, Charles (Chuck), 20, 22, 150, 166n. 4
Murphy, Michael, 98

Nashville (Altman), 67, 97–98, 100–101
Nelson, Ralph, 67
Network (Lumet), 105, 167n. 8
New Hollywood, The, 1–3, 7, 8, 15–16, 17, 25, 37, 56, 67–68, 149, 154, 156, 157
Nichols, Mike, 27, 56, 121
Nicholson, Jack, 3, 7, 22–24, 25, 29, 33, 68–69, 149, 154
Nolte, Nick, 149
Northstar International Films, 167n. 4

Ogden, UT, 10–13

Pacino, Al, 33, 154
Pakula, Alan, 1, 6, 67
Pappe, Stuart, 152
Paramount Pictures, 13, 19–20, 34
Payne, Alexander, 157
Peckinpah, Sam, 14
Penn, Arthur, 67, 154
Penn, Sean, 157
Perry, Frank, 16–17
Persky, Lester, 149
Phillips, Michelle, 22

Pickles, Vivian, 51
Pierson, Frank, 28
Polanski, Roman, 27, 35, 67, 154
Ponicsan, Darryl, 23
post-traumatic cycle of films, 67–68
Pride of the Marines (Daves), 80–81
PSO Productions, 150–52, 170n. 14

Quaid, Randy, 23, 25, 68–69, 154

Rafelson, Bob, 1, 16, 27, 67
Remsen, Bert, 170n. 2
Republic Pictures, 13
Reservoir Dogs (Tarantino), 155, 171n. 19
Reynolds, Burt, 146
Richardson, Tony, 14
Riskin, Robert, 5–6
Ritchie, Michael, 1, 2, 16, 105
RKO Pictures, 13
Robson, Mark, 5, 13
Rolling Stones, the: "Out of Time," 136–7; "Ruby Tuesday," 135; "Sympathy for the Devil," 136
Rosenman, Leonard, 32
Roth, Steve, 150, 151, 170n. 14
Rush, Robert, 17
Russell, Harold, 81
Russians Are Coming, The Russians Are Coming, The (Jewison), 15

Salt, Waldo, 33–34, 79–80, 155, 165n. 13
Sands, Diana, 17, 40, 41
Schaffner, Franklin, 14
Schatzberg, Jerry, 17
Schlesinger, John, 67
Schwartz, Al, 146
Scorsese, Martin, 1, 2, 3, 16, 24, 67, 124, 157, 160n. 23
Second-Hand Hearts (Ashby), viii, 34–35, 37, 143–46, 160n. 26
Sellers, Peter, 7, 35, 117, 167n. 13
Shampoo (Ashby), ix, 2, 3, 6, 7, 36, 42, 58, 59, 63, 134, 155, 171n. 24; awards, 28–29; breakdown of communication as theme, 99–100; collaboration with Beatty, 27–28,
162n. 30; commercial success of, 28; compared with *Nashville*, 97–98, 100–101, 167n. 8; critique of American society, 97–99; critique of television and media, viii, 98–104; editing, 133; mise-en-scène, 130; musical score, 124, 128–33; political viewpoint, 102–4, 129–30; reception of, 28; as satire, 8, 97; screenplay, 26–27
Simon and Garfunkel: "Bookends," 137–38; "Sounds of Silence," 123
Simon, Neil, 149
Simon, Paul, 128
Sinatra, Frank: "Strangers in the Night," 130–31
Slugger's Wife, The (Ashby), viii, 6, 37, 149, 163n. 5
Smight, Jack, 20
Soldier Blue (Nelson), 67
Spielberg, Steven, 67
Stallone, Sylvester, 33
Steadicam, first use of, 31
Steppenwolf: "Born to be Wild," 122–23
Stevens, Cat 61, 65: "Don't Be Shy," 119–21; "If You Want to Sing Out," 121, 127; "On the Road to Find Out," 124–26; "Trouble," 127; "Where Do the Children Play," 126
Stevens, George, vii, 14
Stewart, Melvin, 40, 41
Stone, Oliver, 79, 149–51, 155–56
Storaro, Vittorio, 5
Strauss, Richard: "Also sprach Zarathustra," 113
Streep, Meryl, 94
Sturges, Preston, 157
Sutherland, Donald, 78
Swink, Robert, 13–14
Sylbert, Richard, 27

Tarantino, Quentin, 155–56, 171n. 19
Tavoularis, Dean, 5
Tchaikovsky, Peter Ilyich: *First Piano Concerto*, 63
Thomas Crown Affair, The (Jewison), 17

INDEX

Toland, Gregg, 5
To Live and Die in L.A. (Friedkin), 156
Tootsie (Pollack), 148
Towne, Robert: *8 Million Ways to Die* (screenplay), 151–52; *Last Detail, The* (screenplay), 3, 23–25, 72, 75–76; *Shampoo* (screenplay), 26–29
Truffaut, Francois, 17
Tyner, Charles, 51, 73

United Artists Studio, 29, 168n. 1
Universal Pictures, 13

Veterans Administration (VA), 82, 86
Vidal, Gore: *Kalki* (novel), 148–49
Vietnam War, 2, 17, 31–34, 66–68, 76–95; passim, 96, 102
Voight, Jon, 7, 33–34, 81, 83, 86, 144, 146, 148
Von Stroheim, Erich, 7

Walken, Christopher, 94
Walker, Joseph, 6
Warden, Jack, 27–28, 98, 107
Warschilka, Edward, 14, 65
Welles, Orson, 5
Wexler, Haskell, 14, 15, 16, 18, 30–31, 32–34, 36, 45, 84, 144–46, 148, 162n. 36
Wexler, Jeff, 8, 135, 143
Wilder, Billy, 56
Willis, Gordon, 6, 21, 24, 45–46
Wise, Robert, 5, 13
Wright, Theresa, 81
Wycherly, William, 26
Wyler, William, vii, 13, 14, 47

Yablans, Frank, 150
Young, Neil: "My Soul," 132
Young, Otis, 23, 68–69

Zaentz, Saul, 25–26
Zimmerman, Don, 7
Zinneman, Fred, 80

www.ingramcontent.com/pod-product-compliance
Lightning Source LLC
Chambersburg PA
CBHW071820230426
43670CB00013B/2508